LOVING COMPLETELY

Loving

COMPLETELY

A **Five Star** Practice for Creating Great Relationships

KEITH WITT, PH.D.

INTEGRAL
LIFE
PRESS

This edition published by Integral Life Press, an imprint of Highpoint Executive Publishing.
For information, write to info@highpointpubs.com.

First Edition

ISBN: 978-0-9989840-6-3

Library of Congress Cataloging-in-Publication Data

Witt, Keith
Loving Completely: A Five Star Practice for Creating Great Relationships

Summary: "Acclaimed relationship therapist Dr. Keith Witt presents five key questions that serve as a baseline for understanding why we know so much about intimacy, yet still have to struggle so hard to be consistently fulfilled. He offers clarity and exercises for dealing with the inevitable problems arise in all the common areas of loving relationships."
– Provided by publisher.

ISBN: 978-0-9989840-6-3 (paperback)
Psychology, Relationships

Library of Congress Control Number: 978099898406

Cover design by Sarah Clarehart

Manufactured in the United States of America
10   9   8   7   6   5   4   3   2   1

Contents

Acknowledgements

Books are cocreated like movies, plays, and space stations. Countless people directly and indirectly contribute to unique outcomes. As Isaac Newton said in 1675: "If I have seen further it is by standing on the shoulders of Giants."

I thank all the scientists, visionaries, psychologists and spiritual teachers who continue to influence and enlighten me.

I thank my beloved wife Becky and my children Zoe and Ethan for being my best teachers of love, family, and second tier love.

I thank all my clients and students for sharing their lives, wounds, and wisdom with me.

I thank David Riordan for inspiring and guiding the Loving Completely audio course which gave birth to this book.

I thank Ken Wilber for my Integral awakening and his friendship over the years.

I thank Patricia Albere for opening me into the Universal we space.

I thank Robb Smith for believing in my work and standing for this book.

I thank Jeff Salzman and all my Integral brothers and sisters around the world supporting the evolution of consciousness.

Introduction

This is a different kind of relationship book.

All relationship books describe ideal versions of great marriages, passionate love affairs, effective problem solving, and solid communication skills, but many of us can do this for ourselves already! If asked, lots of people can describe great relationships and cooperative problem solving. I'm sure you can, since you're interested enough in satisfying intimacy to be reading this introduction.

Try it right now. Write or otherwise describe to yourself what characterizes a satisfying relationship and cooperative problem solving.

Now read or consider what you came up with. Pretty good, right? This is probably an excellent description of superior intimacy.

Here's one of mine: *A good marriage is one where both partners continually take care of their marital friendship and marital love affair, and they repair problems and emotional injuries back to shared love quickly and effectively.*

If you, me, and most other discerning individuals can spontaneously define a good relationship—*if it's so obvious*—then why aren't all of us enjoying satisfying intimacy all of the time?

Why is it that 40 percent of U.S. adults report chronic loneliness and *over 60 percent* of self-reported lonely people *are married and live with a spouse?* Why is it that 37 percent of U.S. adults answered "yes" to "Has marriage not worked out for most people you know?" Why are 10 percent more Americans unhappy in their marriages now than thirty-odd years ago?

The answer is that satisfying modern relationships are complicated and demanding in ways that are regularly difficult to understand and deal with.

That's why this is a different kind of relationship book. Not only do I explain why we know so much about intimacy yet still have to struggle so hard to be consistently fulfilled, but I'll tell you what to do about it when the inevitable problems arise in all the common areas such as:

* Sex

* Choosing superior partners

* Self-care

* Communication

* Dealing with crises

* Parenting

* Managing finances with another person

* Balancing personal passions and purpose with the demands of intimacy

* Spirituality

* Sex (I put it in twice to see you're paying attention)

I've spent a lifetime learning, practicing, and generating systems of intimacy, development, and psychotherapy. Every system I've encountered to help people love more joyfully has been useful and exciting, but only provides partial solutions. For instance, the more spiritually-oriented systems are often light on the neurobiological roots of relationships, and the practical, research-based systems are often light on the spiritual and evolutionary aspects of bonding, and so on. Every system has its strengths and weaknesses, but when viewed cumulatively, they yield convergent principles and practices.

The challenge to me as a therapist, researcher, and author has always been, "How do these magnificent interconnected systems of knowledge and practice all fit together, and how can we best learn and embody them to live and love better?"

In general, the shared universe of a fulfilling marriage—what I call the *intersubjective container*—involves successfully maintaining the marital friendship and marital love affair, and continually getting better at receiving loving influence from each other—especially in quick repair of relational injuries such as arguments, misunderstanding, affairs, mistakes, or clueless hurtful acts.

Sounds easy, doesn't it? Stay fulfilled in your friendship and love affair and learn quick, effective repair and you're in for a lifetime of bliss!

But we all know it's not easy, and that creating and maintaining a satisfying modern marriage over time is one of the most challenging and conditional forms of love that's ever existed. This book is designed to help you understand, co-create, and maintain a superior marriage throughout your lives.

Loving Completely starts with a simple foundation of five questions (reflecting five central dimensions of intimacy) to empower you to love others and yourself better *now*. From that point on, I build on each dimension by weaving in neuroscience, social research, wisdom traditions, and psycho-spiritual healing. I also let you know the signs in yourself, your partner, and your relationship that indicate you should seek help from a therapist or another wise counselor—because all of us need help from an expert once in a while.

All relationships, all the time

Why are relationships so important? Because it's all relationships all the time! This includes relationships with the multiple interior aspects of ourselves, with family members, with our lovers and friends, with nature, with spirit, and generally with all the worlds in which we move. The concept of *everything is relationships* is supported by vast bodies of psychological, social, and neurobiological research. Healthy, fulfilling lives *require* joyful intimate relationships in many dimensions.

People are endlessly complex and unique, but we all know there are better and worse relationships. What characterizes them? Even more, how can we best embody better relationships and help others in our lives relate better with us?

Loving Completely organizes relational understanding around the five questions mentioned earlier, reflecting the necessary components of joyful intimacy we can evaluate at any moment with any person. I call these questions the Five Stars, and this book expands them in ways that help you optimize love and health.

What are the Five Stars?

* *Is there erotic polarity, a spark of attraction, between me and this other person?*

* *Does this person maintain their physical and psychological health?*

* *In conflict, would this person be able and willing to do what it takes to get back to love?*

* *Would this person show up appropriately as a parent or family member?*

* *Does this person have deep soul's purpose, while recognizing and admiring what is deeply meaningful to me?*

These questions evoke deep wisdom if you can stay focused on them in yourself, potential partners, or your current partner through different states of consciousness. Self-awareness through different states is one of the keys to blissful intimacy.

We have many marriages.

Let's face the central facts that most modern people will have two or more serious lovers in their lifetime and that our needs change as we change. Young partners tend to create a shared life as they stay together through children, professional development, and life stages. People who meet when they are older are often more formed as individuals with each living a differentiated, complex life. Therapist, author, and speaker Esther Perel calls these marriages of older, formed partners *capstone marriages,* and they do have different demands and characteristics than those of the young couples who co-create a shared life together.

Even if you stay with the same partner from youth onwards, when you cross the threshold into marriage you're signing up for many marriages. We grow and develop individually and relationally from birth to death. The passionate lovers of our early twenties can become the bride or groom of our late twenties. The bride or groom of our late twenties can become the co-parent of our thirties, middle-aged partner of our forties, and life companion till death. Values clarify, bodies age, and we rediscover ourselves and our marriages through children, work, family, financial issues, crises, life demands, and aging. Each new developmental milestone—romantic infatuation, intimate bonding, marriage, children, crises, middle age, and old age—creates a new marriage we have to negotiate for better or worse depending on…everything!

Think of all the countless decisions involved in a shared lifetime! Think of the countless moments of connection with your partner that can support or sabotage love! How can each of us amplify love and minimize suffering during every precious moment of our unique life?

Even more, what causes people to stay and work, or get fed up and leave? What characterizes the long-time happy couples? What can we learn from them to love better right now?

Enter *Loving Completely!*

We can choose great partners! We can be great partners! We can *help others* be better partners! We can help others help *us* to be better partners!

Choosing

How have *you* chosen partners? Sexual attraction? Circumstance? Have you drifted into relationships? Why is it that we're often more likely to research what kind of air conditioner to buy than how to choose who to join our life and future with?

We can *learn* to choose well!

Not only that, we can *learn* how to observe ourselves and our mates in ways that keep us happy and growing, and, *when*—not *if*—we develop problems, we can learn principles and practices to guide us back to love or give us the clarity we need on when and how to leave.

You can see here how *observing* our marital love affair and marital friendship and *observing* how well we repair problems is a necessary first step to *improving.*

We can resolve problems into love.

If you're already in a lover relationship and have problems—which all lover relationships do—how do you evaluate what's happening and choose how to respond? Are you the one who's screwing things up? Is your lover not a good match for you? John Gottman, my favorite couples researcher, has identified four characteristics that are particularly toxic: contempt (the worst), defensiveness, stonewalling, and criticism. Do either one of you resort to contempt, defensiveness, stonewalling, or criticism of the other's character when conflict arises?

What do you believe will make things better? How can *you* be more loving?

Modern science and clinical practice have generated amazing answers to these questions, and we'll explore many in *Loving Completely*.

Staying

My wife, Becky, and I have been happily together for over forty-five years, which is only partly luck! Loving each other, growing together, and maintaining our friendship and love affair are also ongoing *achievements* to which we've stayed *committed*.

In her book *Grit*, Angela Duckworth shows how talent times effort equals *skill,* and skill times effort equals *achievement*. She defines "grit" as "a combination of passion over time for an outcome with persistence in pursuing that outcome through adversity."

Similarly, other researchers have found that "I will do what it takes..." commitments lead to more satisfying and enduring relationships than "I'll stay as long as..." commitments.

Loving Completely explores how grit and "I'll do what it takes..." commitments involve learnable skills you can improve upon to support joyful and enduring intimacy.

Grow your Shadow.

Renowned Swiss psychiatrist and psychoanalyst Carl Jung introduced the concept of *Shadow* as your entire unconscious, the part of you that runs most of your life. Below the surface in our adaptive, unconscious *Shadow selves,* we learn habits, develop reflexive ways of being, and are shaped by life events and our genetic heritage in ways that we are often not consciously aware of.

The most significant relating is unconscious to unconscious—Shadow to Shadow. Sixty percent of communication is nonverbal, mostly out-of-conscious awareness.[1] We are hard-wired for this in many ways. For instance, we all have mirror neurons in our brains that see or hear someone and unconsciously recapitulate their state of consciousness, including their intentionality. If we approach to within three feet of another, our heart rhythms begin entraining each other.

Our nervous systems constantly take in hundreds of thousands of inputs, do information processing revolving around what we want, fear, and habitually think and do, and then generate feelings, impulses, and stories to guide us—all in a tenth of a second. Our conscious selves can reflect on these feelings, impulses, and stories in a half second to a second and a half. Our conscious selves are always a step behind our unconscious Shadow selves.

The material that comes up from our Shadow selves falls into two broad categories: constructive and destructive. *Constructive Shadow* involves healthy habits like saying, "Excuse me," if you jostle someone, or not cutting in line at the post office. *Destructive Shadow* involves unhealthy habits like automatically ordering the third or fourth drink, or raging at yourself if you make a mistake.

Most psychological and spiritual growth involves developing our Shadow selves; aligning with constructive Shadow, and processing destructive Shadow with awareness and healthy choices (I call this dialyzing destructive Shadow) until it transmutes into constructive Shadow.

Loving Completely is designed to help you grow your Shadow by fostering awareness of constructive and destructive Shadow material and providing directions to optimize love and health.

If you want to learn more about Shadow dynamics, I suggest you check out my two books on Shadow, *Shadow Light: Illuminations at the Edge of Darkness,* and *Shadow Light Journal: A Companion Workbook.*

---

[1] Schore 2015

Relationships are for everyone.

Since everything is relationships, this book is for everybody. Whether you're in an intimate lover relationship or not, you'll benefit from the principles and practices that attract you in the pages ahead.

If you are single, you can learn to choose partners better and be a better partner for future lovers.

If you are in an unhappy relationship, you can learn to heal injuries, and also get help determining when it's time to consider leaving.

If you are in a happy relationship, you can learn to appreciate what you both are doing right and get tips on how to love each other better.

If you are LBGTQ, you can rest assured that most of the material in this book applies equally to all intimate relationships, regardless of whether I am using "he" or "she" pronouns.

To help you grow and love, each chapter has exercises for individuals and couples to practice the skills and embody the qualities of happy relating.

We certainly change and develop throughout life, but wisdom and truth aid us at every step. In the twenty-first century we have multiple, well-researched maps to guide us toward health and love in each life stage, in every relationship, and in most situations.

All this is what *Loving Completely* is about.

Special note to therapists

If you are a psychotherapist, you're going to love this book! That doesn't mean that this book teaches you individual or couples' psychotherapy. This is not a therapy manual. Nonetheless, if you do any kind of therapy you will find this book wildly useful.

Why is this?

As I maintain in my books on Integrally-informed psychotherapy, *Waking Up* and *Sessions,* all psychotherapy training systems are variations of therapists effectively learning how to relate, teach, inspire, confront, interpret, and direct.

You notice that "teach" is second only to "relate," and that's by design. Good therapy always progresses from a foundation of the therapeutic alliance toward teaching clients better ways of being and loving. Most therapy involves helping people get to the place where therapists and clients work together to generate, learn, and embody new, better ways of thinking, behaving, and relating. One way or another, every psychotherapy system reflects these core principles.

For instance, Terry Real in his Relational Life Therapy says couples therapists:

* First join by listening and confronting couples with truths of their personalities and individual/relational patterns.

* Then do the trauma work necessary to help clients resolve the blocks they have to growth and positive change.

* As clients become available, then teach them how to love better.

John Gottman teaches people the skills and perspectives that his research has demonstrated to be associated with the "Masters" of relationships (contrasted to the problems he's discovered associated with the "Disasters" of relationships.) These include "blueprints" of conflict resolution, play/friendship/sexuality, and meaning/existential issues—all of which are taught to clients as they are supported by therapists to be open to influence and change.

If you are a therapist, what do you believe are the superior forms of communicating, connecting, choosing, self-reflecting, sexing, parenting, and empathizing that optimize love? How can all the multiple aspects of relationships optimally fit into a good life, which we know includes satisfying relationships, work, purpose, sex, family, parenting, and social involvement?

Loving Completely provides research-based, clinically validated, superior perspectives in all these areas. In other words, when you've successfully co-created those moments where your clients are open to new ideas and behaviors—the "teach" part of relate, teach, inspire, confront, interpret, and direct—*Loving Completely* offers you a cornucopia of proven perspectives and practices you can share.

To the Integrally informed

I have been transformed by Ken Wilber's Integral model, and it permeates my work. To those familiar with his AQAL (all quadrants, lines, levels, states, and types) approach, you'll find me speaking regularly *from* those perspectives, but rarely *about* them. This is by design, since I want this book accessible to everyone, not just the Integrally informed.

That being said, if you are not familiar with AQAL, I suggest you read any of Ken Wilber's many books—I especially have enjoyed *Integral Psychology* and *Integral Spirituality*—and notice how understanding yourself, others, and the universe expands exponentially with the Integral metatheory.

The Big Picture

This part of the book explores some fundamental dimensions of healthy relating, such as how we choose partners, how to have growth mindsets, and training our brains to give up bad habits and establish good ones.

Chapters 1 and 2 start with the Five Stars—how they came into existence and how to start using them *right now* to see more, choose better, and improve your current relationships.

Of course, any change in how we perceive and relate to ourselves and the world requires self-observation, and compassionate self-observation is the best! Chapter 3 teaches attunement as a foundation practice to compassionately observe ourselves, others, and the world.

Once we are attuned, we need guidelines for what to do with what we observe. Chapters 4, 5, 6, and 7 explore training our brains, growth mindsets, and optimally organizing our habits of attention.

Chapter 1

The Five Stars

The five ways relationships work (or don't) is revealed by you asking yourself five questions about everybody, including *you*. I call these five questions the Five Stars.

The Five Star questions came directly from a conversation I had many years ago with my wife, Becky, and our (then) teenage kids, Ethan and Zoe. We were in the kitchen and Zoe asked me, "What should I look for in a boyfriend?" Both Becky and Ethan perked up. We all somehow instantly recognized this as an important moment.

If you are a parent, you know what a rare opportunity this was. Your teenage kid actually asked you for relationship advice! I wanted to give her the best answer I could, so I stopped, relaxed, and opened up to that place most therapists have where they allow healing material to flow from their nonconscious Shadow selves. Suddenly there was that sweet sense of a download beginning (like a wave of insight coming all at once). When that happens you feel it instantaneously, and then have to describe it linearly, one part at a time.

"Well Zoe, first of all, do you have erotic polarity? You need a spark between your feminine and his masculine. (Becky, sensing something good was happening said, "Wait! I want to write this down," as she grabbed a notepad and began furiously scribbling.)

I continued, "Does he maintain his physical and psychological health? If he doesn't, there's always trouble. And, speaking of trouble, if you and this guy had a conflict, would he be able and willing to do what it takes to get back to love?"

We were all focused now, considering what I'd said so far, and I saw them nodding. We are a self-reflective family, and especially so when it comes to relationships.

I continued, "Next, does he show up as a parent or family member?"

Zoe bristled at this one. "Wait a minute! I don't want to start a family—I just want a boyfriend!" she said, and we all laughed.

"Good point!" I said. "But if he can't show up as a parent or family member, he's lots more likely to let *you* down. Not only that, you don't want to practice being lovers with someone who won't show up *appropriately* (not aggressively or codependently) as a parent or family member. Choosing guys like that turns into a nightmare! You *do* want to practice choosing people who will be there for you and others in the clutch."

Zoe got this right away. "Okay, Daddy—I get it! But what else should I look for?"

I realized there was one more crucial dimension. "Does he have deep soul's purpose—something important, even sacred to him? Also, does he appreciate and admire what's sacred to you? You don't want a lover completely into his own pleasures or just your relationship! Both of those will eventually turn you off. He needs to have deeper meaning to feel whole. Along those lines he needs to understand and support what's deeply important to you—like your dancing."

Ethan weighed in, "Are all of these the same for me picking a girlfriend?"

"Absolutely," I replied. "Women and men, masculine types and feminine types, are certainly different, but the questions apply equally."

"Anything else?" asked Becky.

I reached inward and considered whether I should add another dimension, and realized everything else I had to say was connected in some fashion with the Five Stars. "Nope," I responded. "Just ask yourself those questions about a potential lover and you'll do *way* better! *Be* those qualities and you'll do way better!"

Becky put the questions on the fridge, and I began to tell the story to my clients when they asked about dating or evaluating their current relationships. They always wanted a list of the questions and I began keeping handouts in my office. Eventually I began teaching the Five Stars in classes and lectures.

As the years have passed, I have studied lots of intimacy systems, and read hundreds of studies, but have never added or subtracted from the original list, or from the format of *asking*.

The asking is important! Just as Zoe's question in the kitchen accessed my accumulated understanding of intimacy from decades of study and practice, asking the Five Star questions accesses *your* nonconscious Shadow relational wisdom. We observe way more that we consciously know when we interact with other people, and we all have deep intuitive wisdom. Our nonconscious Shadow selves are genius!

Here are the Five Stars again, with a little more explanation:

* **Is there erotic polarity, a spark of attraction, between me and this other person?** We have energetic polarities with everyone we encounter, but some polarities have an erotic tingle. If you're a guy, you probably look at an attractive woman and feel a subtle to huge sexual desire. If you're a woman, you might think, "He's sweet," or feel a pleasant (or maybe uncomfortable) awareness of your body as a certain guy looks at you appreciatively. You may even feel a desire for him to be interested in you, or for you to share who you are with him.

* **Does this person maintain their physical and psychological health?** He or she does not have to be buff, but just needs to seem interested in staying reasonably healthy and happy, and willing to put regular effort into health. For instance, does this person seem like they'd eat healthy food, avoid cigarettes and addictions, and ask for and receive help if they had physical or emotional problems?

* **In conflict, would this person be able and willing to do what it takes to get back to love?** "Able" asks if this person has the depth, knowledge, skills, and maturity to deal productively with conflict. "Willing" asks if this person can manage their own fears, impulses to attack and flee, and resentments so that they can hang in there with you in conflict and work back to understanding and affection.

* **Would this person show up appropriately as a parent or family member?** We all grew up in some family experience. Does this person seem like they'd put themselves second if they were needed by a child? Do they seem like they'd relate well and set healthy boundaries with different family members?

* **Does this person have deep soul's purpose, while recognizing and admiring what is deeply meaningful to me?** We all have some sense of the sacred, and, after the initial romantic infatuation stage of a relationship burns out (as it usually does somewhere from six months to two or three years into a love affair), we usually don't want a partner whose *sole reason for being is to be with us.* Also, we need partners who respect and at least somewhat understand what's important or sacred to us. If I take my relationship with God, spirit, or the infinite seriously, I need you to understand and respect how special that is. If you find a deeper connectedness and sense of unity doing yoga, parenting your child, volunteering for youth soccer, or having integrity in your job, you need me to recognize and honor this special area.

If you deeply explore yourself and your relationship through the Five Stars, you create a detailed map of your personal strengths, weaknesses, and challenges to creating and maintaining satisfying intimacy. *Just this* will make your relationships more conscious and more fulfilling, but there are countless other related ideas and techniques that have helped people grow and love better, and we'll explore a bunch of them in this book.

In the chapters ahead, I suggest you sample the dozens of techniques, practices, and perspectives I've offered that support satisfying relationships. Try out the ones that feel most natural and useful to *you,* and continue the ones that deliver insight, self-love, and enhanced intimacy.

Habits are hard to change, but we can replace bad ones with good ones!

We move through the world governed by beliefs, habits, tendencies, and defenses that we're programmed to learn from birth onward. We habitually look at ourselves and the world in typical ways, all more or less clear/healthy/compassionate. Habits are hard to change because our nervous systems are programmed to cling to previous learning and be suspicious of change.

We usually change incrementally over time, which makes it hard to fully absorb presentations or books that provide floods of information. For instance, one study concluded that we retain 15 percent of a lecture *if we're paying close attention.* Also, as all seekers know, it's hard to apply insights from books, classes, and lectures to *my* life, *right now,* and then keep doing it day after day, year after year.

Because of this, *Loving Completely* is designed to be a series of steps, organized around the Five Stars, and arranged for you to absorb at your most comfortable pace in response to your personal needs and preferences.

~~~~~~

EXERCISE: *For couples*

This is a wonderful book to read with a lover or spouse. Discussing the material and doing the practices will deepen your relationship. I've including couples' components for many of the exercises, and I think you and your partner will benefit from them.

On the other hand, if your partner doesn't want to work through this book with you, or engage in the couples exercises, that's fine! Please don't coerce him or her beyond a simple request.

If you don't want to do all this work and your partner does, that's fine too! Just do your best to support his or her efforts to love themselves and you better.

How the book is organized

This book is made up of seven sections. The first, titled The Big Picture, gives an introductory overview. The next five explore each of the Five Star

questions in four to nine short and accessible chapters that drill down into
the themes, and how to integrate them with your life.

Each chapter invites you to consider different dimensions of satisfying
life and relationship, or specific problems that commonly arise in intimacy,
along with suggested solutions. I'll explain principles, useful practices and
perspectives, and vital research, along with stories relevant to the material.
I'll then suggest various ways to apply this material specifically to your life
and relationships.

All that being said, *please,* always remember, I want you to have *fun!* If
you get bored by anything, skip it! If you do, I predict you'll like the next
chapter better!

The sections and chapters build on each other—they include and transcend each other as you work through them.

Every chapter makes suggestions of activities to do in the day or days
following. When you feel ready, you can move to the next chapter.

To do the exercises, I recommend you set up your phone and/or
computer to take notes throughout your day, and/or buy a journal if you
prefer writing longhand. If you buy a journal, try to get a nice one with a
cover you find appealing. There is some research that suggests writing exercises can be more powerful if done by hand, and you can always transcribe
entries from your phone/computer to your journal, or from your journal to
your phone/computer if you want to do both.

Writing is a way of processing with yourself, as conversation is a way
of processing with another. Any time you *process* personal information, as
when you're discussing or writing about decisions and information that have
originated mostly from your logical, linear, linguistic, literal left hemisphere,
you open yourself up to deep wisdom from your intuitive, non-linear, autobiographical, emotional, sensory right hemisphere.

This is one reason I suggest you recruit people you trust with whom you
can share insights, perspectives, and dialogue. If you're in relationship, it's a
wonderful opportunity for you and your partner to work through this book
together!

If your partner isn't interested, though, there are often multiple people
you trust with different parts of your life. People to share with can include

lovers, parents, friends, family members, or various combinations of different folks. We are social beings and grow much faster when we share with caring others.

That all being said, you might go through different chapters, or the whole book, alone. You might write volumes, or never write a word. I encourage you to experiment and find combinations of activities that help you grow, learn, and become more intimate with people you care about.

Don't feel obligated to do anything! If one of my clients follows through on 25 percent of my suggestions, that's usually enough for significant progress. Try suggestions that appeal to you, and keep doing the ones that seem to deliver insight and progress. If some parts seem irrelevant or not right for you, skip them!

Find your personal rhythm.

Find your personal rhythm while absorbing the material. You may take a day or a week between chapters. If you're unsure what's best for you, experiment. For instance, I learned emptiness practice from a lecture by Daniel P. Brown, and practiced it for six or seven months before I finally bought his book, *Pointing Out the Great Way.* It took me that long to be ready to move deeper into his Mahamudra Buddhist perspectives and practices.

As you progress through this book, expect big insights and transformative practices to emerge that will change your life for the better. *Focused intent and action, in service of principle, and driven by resolve,* is one of the most potent human superpowers, and in *Loving Completely,* I invite and guide you to harness that superpower to grow and have superior relationships with others and the multitudes of your inner selves.

Habits get easier (more habitual!) the more we practice them.

Even though we can hear about a new habit in a few seconds (like writing everything you eat in a food journal), our brains incorporate new habits of attention and behavior slowly through conscious practice. On the other hand, when we practice a new habit enough it becomes automatic—*habitual.* We'll talk much more about deconstructing bad habits and constructing good habits in Chapters 18 and 19. The foundation exercise of *Loving Completely* is cultivating the habit of asking yourself the Five Star questions about other people you see in the world (as well as yourself), and paying attention to the answers your mind and body give you.

~~~~~~

EXERCISE: *Monitoring the Five Stars*

Starting today, ask yourself the Five Star questions about people you meet, your current partner, or even about fictional characters in movies or books, and then record what you noticed, felt in your body, and thought as you asked the questions.

You can do this exercise anywhere. You don't need much contact to have an opinion about another person. One study looked at individuals who met someone briefly for less than a minute, and another group who knew someone for five weeks. When asked to evaluate the other person, people in both groups were equally accurate! Our nervous systems constantly absorb thousands of inputs, and we have multiple channels of social attunement that have evolved over millions of years of being social animals, and several hundred thousand years of being super-genius human beings.

When you ask a question, you stimulate your right hemisphere (where intuitive knowledge and bodily wisdom reside) to respond with intuitive wisdom. That why the Five Stars are questions—they are designed to stimulate and strengthen your social intuition.

If asking all five feels like too much, just ask one or two Stars a day, and record your reactions. You can try different questions on different days. You'll probably discover yourself naturally noticing some Stars more easily than others. For instance, guys are pretty quick at noticing whether erotic polarity exists between them and an attractive woman, but can be less conscious of asking themselves whether she'd be able and willing to get back to love in a conflict.

On the other hand, you can learn to be aware of the presence or absence of all five. I have pulled up at a stoplight, glanced at the middle-aged woman in the Bronco next to me and thought, "I find her attractive, and I'll bet she's a good parent."

We'll explore the Five Stars in greater detail in future chapters. Right now, just ask yourself these questions about as many people you encounter as possible, and be curious and interested in your answers.

What do you think as you ask? How do you feel in your body as you ask? Remember to write down what you remember.

* *Is there erotic polarity, a spark of attraction, between me and this other person?*

* *Does this person maintain their physical and psychological health?*

* *In conflict, would this person be able and willing to do what it takes to get back to love?*

* *Would this person show up appropriately as a parent or family member?*

* *Does this person have deep soul's purpose, while recognizing and admiring what is deeply meaningful to me?*

EXERCISE: *Sharing with a partner*

After your first day's entries, try sharing them with someone you trust (your current partner if possible), and pay attention to how you feel during the conversation. Do you feel awkward? Closer? Tense? Does the conversation lead to conflict, or to deeper intimacy? Record in your journal what you notice after your talk.

EXERCISE: *The Five Stars in me*

Over the next few days, observe the Five Stars in yourself. Ask yourself: Am I supporting erotic polarity with my partner? Am I maintaining my physical and psychological health? Am I able and willing to get back to love through conflict? Am I showing up as a parent or family member? Am I recognizing and honoring what my partner finds important or sacred? Write about what you do well and do poorly in your journal, and add any ideas you have about improving problem areas.

Each evening tell your partner what you've discovered about yourself and listen with acceptance and no criticism or advice to what your partner has discovered. Pay special attention to when you slip up (and you will slip up!) and find yourself criticizing or advising, and apologize immediately! Quick apologies are wonderful for relationships!

Chapter 2

Choosing Partners

Most of us choose intimate partners through sexual attraction, opportunity, someone else's interest in us, or simply our relational programming influencing who we're wired to be drawn to. How have you chosen relationships in the past?

For instance, at 19, I chose my first serious girlfriend, Mary, because she was an attractive woman who walked out of a statistics class at the same time I did, said "Yes!" when I offered her a motorcycle ride, and also was interested in having fun sex with me. That turned into a three-year relationship that could have produced marriage (she asked me once), children (it turned out she wasn't pregnant), and a miserable life (we ultimately were too different to stay together, and she left me, thank God!). In retrospect, my decision was basically, "She's attractive, shares my counter-culture values, and wants me."

At 23, I asked Becky out because she was cute, I knew her from a counseling class we'd shared the previous year, I randomly ran into her in the Isla Vista Bank of America parking lot, and she seemed to like me. I stayed because she was sweet and it never felt right to separate. As of this writing, we've been together for forty-five years.

In retrospect, my unconscious was screaming at me that she was perfect to be my life partner, but my ignorance, naiveté, and psychological wounds kept getting in the way in the conflicts that plagued our first eight years. (And Becky had her own wounds to deal with!) Throughout that time, our shared value of working on growth and love kept us struggling together rather than leaving each other and finding someone new. We had I'll-do-what-it-takes commitments and growth mindsets, both of which we'll be exploring in the chapters to come.

~~~~~~

EXERCISE: *Choosing partner style*

Remember how you met your last two lovers. Most of us in the modern world will have had two or more serious pair-bond relationships in our lives. How did you choose and keep choosing? In other words, did you approach these partners, or were you approached? Why did you choose him or her or say "yes" to his or her overtures? What kept you together when inevitable problems arose? If you broke up, what was your contribution? Write in detail the stories of these two love affairs.

After a day or two, read what you've written and look for insights about how you choose or are chosen. Write what you like and dislike about what you've discovered, and what you want to keep and change about how you choose and are chosen.

Ask your partner how they have chosen or been chosen, and listen with interest as they describe their choosing style. Write about your conversation afterwards.

Relational drives

"Falling in love" is a definable neurological-relational-evolutionarily-determined state we'll explore more deeply in future chapters. For now, just know we have at least three separate but interconnected sexual/relational *drives* programmed into us by evolution.

The first is **lust.** This is attraction/desire that might be impersonal (guys can respond physically to an hourglass shape painted on a wall), or intertwined with personality characteristics you're drawn to erotically.

The second is **romantic infatuation,** where we fixate romantically/erotically on a specific other person. This is the falling in love experience that has such luminance and prominence in all human cultures.

The third is **intimate bonding,** where the other feels like "family." This is often when people marry, have children, or more deeply intertwine their lives, generating family feelings and states that show up differently at different developmental stages.

~~~~~~

EXERCISE: *How you fall in love*

Look back at your falling-in-love stories. How did you bond with your first lover (or lovers)? Was it sexiness? His or her interest in you? Availability? His smile? Her laugh? The world he lived in? The world she lived in? In retrospect, which of the Five Stars did you consider and which did you not consider as your love affair progressed? Write about what kept you connected enough to fall in love.

~~~~~~

EXERCISE: *Sharing with your partner*

Try sharing your insights with your current partner. Be aware of how you feel and what you think or remember during the conversation and write about the conversation in your journal.

Ask your partner how he or she progressed into the major love affairs of their life and listen with interest and support. Write about your conversation afterwards.

~~~~~~

EXERCISE: *Lust, unconscious programming, and our drives to bond*

We'll explore all of these in future chapters, but for right now, compare your previous ways of evaluating potential lovers with what you've experienced with the Five Stars since you first read them is this book.

Which evaluation dimensions (the Five Stars and others, like being set up by friends, or going for whomever is available) come most naturally to you, and how do they intersect? Write down your answers.

~~~~~~

EXERCISE: *Expanding awareness of attractions and the Five Stars*

Observe your attractions and relationship behaviors for the next two days as you do the Five Star practice and also cultivate memories of your previous attractors. If you're single, who are you drawn to? If you're in a relationship, who would you go for if you were single, and what lights you up about your current partner? How has this changed throughout your life—say from age 15 to 25, to 35, to 45, to 55, to 65? How has it stayed the same? Write about your insights and observations.

Read your journal entries from this chapter, and write how the Five Stars and your previous attractors intersect and diverge. Share this with a partner.

Chapter 3

Attunement as a Foundation Practice

All of us like to be alone sometimes. Introverts are especially nourished by alone time, but extroverts crave solitude too—just ask your most extroverted friend if he or she ever craves time just with themselves.

That being said, like all mammals we are a social species, conceived in, raised with, and needing relationships with others. Evolutionary anthropologists believe that the big expansion of brain size in humans two to three million years ago was *in response* to larger, more complex tribal groups of up to 150 (to this day, most of our brain is dedicated to social engagement with others). That "150" is called the "Dunbar number" after British anthropologist Robin Dunbar who found that human communities naturally calve off from each other as they approach the 150 limit.

Being highly social, we have natural instincts to communicate and connect in most states of consciousness—safe, unsafe, loving, angry, happy, sad, sexually aroused, etc. Social connection is mostly good, but sometimes can devolve into disastrous. As anyone who has just had a fight with a friend or lover can tell you, there are better and worse ways to connect!

How can we optimize social engagement and stay away from destructive conflicts? One answer is *attunement,* which is being aware *with* acceptance and caring intent of sensation, emotion, thought, judgment, and desire in ourselves and others.

Attunement is one of the best methods to optimize connection. Let's check in with a couple I once worked with—Hal and Judy—who demonstrate the hazards of mis-attunement and the values of learning attunement.

Hal and Judy are in their mid-thirties, have been together ten years, and have two small children. They come into a session obviously angry with each other. Judy says in a frustrated tone, "Hal is disconnected from the family. He won't talk."

Hal responds contemptuously, "She always gets too emotional and unreasonable, so why should I?"

How attuned are Judy and Hal right now? Not much!

Hal and Judy *are* communicating, but they are *not* attuned. Interpersonal attunement is awareness with acceptance and caring intent of what you and another are sensing, feeling, thinking, judging, and wanting right now.

How would they think and act differently if they were attuned? Attuned communication can take many forms, but one example would be:

Hal and Judy come into the session obviously angry with each other. Judy says in a frustrated tone, "Hal's disconnected from the family. He won't talk when we have a problem. I ask him to talk about what's wrong and he says, 'No!' almost every time. When he refuses to process with me, I start thinking bad thoughts and can't remember how distressing it is to him when we argue."

Hal responds thoughtfully, "Judy's right. I don't like to argue, and when Judy feels unheard she often gets so emotional and unreasonable that all I can think of is getting out of the room! I can see how it makes things worse, but I just feel so overwhelmed at the time."

In this second example, Hal and Judy are observing their own and each other's feelings/thoughts/impulses with that acceptance and caring intent— they are attuned.

Attunement strengthens the prosocial, self-reflective, and empathic circuits in your brain—especially in the prefrontal cortex, insula, and cingulate, which are the centers of self-identity and self-control circuits.

Attunement and mindfulness

Attunement is a central component of all mindfulness approaches.

Another name for attunement is *mindfulness.* Mindfulness has been defined by Jon Kabat Zinn, the founder of Stress Reduction Clinic and the Center for Mindfulness in Medicine, as being aware with acceptance and caring intent, with compassionate judgment, on purpose, in the present moment.

Mindful awareness changes everything!

For example, a woman named Jane came to see me because she was depressed. As I asked her about her life, it quickly became obvious that she instinctively responded negatively to any question:

* "How are you with your kids?" "I'm too tired and detached."

* "How are you with your work?" "I procrastinate too much."

* "How are you with your husband?" "I think I'm almost always a disappointment to him."

* "What gives you pleasure?" "Nothing much anymore."

She reflexively kept making cases for her life being shameful, bad, and hopeless—a signature worldview of many depressed people. She was unable to be aware of these instinctive critical judgments as a *habitual response style,* never mind having acceptance and caring intent. She hated her critical judgments, but also hated herself for making them! A breakthrough occurred when she realized her negativity was a habit that had burdened her for years. As she became consistently aware with acceptance and caring intent of her depressed explanatory style and her anger at her emotional pains, she began to feel lighter and reach for more compassionate understanding of herself and others. This compassionate self-observation helped her understand how her negative thoughts/feelings/beliefs were bad-habit distortions rather than indictments of her character. Attunement helped wake her up out of her chronic depressive-trance.

EXERCISE: *Compassionate understanding of my blocks to
             self-acceptance*

*Where is it hard for you to accept yourself with caring intent? Write down
your answer in your journal. Now write your most compassionate understanding of yourself in this area. Notice how your feelings shift as you
reach for deeper perspectives.*

*Ask your partner where it is hard for him or her to accept himself or herself
with caring intent, and what his or her compassionate understanding of this
is. Listen with interest and write about your conversation.*

As I've previously mentioned, one of the most powerful forces in the
world is human focus, intent, and action, in service of principle, and driven
by resolve. This superpower is amplified by attunement.

EXERCISE: *Attunement*

*Let's practice attunement—I'll guide you through attuning to yourself,
others, and nature. For more on attunement, you can check out two of my
previous books,* The Attuned Family *and* Integral Mindfulness.

We start with the breath

Sit comfortably and breathe deeply.

*All meditation and mindfulness practices start and end with the breath.
Sit, relax, and send your attention to your breath. You breathe in; you
breathe out. Feel yourself drawing air deep into your belly, pausing, and
then allowing it to flow out—an endless cycle we began at birth and will
continue to our last breath.*

*The slower you breathe out, the more you self-soothe. Our out-breath acti-
vates our tenth cranial nerve, the parasympathetic vagus, which increases
heart rate variability (how in tune with the present moment your heart
rate is) and calms you down. An exhale of ten to fourteen seconds generally calms us super-efficiently, so it's often a good idea to start an attune-*

ment (or any contemplative practice) with three or four deep breaths and slow exhales.

Focus on breathing can be a mindfulness practice in itself. At the end of breathing in, just before you breathe out, be aware of your body. At the end of breathing out, just before you breathe in, be aware of your body. This is a central feature of many meditations. If you do just this on a regular basis, your brain will actually change shape. For example, the anterior cingulate cortex (in your frontal lobes) gets activated when you direct your attention, and regularly activated brain areas grow over time, increasing both white and gray matter. Mindful breathing stimulates the growth of more neurons, neural networks, and myelination in the anterior cingulate cortex, the frontal cortex, and other brain areas having to do with attention, self-observation, self-soothing, morality, intuition, and decision-making.

Sensation

Breathe in and breathe out—into your belly and out from your belly. As you breathe in and out, be aware of the sensations in your body with acceptance and caring intent. Are you hot? Are you cold? Do your feet hurt? Are you tense or relaxed? Whatever the sensation, experience it with acceptance and caring intent.

Feelings

Now, as you breathe in and out, aware of sensations in your body, be aware of what emotions you might be feeling right now. Are you feeling happy? Sad? Are you feeling angry? Irritated? Depressed? Anxious? Are you feeling joyful? Turned on? Ashamed? Guilty? Embarrassed? Are you feeling a little self-conscious? Self-satisfied? Notice how feelings come and go, rise and fall, and just observe your feelings with acceptance and caring intent.

Thoughts

As you breathe in and out, aware of sensations and emotions, be aware of your thoughts. Thoughts come and go. Sometimes we focus on them, sometimes we don't. Right now, just be aware of thoughts coming and going with acceptance and caring intent. If you start following or elaborating on a thought—you know, "We're going out tonight with Ray and Jillian. I wonder if they've spoken with their son who just got married, who..."—try and catch the thought as early as possible, accept it with caring intent, but allow it to pass without pursuit or elaboration, and return to your breath going into your belly and out from your belly.

Judgments

As you're aware of breath, sensation, emotion, and thought, direct your attention to your judgments (both positive and negative) with acceptance and caring intent. What judgments do you have right now about yourself? About me? About this book? About other people? Try not to elaborate, explore, or pursue the judgments you discover, instead just be aware of them with acceptance and caring intent, and then return to your breath.

Try to observe your judgments with interest. "Oh, I look fat in this shirt." Fine. Be aware of that distress, that shame, with acceptance and caring intent. "Oh, I really like my new hat." Be aware of liking your new hat and believing you look good in your new hat with acceptance and caring intent.

"I think the lady next door is nasty and selfish." OK, be aware of your critical judgment with acceptance and caring intent. "I think Jeff at work is really sweet." Be aware of that judgment of him being sweet with acceptance and caring intent.

As you can see, judgments can be negative or positive. If I think you're a nice, attractive, or charming person, or I'm a nice, attractive, or charming person, those are judgments—positive judgments. If I feel embarrassed or ashamed of forgetting my dental appointment, or irritated at you for forgetting to come to our 10:00 breakfast meeting at the coffee shop, I'm caught up in negative judgments of me or you. Whatever judgments you have, positive or negative, observe them with acceptance and caring intent, and return to your breath.

Desires

And now, breathing in and out, aware of sensation, emotion, thought, and judgment, be aware of what you desire, what you want right now, with acceptance and caring intent. Do you want to stand up? Do you want to sit down? Do you want to eat something? Drink something? Do you crave the company of a particular person? Do you want to avoid a particular person? Without pursuing them or elaborating them, just be aware of your desires with acceptance and caring intent, and return to your breath.

Awareness of breath, body, emotion, thought, judgment, and desire with acceptance and caring intent is attuning to yourself. It is mindful awareness of you.

Sitting attunement

You can sit and do this for five or ten minutes once or twice a day; and as time passes, you will expand your abilities to calm yourself, be self-reflective, make good decisions, and be empathic.

Living attunement

You can also attune to yourself working in the garden, riding on a bus, exercising, or going to sleep. You can do it all day long. The more you do it, the better!

Attuning to others

To attune to others, look at someone (if they're not around, you can send him or her your attention) with acceptance and caring intent. What do you imagine he or she is currently sensing, feeling, thinking, judging, or wanting? Now you're attuning to them. Couples who do this tend to be happier. The practice makes you more generous and empathic in general, because as you more habitually attune to another, that person less and less frequently disappears from your awareness. Couples tend to do well when they stay compassionately aware of each other's lives even when they aren't actually together.

Next time you're with someone, imagine with acceptance and caring intent what he or she is sensing, feeling, thinking, judging, and wanting. As you do this, you attune to them.

Try it right now with somebody you love who's not around. Think about where he or she is and what they're doing. Are they sitting? Standing? Walking? Driving? Hanging out with a friend? With acceptance and caring intent, imagine them sensing, feeling, thinking, judging, and wanting at this moment. How does this feel? I always get a warm glow attuning to people I love who are not currently with me.

Mothers naturally attune to infants, and most happily married couples do a lot of mutual attunement. Friends tend to attune to one another, and this is one of the reasons that if you want to be a happy person, it's a good idea to live next door to a friend. People who live next door to a friend tend to be about 35 percent happier than people who don't.

Attuning to nature

You don't have to limit your attunements to yourself and other people. You also can attune to nature. If you're not outside, there's probably a window near you. Look out into nature. Be aware of what's happening out there with acceptance and caring intent. It doesn't matter if it's comfortable or uncomfortable. It doesn't matter if it's sunny or dark, cloudy or rainy, muggy or invigorating. Just be aware of nature. Direct your attention toward nature and be aware of nature with acceptance and caring intent. Cultivate a sense of oneness with a blade of grass, a bird singing, or a whole ecosystem. This is attunement to nature.

You can practice attunement all the time

I love attuning. I find attunements simple, potent, and easy to do. I encourage you to practice attuning to yourself, others, and nature as you progress through your day, hanging out with friends or family, at work, or moving through the world.

You also benefit from sitting daily for ten or twenty minutes attuning to yourself, others, and nature. Find some combination of attunement practices that works for you, because the important thing is to find what *you* like and to do it a lot! The more you practice, the more habitual attunement becomes, and what a good habit it is!

EXERCISE: *Attunement in action*

Sit for at least two minutes a day practicing attuning to yourself. Try attuning to yourself and the people around you whenever you have a moment of free attention—driving in the car, sitting in a room, hanging out with your friends or family. Each night write about your experiences and insights. After the first night, share your entries with another person and stay attuned to yourself and him or her during the conversation.

~~~~~~

EXERCISE: *Couple attunement*

If you are in a relationship, sit comfortably and first attune to yourself and then your partner. Notice what it's like to focus on your and your partner's sensations, feelings, thoughts, judgments, and desires with acceptance and caring intent. Write about your experiences and share them with your partner.

After practicing attuning to yourself and your partner for several days, start noticing when you are not attuned to yourself or your partner. Write in your journal when and how this happens, and then share what you've written with your partner. Write about that conversation.

Chapter 4

Train Your Brain

Our brains are wired to learn and relate, motivated by drives to survive, thrive, have position on personally important social hierarchies, and to defend. Using our superpowers of focused intent and action, in service of principle, and driven by resolve, we can train our brains to be more powerful, happy, and prosocial.

Think for a moment about how the universe started over thirteen billion years ago with a mysterious smaller-than-an-atom *something* exploding into undifferentiated plasma that, somehow, eventually produced this conversation.

Why and how did plasma turn into hydrogen, turn into suns, turn into elements, turn into more suns and planets, turn into our earth, turn into life, turn into people, turn into language, turn into writing, turn into computers, turn into us relating now? It wasn't just random! Randomness doesn't turn plasma into self-aware beings who can think about plasma!

The universe came into being with self-organizing characteristics— the natural law—like gravity, the speed of light, electromagnetism, and *chaos theory*.

Chaos theory dictates that complex systems naturally self-organize toward greater complexity. A complex system is a group of differentiated parts that are linked, energized from the outside, arranged hierarchically, capable of chaotic behavior, and don't get lost in rigidity or chaos.

Our brains, bodies, relationships, and families are complex systems—they are differentiated parts that are linked, energized by us and the world, arranged hierarchically in social structures, and (God knows!) capable of chaotic behavior!

In human systems, we can optimize development by linking parts with compassionate understanding and acceptance. We link the different parts of ourselves by identifying them (happy self, angry self, mature self, immature self) and focusing on them with acceptance and caring intent. We link different parts of our social systems by attuning to everyone in the system. These systems grow faster when we link differentiated parts with attuned awareness and compassionate acceptance. Compassionate acceptance helps these linked differentiated parts not get lost in chaos or rigidity, but instead self-organize to greater complexity.

Remember Hal and Judy from Chapter 3, who in the first example came in angry and mis-attuned, and in the second attuned? In the first example, Judy was saying, "Hal is disconnected from the family. He won't talk."

Hal was responding contemptuously, "She gets too emotional and unreasonable." Their hostility and mis-attunement separated them. They were frozen and unable to become more complex.

Then they expressed the same feelings while attuned to each other, and the interaction changed dramatically. They connected to themselves and each other with acceptance and caring intent, and this allowed them to support more complexity.

Two people in interaction are a complex system—they are linked energized parts, capable of chaotic behavior—but angry distortions disconnect us. Angry distortions push us toward rigidity where no one is willing to give up his or her hostile story, and chaos where our couple system becomes incoherent and mis-attuned.

How do we link hostile Hal and Judy? Through attunement. How can this happen? Here's one way:

Keith: "You two are in rigid negative stories and are resisting caring influence."

Judy, somewhat outraged and self-righteous, "What do you mean? I'm just taking a stand for connection! Hal refuses to listen! He's the rigid one here!"

Keith: "Really? I'm not hearing you acknowledge any validity in his concerns about you being too emotional and unreasonable."

Hal, feeling vindicated, "Yeah! You never listen to my feedback!"

Keith: "Okay, Hal. I'm not hearing you validate Judy's point about you being disconnected. She's a pretty sensitive person and is rarely 100 percent wrong about anything." Both look a little abashed. I continue, "Try telling the other person what's *right* about what they're imagining and wanting."

Judy, visibly softening, "Well, I do sometimes get upset and unreasonable when I'm frustrated."

Hal relaxes his shoulders and takes a deep breath, "Thanks for that! Judy's right about me isolating myself from her and the kids when I'm stressed."

Keith: "Look each other in the eyes and try to feel into the other person's body and spirit right now." They do this. "How do you feel?"

Judy: "I feel closer and warmer."

Hal: "Me too."

Keith: "As you attune to each other like this, your relationship becomes more complex—more engaged and flexible. Can you feel it?" They both nod and smile.

Acceptance and caring intent *connects us*—we become attuned, coherent, and integrating toward greater complexity.

This is how it almost always works in intimate relationships. Deeper understanding and increasing compassion leads to greater complexity and more love and wisdom.

The evolutionary impulse

Complex systems such as brains, families, tribes, and businesses, where there are differentiated parts linked, energized (input enters from the outside), arranged hierarchically, and capable of chaotic behavior, are the visible manifestations of the evolutionary impulse. Let's look at some more examples.

Complex systems can become rigid like rocks, chaotic like smoke disappearing in the wind, or integrated into progressively deeper coherence. We can see these characteristics in good and bad conversations.

If you yell "Yes!" and I yell "No!" endlessly, we are locked in a rigid exchange.

If you scream without listening to me as I scream without listening to you, we are lost in chaos.

If we attune, listen with interest, and receive influence from each other, we both grow, we feel good, and *we appear* much simpler than the two other scenes, but actually are engaged in much more complex behavior. You can see this in the conversation I had with Hal and Judy

If a system doesn't become frozen in rigidity or lost in chaos, the natural evolutionary progression is homeostasis, into disruption, into disorganization, into reorganization at a more complex and coherent level. Every particle in the universe is biased to self-organize to greater coherence and more complexity, if given the chance. This universal force is *the evolutionary impulse.*

As complex systems receive input from themselves and from the outside (energized), they have a tendency to keep reorganizing toward greater complexity, which looks like more simplicity. Consider another example of Hal and Judy arguing about his surfing and biking. Here they are lost in rigidity and chaos:

Judy: "I hate how you're always gone!"

Hal: "I told you before we got married that I'm going to surf in the winter and bike when there's no surf. You agreed!"

Judy: "I didn't agree for you to be gone all the time!"

Hal: "First of all, it's not all the time! Second of all, get used to it!

Judy: "I hate you!"

Now here they are starting at the same place but attuning instead of getting lost in rigidity or chaos:

Judy: "I miss you when you're gone surfing or biking."

Hal: "You know how important surfing and biking are to me. I try to be home with you and the kids as much as I can."

Judy: "I know surfing and biking are great for you, and I want you to be happy! It's just that I've been getting lonely recently, and angry when there's a kid problem and you're gone."

Hal: "I'll stay home more this week and see how it works out."

Judy: "Thanks! I super-appreciate it!"

A couple like Hal and Judy creatively resolving an issue when they're angry look and feel much simpler than the same couple lost in a vitriolic argument, but they are actually acting in a much more coherent and complex manner.

Since complex systems described in chaos theory are non-linear, occasionally a little bit of input can tip the system into a major reorganization. This means you can sometimes put in a lot of effort and feel no results, or experience a little push (like a random comment or a sudden insight) and feel a major change. That's the magic of complexity theory and evolution in general.

Offering your mind, body, and relational systems as many bits of influence (and as many healing opportunities) as possible increases your chances of having such transformative experiences. As complex systems, we always have the capacity to completely reorganize if we get just the right input at just the right time.

EXERCISE: *The Five Stars and me exercise*

As you do the Five Star exercise the next few days with other people, expand it to focus much more on yourself.

When are you feeling erotic polarities with others, taking better/worse care of your physical/psychological health, able/willing to get back to love in conflict, showing up as a parent or family member, or being true to your deepest purpose?

Notice what parts of yourself you deny and judge (denial and critical judgment block linkages of the differentiated parts of your personality/nervous system), and what parts you notice and accept (creating attuned linkage between parts of your personality/nervous system, thus supporting integration and evolution).

For example, say you notice yourself getting angry with your son and refusing to do what it takes to get back to love—clearly a bad habit for a parent. You can either get lost in shame (I'm a bad parent!), try to shift the blame (he deserved me telling him he's a loser!), or otherwise avoid looking with acceptance and caring intent at your character flaw—all of which block integration. Alternatively, you can compassionately observe yourself resisting getting back to love, and consider making another choice next time you're angry.

Write about your insights, and share them with another.

Experiment with cultivating compassionate acceptance of all your inner voices, figures, memories, and experiences and write about your efforts. Share this with another.

Chapter 5

Growth Mindsets Create Happiness and Success

Our attitudes toward challenges, learning, and mistakes have huge impacts on our development. These attitudes toward who we are and how we meet challenges are called *mindsets,* and most people lean toward one of two kinds—*growth mindsets* or *fixed mindsets.*

Social scientist Carol Dweck was in the sixth grade when her teacher lined all the kids in her class up in order of their IQ test scores. This so righteously pissed her off that she made a career out of proving that most intelligence is a function of effort and progress—what she calls growth mindsets.

Growth mindsets favor effort and progress and don't mind mistakes much, while fixed mindsets want to do everything perfectly the first time or not do it at all.

People with habitual fixed mindsets don't like challenges or mistakes—challenges and mistakes make them feel stupid and inadequate—so they try to avoid them. People with habitual growth mindsets love challenges and don't mind mistakes—they see mistakes as opportunities for growth, and effort and progress are more important to them than outcomes.

Growth mindsets are superior by every measure. *What do they look like in action?*

You're talking to two eight-year-olds, Danny and Aaron.

Danny says, "Give me lots of easy puzzles because I feel bad when I can't do the hard ones—it makes me feel stupid when I make mistakes."

Aaron says, "Give me the hard puzzles because I like figuring them out and I'm bored with the easy ones."

Which kid do you think is going to achieve more in school and in life?

It's most likely Aaron because he has a growth mindset.

Growth mindset people tend to think, *"I want a challenge, give me a more difficult task."* Growth mindset kids and adults aren't afraid to fail. They like getting gradually better in challenging activities like sports, playing the piano or guitar, writing poetry, or anything else.

Interestingly, out of a hundred variables studied by the makers of the SAT test for college admissions, one predicted success during and after college more than any other. That crucial variable was a student spending two or more years on two or more activities where he or she got better at the activity over time. In this case, effort and progress orientation predicted success.

Fixed mindset people tend to be anxious perfectionists and think, "I want something I can do well right now." Fixed mindset kids and adults find failure shameful and want to avoid it. They feel stupid if they can't do something well right now.

Kids diverge wildly at the age of 11 with very different developmental probabilities, depending on whether they have fixed or growth mindsets. Growth mindset kids and adults tend to do way better in school, work, and relationships.

You can see how this applies to marriage. Even if we start out as Five Star candidates, intimacy requires monitoring and adjusting to multiple processes of growth, communication, development, and problem-solving throughout a lifetime. We want to maintain the marital love affair, the marital friendship, and have progressively more effortless repair of emotional ruptures and injuries. To do this we need to receive caring influence from our spouse, others, our self-observations, and the world.

Fixed mindsets resist influence—even caring influence designed to make them stronger, healthier, and happier. Growth mindsets embrace caring influence—any opportunity for progress is welcomed, and security isn't in appearing perfect, but rather in commitment to lifelong growth and progress.

EXERCISE: *Mindsets in lovers*

Imagine you are a woman with a new lover who is a fixed mindset guy— he can't be wrong about anything. He takes offense when you want to talk about him tuning you out sometimes, and easily goes into a shame/humiliation/rage cycle when he feels caught in a mistake. When you suggest ways of improving your relationship, he says, "Everything's perfect! Why do we have to change anything?" Write your feelings, thoughts, and judgments of yourself and him in this imagined relationship.

Now imagine yourself to be the same woman with a growth mindset guy who wants to grow and receive influence from you about a problem. You talk to him about tuning you out and he says, "You're right. I just turned into a jerk when I wouldn't listen to your side of the story about me spacing when you talk about your job. I want to do this better and I'll work on improving." Write your feelings, thoughts, and judgments of yourself and him in this imagined relationship.

Which guy is more attractive to you if you're a woman, or more admirable if you're a guy? Let's face it; the second guy has a growth mindset about getting better at listening to your side of the story, and a relationship with him is going to have a much higher probability of success and improvement!

EXERCISE: *Your areas of fixed and growth mindsets*

Observe and record how you respond to difficult situations over this coming week. You will probably find examples of both fixed and growth mindsets. Especially pay attention with your partner and children (if you have kids). If you're caught in a fixed mindset, reach for "Effort and progress is what I want," and set your intent to receive and act on caring influence from what's valid about the other's position. Record and share your insights with someone you trust (hopefully your partner), paying attention to what mindsets you enter and exit during the conversation. If you notice yourself shifting from a fixed mindset to a growth mindset in a stressed situation, congratulations! You just practiced the human super-power of accelerating your own evolution with focused action and intent, in service of principle, and driven by resolve.

Chapter 6

Attention

Wherever you are right now, look around. What do you see? A room, a window, a person? How do you feel about what you're experiencing? Interested, bored, indifferent? Now, direct your attention to some aspect of you that you're proud of—perhaps your dedication at work or your love for your children. How do you feel about yourself as you do this? Now, direct your attention to some aspect of you that is distressing or embarrassing. How do you feel about yourself as you do this?

How we direct attention actually determines the nature of the world we live in. Deliberately directing our attention utilizes circuits in our brains called the *executive attention network,* and most of us don't recognize directing attention as one of our human superpowers.

Let your gaze wander from where you are right now and notice what captures your attention. Let your gaze linger more than a second and notice that you might start to create a story about what you're looking at. I'm looking at a chart on my wall called "Trauma into Transcendence" and I'm creating a story of gathering my trauma materials together and writing a book called *Trauma into Transcendence.* We can't help creating stories about what we focus on; we just do it automatically because humans are the story-generating and story-telling species.

What is the neurobiology of attention? Our nervous systems receive hundreds of thousands of inputs every second, then *choose* seven (plus or minus two) items, and our brains turn these into a story with emotions, impulses, and perspectives. This is how our adaptive unconscious—what I call our Shadow self in my book *Shadow Light*— helps guide us through life.

Here's an example of a distorted, defensive story. I run into you at the store and, as we talk, I realize you've forgotten my name. I get distressed and conclude that since you forgot my name you don't like me. "Oh no! Maybe I'm not likable!" "Maybe you heard a bad story about me and think I'm a jerk!" (This is why you never want to let yourself fantasize about why someone might be upset with you!)

If I'm attuned to myself—observing feeling, thought, judgment, and desire with acceptance and caring intent—*I can direct my attention* to clean up my anxious paranoia. I can send my attention to compassionate understanding and change my anxious story into a prosocial story—you forgot my name because names are hard to remember, I think you're a nice person, and your non-verbals were all friendly toward me in the store, so it seems probable we like each other. I have *deliberately* directed my attention to use my story-making instincts to create a pro-you, pro-me, pro-us story.

Directing our attention toward choosing and cultivating what stories we feel best serve love is one of our best human superpowers.

Your state affects my state affects your state—mirror neurons and social intersubjective fields.

Say you call me for a therapy session and come into my office in emotional pain. I look into your eyes with love. You look back cautiously, but hopefully. If I project a trustable presence, you will open further to letting me help you. Perhaps your wife left, or your husband cheated, or your daughter died. No matter how horrible your state of pain, my state of compassionate attention helps at least somewhat. We resonate back and forth as we automatically seek coherence, unconscious to unconscious, Shadow to Shadow. This process is organized around our instincts to empathize and relate, which are supported by mirror neuron systems in our brains—mirror neurons being brain cells specifically dedicated to automatically recapitulating in us what we perceive to be another person's states and intentions.

In the above example, the powerful empathy process revolves around me directing compassionate attention at you, and you responding by receiving my warmth and concern.

We are social beings with exquisite sensitivity to social cues and incredible responsiveness to each other for better or worse. The good news is that we are genetically biased toward prosocial coherence when in the presence of another—we all basically want to share, be fair, and care for one another. The bad news is that when we feel threatened (either by another person or by our own traumatic memories or bad habits), we tend to direct our attention to real and imagined problems and negative destructive stories.

~~~~~~

EXERCISE: *Directing attention*

* *Look at your hands and attune to how you feel/think/judge/want.*

* *Allow your gaze to wander around the room and fix on some object. Attune to how you feel/think/judge/want.*

* *Widen your attention to the whole room and attune to how you feel/ think/judge/want.*

* *Send your attention to another place on earth. Where do you go? What do you feel/think/judge/want as you go there?*

* *Remember a moment from the last walk you took.*

* *Imagine yourself eating dinner tomorrow night.*

* *Fantasize yourself in a pleasurable place and attune to how you feel/ think/judge/want.*

* *Remember a time you did something generous and caring for another person.*

* *Direct your attention to your partner's desire to feel fulfilled in your friendship and love affair. How do you feel as you do this?*

Direct your attention to what you most dislike about your partner. How do you feel as you do this?

Notice the power you possess to direct your attention anywhere and anytime.

What do you conclude about yourself from this exercise?

Write about this and share it with someone you trust.

Directing attention is a superpower!

The fact that we control where to send our attention is amazing! We can use it any time! You can direct attention to compassionate understanding, to what you are grateful for, or proud of, to whom you love and what you love about them, to your strengths and how cool they are, or to your weaknesses and how you intend to improve (with a growth mindset!).

The more you consciously direct your attention to prosocial and compassionate directions, the more you develop the habit of using attention to support health and growth. The more you direct compassionate attention to understanding and dealing with your partner, the better your attunement and the more well-loved your partner is likely to feel.

I suggest you do this all the time!

Chapter 7

Habits of Attention

Brains never stop generating consciousness and relationships with self, others, and the world. We focus on something, we daydream, we night dream, we remember, we fantasize—consciousness is always doing something.

The executive attention network is us deliberately directing our attention, but brains also have habits of attention—places they instinctively go when not otherwise engaged. Two major categories of where attention naturally goes—instinctive attentional states—are attractor states and default modes.

Attractor states and our default mode

Close your eyes and just attune to what you're feeling and thinking. What images, sensations, memories, or judgments show up?

Think back to previous chapters in this book. What images, sensations, memories, or judgments show up?

States our brains naturally generate in certain situations (like thinking about past chapters of this book) are *attractor states,* and states that just show up when nothing much is going on are *default modes.*

Attractor states are where we naturally go in the presence of certain cues.

Attractor states are how you habitually think and feel when cued by different situations. When I see my wife, Becky, smile, I naturally feel warm and loving toward her. I don't *decide* to feel this way. It's an attractor state that naturally occurs when Becky smiles. I get irritated when I think about health insurance companies and American pharmaceutical companies. I don't decide to get pissed when reminded of these two exploitative American monopolies—it's an attractor state that shows up when I'm reminded of them. (I work at compassionate understanding of these industries with an effort-and-progress growth mindset, but it's hard slogging!) As you can see, attractor states can be way better (self-love, compassionate understanding), or way worse (self-loathing, contempt for others).

When our nervous systems read "safety," we tend to have attractor states of relaxed social engagement. When our nervous systems read "threat," we tend to have attractor states of defensiveness and distortion. As we'll see in chapters to come, these defensive states are major obstacles to love and happiness.

Default mode is like daydreaming

The default mode includes particular kinds of attractor states of where your consciousness goes when you are not particularly engaged in anything else. Woolgathering, daydreaming, spacing out—there are a lot of terms for the default mode—and in many ways our default mode determines how happy, satisfied, attuned, or uncomfortable we are at any given time.

Why are these default modes so super important? We spend up to 20 percent of our waking hours in default-mode daydreaming, and there are three major kinds of default mode: *positive constructive, negative dysphoric,* and *disorganized scattered.*

* **Positive constructive daydreaming** involves naturally considering relaxing and enjoyable memories, sensations, or anticipations, or happily solving problems that exist or may exist in our lives.

* **Negative dysphoric daydreaming** involves naturally going to unhappy feelings and distressing, shameful, or irritating thoughts, images, memories, or anticipations that can arise to torment us when

we're not doing something else. For example, people high in *rejection sensitivity bias,* being hyper-focused on social approvals and disapprovals, tend to be less happy, connected, healthy, and successful.

* **Disorganized scattered daydreaming** is chaotic and unfocused thinking, accompanied often by anxiety, depression, or confusion. Worrying about going to the dance, while wondering if your date likes you, while fearing you're unattractive, while feeling distress in your heart area, while trying not to think about it is one example.

You can see how, in relationships, we're going to have trouble if our default modes are negative dysphoric or disorganized scattered, and we're going to do better if our default modes are positive constructive.

Examples of positive and negative attractor states and default modes

A positive example of a healthy default mode is reflected in the sayings, "Life is good," and "I am the captain of my ship." You walk through the world feeling powerful and grateful. A negative example of an unhealthy default mode is, "Life sucks and I am a helpless victim." You walk through the world feeling weak and scared.

Positive attractor states are healthy states we naturally enter when cued by life events. Here are a few examples:

* You're a guy, see a beautiful woman, and go into zero-in-on-the-babe mode (this is positive if you and she aren't cheating on anyone).

* You're a mom, see a couple playing with their one-year-old, and go into zero-in-on-the-adorable-baby mode.

* You're a surfer, see a coastline, and go into zero-in-on-joyfully-checking-out-the-waves mode.

* Your husband or wife says, "I love you," and you feel warm and loving.

How can I train my executive attention network, attractor states, and default modes to be pro-growth, pro-social, pro-health, and pro-love?

The right hemisphere is the center for habits. It learns slowly.

The left hemisphere is the center for conscious attention. It can learn a new routine quickly, but usually needs multiple repetitions to turn the new behavior into a reflexive habit programmed deeply into the right hemisphere.

We can practice emotions or attitudes like gratitude, suspicion, loving kindness, or contempt, either when we're aimless/alone (which trains our default mode), or in particular situations (which creates attractor states).

Clearly we want to practice positive default modes and attractor states and replace negative ones with positive ones. We *especially* want to do this in our intimate relationships!

As you read the rest of this book, notice how almost every suggested exercise involves cultivating positive default modes and attractor states, while interrupting negative ones with attunement, compassionate understanding, and positive intent to transform them into positive states.

~~~~~~

EXERCISE: *Cultivating positive attention*

Observe and record where your attention goes throughout today and tomorrow, and write how you feel as it zeros in on self, people, objects, or processes. What habitual thoughts or impulses do you have during these moments? Which ones do you want to cultivate, and which ones do you want to change? Write them in you journal, and then share them with someone you trust. If you share with a romantic partner, share the good habits you are cultivating that involve that person, as well as the bad habits that you are working on replacing with those that are good. This is essentially telling your partner, "I intend to put in regular efforts to love you better."

Chapter 8

Integrating the Big Picture

We started this "Big Picture" section with the Five Stars. Have you continued to ask yourself the questions about others and yourself or have you stopped asking?

If you've stopped, are you willing to start consciously noticing the Five Stars again? If not, why not? Write your answers in your journal.

Promising to change can be a two-edged sword!

Be careful about resolving to improve, and then procrastinating or forgetting your way out of your resolves.

I once worked with a man named Benny who kept promising his wife, Emily, he would change. He would follow through, he'd get a job, he'd stop drinking, he'd start working out, he'd buy the decorations for the party—and then he'd procrastinate and rarely follow through. Eventually Emily started to despise him, and they eventually divorced. When you make commitments and consistently blow them off, there are consequences!

EXERCISE: *Keeping yourself on track*

Review your journal entries and experiences from Chapters 1 through 7. What aspects of the material were most useful to you? Record your insights.

What strengths did you discover about yourself? Record your insights.

What weaknesses/vulnerabilities/areas-that-need-attention did you discover? Record your insights.

What ideas do you have at this moment about what to do to improve weak areas and celebrate your strengths? Growth mindset, effort, and progress is the standard to reach for. Record your insights.

Share these with your partner. Try reading them every day for two weeks, absorbing your insights, learning from your victories and vulnerabilities, and making efforts to change your habits and train your brain to love yourself and others better.

THE FIRST STAR

. . . .

Is there erotic polarity, a spark of attraction, between me and this other person?

The reason erotic polarity is the First Star is that almost all intimate partner relationships involve a love affair, often from the very beginning.

After survival, lust and sex are primary drives. Since the number-one guiding purpose of our genes is to reproduce themselves, we have multiple sex-related drives, all pushing us to find a suitable mate and make babies now!

Who I'm attracted to, how I position myself in social hierarchies, what my gender orientation is, who I trust, how jealous I get when my partner relates to others, and how far I fall if I lose my mate are all intertwined with erotic polarity.

In this part of the book, I'll define erotic polarity, talk extensively about masculine and feminine aspects and essence, and explore men's and women's sexual arousal systems—similar, but also wildly different in significant ways.

I'll discuss secret affairs, why to not have them, and what to do if you or your partner gets tangled up in one.

Throughout this part, I encourage you to keep looking for yourself and your partner in all the perspectives. I've never found two people to have exactly the same sexual or relational wiring, and so it behooves us to be curious about exactly who we and our partners are when it comes to erotic polarity, sexuality, arousal, and all the sexual drives like lust, romantic infatuation, intimate bonding, and jealousy.

Chapter 9

Masculine/Feminine Aspects and Essence

When a man's sperm penetrates a woman's egg and fertilizes it, a little electromagnetic field comes into existence. This field expands and continues until death. At the moment of fertilization—when that electromagnetic field associated with *this* unique being comes into existence—gender is established, though you would need genetic analysis to determine whether that little being will grow to be a boy or a girl.

At eight weeks, an enzyme is released in a female fetus that makes her brain immune to estrogen. This enzyme is absent in a boy fetus. Weirdly, estrogen then *masculinizes* the little boy's brain (evolution works in mysterious ways) and from then on, boys and girls are *different*.

This is not cultural, though culture will have a lot to do with how boys and girls self-identify and grow. Boys and girls are hard-wired to be different morally, motivationally, in stress responses, in competition and aggression, sexually, parentally, socially, and neurobiologically.

For instance, check out the following excerpt from an article by Hailey Branson-Potts from the *Los Angeles Times* on September 19, 2017:

A Yuba County strip club, feeling particularly philanthropic, used its abundant assets—topless ladies—in a weekend carwash to raise money for two sheriff's deputies who were in injured in a shootout at a Rastafarian pot farm last month.

The police were actually at the farm *protecting* the Rastafarians from a crazy employee who started pulling up plants and waving a gun around. Besides just reflecting how much the world has changed since the fifties when I was a boy, the point I'm making is that we all are making endless gender assumptions about the masculine and feminine characters in this story. The strippers might have been guys, but they weren't. The cops might have been mostly women, but that's statistically unlikely in Yuba City, where the preponderance of police officers are male. It's a sweet story that the strippers did a topless carwash for the cops, but it would be a weird story if the cops did a topless carwash for the strippers.

Men and women, masculine and feminine, are *different*.

Of course, our similarities outweigh our differences. After all, we men and women are first and fundamentally *human*. But, that being said, more masculine humans are different from more feminine humans, and this usually tracks through male and female (with lots of room for LBGTQ variations).

To maintain the delicate and powerful container of the marriage, partners need to attend to the marital friendship, the marital love affair, and make efficient repair of injuries. The marital love affair at its most fundamental level runs off the energetic dynamic of one partner's masculine sparking with the other partner's feminine.

You're a 28-year-old heterosexual guy who walks into a party. After you greet the host, you look at the crowd of thirty or forty men and women. First of all, unless you are truly bisexual (a rare orientation where you can be in a bonded sexual relationship with both men and women—more common in women than in men), you are going to relate differently to the attractive women than the attractive men. They will *feel* different to you. Some of them will attract you, more or less. On which women do you fix your attention, and why *this one,* and not *that one?*

You're a 28-year-old heterosexual woman who walks into a party and checks out the crowd. Once again, you are going to relate differently to the attractive men than the attractive women—they will *feel* different. You're sitting with a friend and three guys are glancing at *you* from different parts of the room. You like the attention of one guy, dislike the attention of another guy, and only notice the third when your friend points him out. What is it about these guys that resulted in your different reactions?

This doesn't just happen at parties. It happens all the time and it has *eroticism* in it.

Masculine and feminine aspects and essence

All of us have masculine and feminine traits or aspects, but, especially in the sexual occasion, we are usually more masculine or more feminine—which usually tracks through male and female.[1]

Let's start with sex. Sex is like dancing, where there is usually a leader and a follower. Just like dancing, the lovemaking leader is often the guy, while the follower is often the woman.

Masculine presence

In general, the masculine is more frequently the leader in a sexual encounter, directing the process of lovemaking toward deeper pleasure in his lover and generally being turned on by her progressive arousal. A common complaint I've heard numerous times from guys in sexually conflicted relationships is, "She doesn't seem to enjoy sex that much!" Similarly, when I've said to men or couples over the years, "The masculine gets off on his feminine partner's pleasure expressed through movement, breath, and sound," the guys have responded with variations of, "Yes! That's exactly right! It turns me on when I can see that she's turned on."

Trustable masculine presence amplifies erotic polarity with a feminine partner. Masculine presence in relationships involves an attuned, confident man, solidly committed to his principles and integrity, aware of his surroundings, and focused in a supportive, non-anxious way on his feminine partner, communicating to her verbally and non-verbally, "I know you deeply and want you." This form of attention tends to relax and open more feminine people to pleasure through the body—it *feels* good.

Feminine radiance

In general, the feminine is the follower in the sexual occasion, allowing herself to relax into deeper pleasure (experienced as erotic radiance by the masculine) as her lover offers trustable intimate attention and direction. Common complaints I've heard from women over the years are, "He's not connected," and, "He's not attuned to me when we make love." When I've suggested to women that they yearn for their guys to be more trustable, present, confident, and attuned to directing them into deeper pleasure, I often get back some version of, "Yes! I love it when he's confident, into me, and guiding us into a good time!"

Feminine radiance attracts and nourishes the masculine. Feminine radiance in relationships is women feeling love and pleasure through their bodies. Women who feel full and happy tend to radiate what literally feels like light to masculine people. President Clinton said Monica Lewinsky "lit up the room," when describing his attraction toward her.

A central feature of solid erotic polarity in relationships are feminine partners *contracting* when their masculine partner acts badly or collapses into less than his best self, and *expanding* into love through the body when he's being present and his best self. This love through the body is expressed through expression, movement, breath, and sound.

Erotic intersections

Every man will have an array of specific forms of feminine radiance that most turn him on with his feminine partner—like smiles, lingerie, affectionate touch, or intimate conversation. Every woman will have an array of specific forms of masculine presence that most turn her on with her masculine partner—like confident touch, loving expressions, gifts, focused attention, special events, or anticipating her needs.

Consciously supporting the erotic polarity in your love affair means being alert to the intersections between what most lights up your partner or what shuts them down. This helps you cultivate what is mildly to strongly pleasurable for you to provide, while always working on reducing what shuts your partner down. Two partners alert to the erotic polarities of their relationship are always adjusting these forces to improve their erotic polarity. This is an especially crucial activity during the intimate bonding stage that often arrives after romantic infatuation, when sexual urgency diminishes and defensive patterns are more likely to emerge.

The loss of erotic polarity during intimate bonding is one of the main complaints of couples entering therapy. I've found many men and women to be shocked at the idea that erotic polarity is a *responsibility*. This responsibility can (and should!) be consciously taken on and improved by knowledge of masculine/feminine aspects/essence, along with the principles of masculine presence and feminine radiance.

I often tell couples who understand Eastern practices and thought, "Masculine and feminine practice, as well as erotic polarity, are yogas that we can and should include in our daily and weekly routines."

Wait! I like both!

At this point lots of people say, "Well, I like both masculine and feminine! I like to lead *and* follow." To which I respond, "Of course! Me too! We all have both masculine and feminine aspects. I love being the follower in sex, but I'm mostly the leader."

I often go on and ask, "If you made love a hundred times in *exactly the way you wanted*, how many of those times would you be the follower or the leader? If you'd be the leader more than the follower, you almost certainly have a more masculine sexual *essence*. If you'd be the follower more than the leader, you almost certainly have a more feminine sexual *essence*.

Interestingly, the most universal sexual fantasy—present in straight, gay, bi-, and trans- relationships—is the dominance/submissive fantasy: essentially leader/follower.[2]

~~~~~~

EXERCISE: *Sexual essence and erotic polarity*

I invite you to participate in the following experiment. Remember the last time you had hot sex with another person. Who was your partner, and what were you feeling for that person? What was the environment? How did your partner act to support the passionate encounter? What did you contribute to this passionate encounter? Write about all this in your journal.

Now read what you've written. Probably one of you was in a more a trustable presence, feeling into your partner, opening him or her with pleasure, and hungering to penetrate and release into ecstatic explosion and then sweet emptiness. Probably one of you was more relaxing to trustable direction, opening and expressing love through your body, voice, and movement; yearning for fullness; and feeling trust and devotional love for your partner.

Discuss what you've observed and discovered in this exercise with your partner, and then write about the conversation. Be curious and respectful about your partner's insights about his or her masculine/feminine essence/ aspects and how you two create and sustain polarity together.

Don't worry if the conversation creates conflict! If you two can't productively discuss this material after several attempts, find a therapist you both like to process it with you.

Some version of leader/follower seems to fit most hot sexual encounters. These are the two poles of an energetic polarity that lasers back and forth, creating progressively more energy, until there is release and resolution, often with orgasms. Spiritual teacher and relationship expert David Deida calls these poles the masculine and feminine, and teaches how understanding and enhancing the polarity between them supports personal meaning and fulfillment, relational health, passionate sexuality, and spiritual growth.[3]

Masculine types of people tend to suffer when they are not true to their deepest masculine needs, purpose, and responsibilities, and this can inhibit satisfying polarities with feminine partners.

Feminine types of people tend to suffer when they are not true to their feminine heart, which can compromise satisfying polarities with masculine partners.

We all have both masculine and feminine aspects in us.

A wide open, non-conflicted individual can fully inhabit any point on the masculine/feminine continuum. This continuum ranges from deepest, ever-present witness consciousness on the extreme masculine pole (the unchanging "I" that remains subjectively the same from birth to death), to being fully in the flow of life, love, change, nature, and sensation on the extreme feminine pole.

A more masculine person, when fully relaxed and open, will more frequently inhabit the masculine side of this continuum. A more feminine person, when fully relaxed and open, will more frequently inhabit the feminine side of this continuum. Men and women can be either more masculine or more feminine in their deepest essences, and masculine and feminine people usually have areas of their lives where they need to activate their non-dominant side.

One example could be a man who is hard driving, on a mission, and goal-oriented at work, but sexually prefers to more often be the "bottom" where he receives direction, opens with pleasure to a trustable presence, and expresses devotional love through his body.

Another example could be a stay-at-home mother who enjoys being a radiant wellspring of love, who is opened erotically farther than she can open herself by a trustable man, but also has to animate her goal-oriented, hierarchical, structured masculine self to organize her household, get her children to school and appointments consistently, and engage in disciplined self-care in exercise, diet, medical treatment, and social organization.

We want *harmony* with our masculine/feminine aspects, not *balance*.

There often is a fallacious assumption that we want "balance" between our masculine and feminine aspects, as if we are optimally 50/50. This is not consistent with biology, evolutionary drives, or our native eroticism, so *let's just let the balance thing go!*

What works best is to be a healthy version of whoever we uniquely are! There is a reason why "type" is one of the core dimensions of the Integral metatheory for maximum understanding of the universe (along with quadrants—subjective and objective understanding of individuals and groups—developmental lines and levels, and states of consciousness). Human consciousness creates endless diversity and variations in all forms of being human—body, love, work, family, sexuality, meaning, spirituality, community, etc. In previous eras when we had to conform to cultural standards or risk persecution (which includes most cultures before the twenty-first century and even many now), people had to suppress, repress, or hide their differences from what they believed were cultural norms. Sexually, we've all seen this through our lifetimes—gay or trans- people persecuted, women discriminated against, non-traditional sexual relationships vilified, childhood sexuality denied, and sex education hijacked by religious fundamentalism.

I was speaking to a group of 300 Brazilians near Sintra, Portugal, in April 2017, and asked for a show of hands of anyone who felt normal sexually. Only a handful of hands were raised! Most of us assume intuitively we don't perfectly match what we believe are cultural sexual norms.

Today in post-modern society, individual sexual differences are more acknowledged, normalized, and often supported. This gives us the potential to deeply explore and accept our own and our partner's unique sexual aspects and essence. A fulfilling marital love affair now can become more practical and less formulaic—less morally constrained, and more focused on shared pleasure and fulfillment by two unique individuals looking to understand their sexual essences and aspects and maximize satisfying erotic polarity.

Masculine and feminine are lines of development as well as types of individuals.

Masculine and feminine types develop similarly, but differently, and thus, in my opinion, constitute different lines of development as well as types of person.

Carol Gilligan has shown that, morally, women develop from selfish, to care, to universal care, to both universal care and universal rights, while men develop from selfish, to rights, to universal rights, to both universal rights and universal care.[4]

David Deida has observed how a man can develop relationally from first stage macho jerk (who, egocentrically, is mostly in relationships to gratify his own needs), to second stage 50/50 egalitarian flow boy (often sexually tepid, dedicated to pleasure in the moment, unwilling to commit too deeply, but sold on the idea of fairness and clear communication), to third stage presence (serving his deepest purpose, his feminine partner, and the world in each moment as best he can).

Similarly, Deida has observed how a woman can develop from first-stage radiance for egocentric strokes, to second stage 50/50 egalitarian career girl (often sexually tepid, not relying on a man, and considering fairness and clear communication the answer to most relationship problems), to third-stage erotic radiance, devotional love, and free flow of emotion (giving her best gifts of radiant love to the world).[5]

Since we have both masculine and feminine aspects in each of us, both masculine and feminine lines develop in each person to some extent throughout life. This echoes Carl Jung's conviction that human adult development, or "individuation," involves the gradual integration of animus (the masculine), anima (the feminine), and Shadow (all those constructive and destructive parts of us we're not consciously aware of such as our violent selves, selfish selves, irrational selves, altruistic selves, or transcendent selves).[6]

POLARITY

✳ MASCULINE

- ◆ Trustable presence
- ◆ Deep soul's purpose
- ◆ True to principles
- ◆ Deepening consciousness
- ◆ Penetrating
- ◆ Seeks emptiness
- ◆ Drawn to feminine light

✳ FEMININE

- ◆ Trusting, devotional love
- ◆ Wellspring of love
- ◆ Love through the body
- ◆ Clear channel of emotion
- ◆ Opening, yearning
- ◆ Seeks fullness
- ◆ Wants to be seen as light—drawn to masculine presence

HOT SEX

✳ DEEPENING SPIRITUALITY

- ◆ His mission to open her to pleasure, love, deeper spirituality
- ◆ Un-recoiling in the face of anything

- ◆ Resolute acceptance of death

- ◆ Open me farther than I can open myself

- ◆ Show pleasure in his integrity

- ◆ Show suffering in his collapse

As you look at the polarity chart, which side do you most identify with *in the sexual occasion?* That probably reflects your deepest sexual essence. The items on the other side that you identify with probably reflect your masculine or feminine aspects.

Hot sex is usually the outcome of two partners supporting erotic polarity by embracing and fully inhabiting the various aspects of their masculine/feminine types and maintaining erotic tension between masculine and feminine. People can shift from masculine to feminine poles in life and in lovemaking. In lovemaking, as long as both partners are artfully inhabiting complementary poles, erotic polarity is maintained and enhanced.

~~~~~~

EXERCISE: *Sexual aspects*

If your deepest sexual essence is more masculine, what parts of you are more feminine, reflecting your feminine aspects? Write about these in your journal.

If your deepest sexual essence is more feminine, what parts of you reflect your more masculine aspects? Write about these in your journal.

Share this with someone you trust while attuning to yourself. What emotions do you experience as you talk? Intimacy? Love? Shame? Guilt? Excitement? Arousal? Irritation? Joy?

Write any observations and insights from your conversation in your journal. Share them with your partner or someone else your trust, and then write about your conversation.

Chapter 10

Erotic Polarities

We naturally create *energetic* polarities with other people, creatures, objects, or even ideas. If I look at a baby, I usually feel loving and protective, and these feelings intensify if the baby smiles at me, amplifying the energetic exchange.

If I encounter an attractive woman, I project my interest either obviously or subtly, she responds in some fashion, and there is an erotic quality to the energetic exchange (at least to me, but, since communication tends to be reciprocal, often from her also if my attention feels clean and healthy to her). This is an *erotic* polarity. Often it doesn't *feel* sexual, but there is a different quality to the "we space"—the *intersubjectivity*—between me and an opposite-sexual-essence person and a same-sexual-essence person. Masculine and feminine people create erotic polarities whenever they're around each other—and they can manage them way better or way worse.

For example: Allan and Dorothy come to a therapy session lamenting, "We never have sex."

I ask, "Do you ever talk about sex?"

Alan answers, "Hardly ever. It always devolves into fighting and feeling bad."

I go on, "When do you feel sexual sparks between you?"

Dorothy looks a little spacey as I ask this question, but she speaks from her feminine heart, "I don't know. It just happens sometimes," as Allan nods.

Allan and Dorothy have little conscious access to erotic polarity—sometimes it happens, sometimes it doesn't, and they either fight or get dissociated and spacey when they try to talk about it.

~~~~~~

EXERCISE: *Polarity*

When was the last time you looked at someone with desire? How did you know you were titillated? What did you feel in your body? What did you think? What was it about this person that did it for you? Write about this episode in your journal and attune to how you're feeling, thinking, judging, and wanting as you write.

Visual vs relational desire

Guys tend to be more visual/erotic, so, if you're a guy, it was probably a woman or an image of a woman that sparked your desire.

Women tend to be more relational, but also are visual. If you're a woman, when was the last time you felt that pleasure of, "He's an attractive guy. Yum!"?[7] Becky walked into me watching *Hell or High Water,* saw the Chris Pine character driving a truck down a country road, and immediately said, "He's cute!"

These are *erotic polarities* and, if someone encourages your attention, that's a *mutually reinforcing* erotic polarity, *which accelerates super-fast!* We're talking freight trains here! If Becky was magically transported into Chris Pine's truck, and he was present and interested, she and he would unconsciously start talking themselves into a sexual encounter *now.* They might not do it, but the flirtation would accelerate *quickly.*

This is innocent! We have lots of drives associated with sex.

* Lust is the simplest—an attractive other is around and we start talking ourselves into them as a sexual partner (either real or imagined).

* Romantic infatuation is more complicated—we fixate on one person to the exclusion of others for the six-month to two- or three-year romantic infatuation joyride.

* Jealousy is another sex-related drive—someone is interested in our partner and we want to drive them away and protect our territory. Over 25 percent of the murders in the U.S. involve love triangles!

* Infidelity is a sex-related drive. Yes, unfortunately we have the drive to cheat on our spouse with another attractive other if we have the opportunity—opportunity is the number-one cause of secret affairs.[8]

Sexual polarities are different from the energetic polarities we experience with everyone and everything else. We have energetic relationships—polarities—with people, ourselves, nature, the world, and the universe. Any connection with people and objects has an energetic component. When that component is informed by our sexual aspects/essence and is *erotic,* there are sparks of erotic polarity between masculine and feminine energies.

We're sometimes trained by sexually repressive aspects of our culture to dissociate from awareness of erotic polarities, like Dorothy in the previous example, who spaced out when I asked her when she felt sexually charged with Allen. These *dissociated responses* can cause unexpected results, both positive and negative.

How can a dissociated response be positive?

Sometimes a dissociated response can turn out to be healthy! Healthy results of dissociated erotic polarity might be enjoyable attractions, enlivening flirtations, or virtuous love affairs surprising us as we move through our life. For instance, a woman with whom I worked attended a business meeting with a male colleague. They shared a taxi home, and she liked him a lot. She kissed him lightly on the cheek before she got out. He was so staggered by the wave of desire that rushed through him that he couldn't get out of the taxi to see her to her door. This turned into an outstanding love affair that benefitted both of them enormously.

How can a dissociated response be negative?

It's often risky not to be aware of what's happening or what we're doing, and dissociated erotic polarity can result in a lot of negative consequences. Distressing flirtations (to one or both people), distracting attractions that harm other relationships, sexual harassment experiences, or devastating secret affairs are all examples of dissociated erotic polarity run amuck. A woman I worked with liked her boss, enjoyed his company, and helped him out for several months on a particularly challenging case. One night, after a brief was finally filed, they looked in each other's eyes and found the other irresistibly attractive. Both were married with children and chaos ensued.

In general, less dissociation and more presence is better!

Encouraging news: Out of twenty-nine countries, the U.S. was number two in sexual satisfaction (following Austria, with poor Japan and Taiwan coming in last). This suggests that the U.S. is getting less dissociated with sex as we speak.

Discouraging news: Out of twenty-six countries followed over the last thirty years, seventeen of them have increased happiness levels—but not the U.S. Also, the U.S. has the highest divorce rate in the world. So, it appears that, on balance, the U.S. has become more miserable and more divorced through the dawning of the twenty-first century!

Masculine presence

In general, a man who is centered, confident, unafraid, attuned to himself and whoever is around him, and resolved in his current purpose is *present*.

When a present masculine person turns his attention on a feminine person with interest, appreciation, and no shame or fear, it tends to increase the erotic polarity between them. Some men are very good at this. Paul Newman in his time, Brad Pitt, Justin Timberlake, and Ryan Gosling are famously good at this. If a man is particularly present with a woman, it can be pleasurable, but also disorienting.

Back in the 1990s, a woman walked into an ice cream store in New England one day and ordered a couple of scoops on a cone. As it was handed to her, she noticed that the man standing next to her was Paul Newman, who was relaxed, friendly, and present. He made polite conversation as she paid, thrilling her no end. When she turned to leave, she realized that she was no longer holding her ice cream cone. As she looked about in confusion, Paul Newman smiled at her and said, "You put it in your purse."

Feminine radiance

When a feminine person feels full and happy, there is a kind of light that emanates from her. This is *feminine radiance*. If she is current in her emotion—emotionally attuned to now—and feeling love through her body, her feminine radiance naturally attracts the masculine and amplifies erotic polarity. This is especially true if she's happy.[9] Like masculine presence, some women are particularly good at this.

Back in the late 1980s, I was getting out of my car at the beach to go take a run, when a beautiful woman I casually knew named Cheryl saw me and said "hi" in the parking lot. She was especially happy and radiant that afternoon, and I could feel our polarity intensifying, which was somewhat disorienting. I tried to stay present and appropriate but, as I was putting my wallet in the trunk, I threw my keys in after my wallet and shut the hood, locking myself out of the car. I had to call a taxi to take me home.

~~~~~~

EXERCISE: *Sexual attractions and repulsions*

Observe and record in your journal your sexual attractions and repulsions as you go about your day. Can you intentionally intensify or reduce the energetic polarity if you focus on it? Try it a few times and write about your efforts in your journal.

As you describe these polarities, what does it tell you about you and your sexuality? Write your insights.

Try sharing this with someone you trust.

Is the person you share with someone with whom you have sexual polarity with, or someone with whom you have no sexual polarity?

If you're sharing with your partner, are you able to have a conversation that feels safe and supportive, or does it trigger conflict? If you can't resolve conflict that arises, find a therapist to help you both.

Are there people you wouldn't want to share these erotic polarity journal entries with, and why not? Write about that—who they are and why you wouldn't trust them with this information about you.

Write about all this is your journal, looking for insights about how you are programmed, and share everything with someone you trust.

~~~~~~

EXERCISE: *Adjusting your erotic polarities*

If you're a woman, and a guy is extra friendly and touchy, you can pull back physically and psychologically to create a feeling of more distance, or you can lean in, look into his eyes, smile, use his name, and open your heart to create more erotic charge.

If you're a man, and a woman is extra smiley and touchy, you can adjust your expression, body, and energy to be more reserved, or you can address her by name, compliment her expression and outfit, smile, lean in, and radiate approval and presence to increase the polarity.

If you smile, make eye contact, casually touch, address someone by name, and generate warmth at another person, it tends to intensify your erotic polarity.

These capacities get more refined and robust with conscious practice.

In the week ahead, try noticing and adjusting erotic polarities to serve the highest good—so you and others feel pleased by your giving and receiving of attraction, rather than distressed or intruded upon. Write what you discover and share with somebody you trust.

Conscious polarity

In my book, *Integral Mindfulness: from Clueless to Dialed-In,* I maintain that being attuned and organized to serve the highest good is being *dialed-in.* With polarity, awareness of my and your sexual aspects/essence and the polarities between them gives me opportunities to adjust them to serve the highest good for you, me, and everybody. This is critical in loving relationships because we want to maintain and enhance erotic polarities with our chosen partner, and moderate the ones with others to help people feel attractive and seen, instead of uncomfortable and intruded upon.

Author Gary Chapman, in his best-selling book, *The Five Love Languages*, suggests that people are wired to be lit up by different love languages—gift giving, quality time, words of affirmation, acts of service, and physical touch.[10] If you and your partner rank order your top five favorite ways of feeling loved, they'll probably include variations of these themes. Also, you two probably won't have the same lists or the same order of importance in your lists. This is important because we tend to assume that our partner *knows* what we like best, and assume *we* know what he or she likes best. Sometimes we do, and sometimes we don't, and the best way to find out is to have a fun conversation!

EXERCISE: *Couples favorites*

Sit down with your partner and ask him or her a series of questions about his or her favorite movie, flower, activity, tree, place, form of caress, book, etc. Listen with interest to his or her answer and then answer the question yourself. Comment on what you knew and didn't know about these preferences.

Encourage your partner to do the same; ask you about your favorites and then listening with interest.

After you do this for a while, monitor how you're feeling between you, the quality of your intersubjectivity. Comment on it to your partner and write about it in your journal.

Erotic polarity needs conscious attention.

Erotic polarity needs conscious attention in long-term relationships because romantic infatuation fades after six months to a few years. Some of this is habituation, where we normalize what we routinely experience, including loving contact. Probably more significantly, in the ancient tribes, it would not serve the tribe to have two individuals crazy intoxicated with each other all their lives. Whatever the genetic roots, we are wired to have falling in love transform into intimate bonding. This intimacy makes us feel like our family of origin did when we were growing up, but is less erotically urgent.[11]

If you are the more masculine partner, conscious attention to polarity involves consistently mobilizing your focus and presence so that your feminine partner feels consistently known, claimed, and opened by your trustable attention.

If you are the more feminine partner, conscious attention to polarity first involves consistently cultivating love, pleasure, and fullness in your heart and body. A happy, full, feminine person is radiant, and masculine people feel this literally as warmth and light. Feeling your love, you can offer it to your partner with love when he's being his best self through comments (such as "I love you right now!"), but more importantly through movement, breath, and sound anchored in attunement and current emotion, not past traumas or distress. A caress on his arm, a warm smile, an appreciative nod when he's being excellent, or a loving hug when he walks in the door are all examples of this.

Erotic polarity is a resource in a long-term relationship that requires cultivation and attention, especially when aging, children, crises, work, and life problems seem to conspire to demand our time and distract us from self-care and care for our partner.

Just monitoring your erotic polarity with a partner regulates it and enhances it *if your conscious purpose is to establish and maintain erotic polarity.* Conscious intent is a big deal! This once again reflects a core human superpower: that focused intent and action, in service of principle, and driven by resolve can create miracles in every arena, including erotic polarity.

Promoters and resisters

Often in couples there will be one partner who wants sex more frequently or more urgently—the *promoter*—and a partner who's satisfied with less frequency, makes fewer overtures, and habitually chooses other activities over sex—the *resister.*

The promoter/resister dynamic becomes amplified as couples pass from sexually charged romantic infatuation into more everyday life intimate bonding. It is especially evident after women give birth and care for babies, where husbands find wives more attractive than ever, while fatigue, responsibilities of nursing and infant care, and hormonal shifts tend to make women less interested in sex.[12]

Renowned psychologist John Gottman's research on couples yielded an interesting fact about sexual fulfillment. Couples where one partner said "No" to an overture for sex and the other responded with love (not neutrality, hurt, or criticism) tended to report mutual sexual satisfaction where they both experienced their marriage having "plenty of sex."[13]

I think this statistic is the tip of an iceberg, revealing other complex dynamics below the surface. I've observed with many couples that if a promoter can gladly hear a "no," it generally reflects confidence that sex is available and will happen soon. In other words, both partners are consciously committed to mutual sexual fulfillment. This could somewhat explain other research on happy couples where two thirds of the women and one third of the men reported having sex when they didn't feel like it because they knew it was good for their relationship.[14]

An interesting sidebar on promoters and resisters in gay relationships is that in one set of studies lesbian partners both thought they resisted sex more than their partner, while gay male partners both believed they initiated sex more than their partner.[15]

~~~~~~

EXERCISE: *Maintaining erotic polarity in couples*

I suggest you notice the things you do that seem to warm your partner and make him or her feel cozy, sexy, or affectionate. Smiles, casual touches, sexy jokes, clothes they like to see you in, sexual favors, words they like to hear, and caring actions are all examples. I suggest you write these in your journal in as much detail as possible.

Now think of the things you do that drive your partner away or shut him or her down. Write those in detail in your journal.

Receiving love is just as important as offering love! Write your favorite ways of receiving love from your partner in as much detail as possible.

On the other hand, what are the things your partner does that drive you away or shut you down? Write these down in your journal in detail.

Share everything you wrote with your partner and write about your conversation. If this conversation doesn't help you feel closer and a little sexier, have another conversation, and, if that one doesn't, make an appointment with a good couples therapist to help you two use this material to maintain erotic polarity and love each other better.

Chapter 11

Relationship Stages and the Pair Bond

We are *driven* to relate! Over sixty-five million years of evolution guiding mammals to hunger for security in kinship groups, five million years of humans seeking a pair bond with a special man or woman, and biological mandates to care for children—especially *our* children—are all genetic imperatives manifested in our instincts to relate. These are primal, primitive, urgent drives, and to have happy healthy lives and good relationships, we need to take our drives seriously!

Humans are unique.

Why are we wired this way? Why are human women *the only mammals* who are biologically sexually receptive 100 percent of the time?[16] (Please don't give me a hard time about this! Every woman I know is *absolutely* not sexually receptive 100 percent of the time, but *as a species* there is no time where women are biologically not able to have arousal and orgasm.) Why do humans have infinitely more variations on the themes of relationship, sexuality, and family than any other species? Why has the pair bond evolved into the modern marriage—the most conditional and powerful love that the world has ever seen?

Five million years ago on the savannahs of Africa, our ancestors came down out of the trees, and women lost the capacity to easily carry their infants and toddlers on their backs and jump onto the nearest branch when danger threatened. A woman who had a male focused *exclusively* on protecting her and her children had a huge survival advantage, and so the *pair bond* evolved in humans, where attraction leads to lust, lust leads to falling in love with a particular person, and falling in love leads to children and family. The pair bond gave such an advantage that every human on the planet is now programmed to seek it.[17]

The pair bond is created and anchored by instinctual drives—the most prominent ones being lust, romantic infatuation (falling in love), intimate bonding into a nuclear family, jealousy (where we automatically protect our territory and attack rivals), and desire to cheat when possible (to extend our genome and create insurance that I will have a mate if my partner is lost through injury or desertion). All of these drives involve sexuality in one way or another. As humans have evolved physically and socially, so has the pair bond evolved into its current most powerful and fragile form—the modern marriage.

The modern marriage is conditional love.

The modern marriage is powerful because an egalitarian union between two educated, self-aware partners with equal power in sex, money, child rearing, and social engagement can accelerate each partner's personal and relational evolution. This occurs through giving and receiving loving influence and synergistically combining the forces of two autonomous but connected adults in dealing with the incredible challenges of life in the twenty-first century.

The modern marriage is fragile, because to establish and maintain the marital friendship and love affair, and to effectively repair the inevitable injuries and ruptures to the relationship, partners need to cultivate transparency, authenticity, and fidelity, and be committed to both growth and receiving caring influence throughout a lifetime. This requires *extraordinary* vulnerability, trust, and emotional sensitivity. A five-minute tirade can break trust and create doubt about emotional safety for days, weeks, months, or *years*. One secret affair, even a one-night stand, can destroy an established relationship (and does in 30 percent of secret affairs).[18]

Take the opportunity now to explore more deeply these instincts, and how you are currently managing your lust, romantic infatuation, intimate bonding, jealousy, and cheating drives.

Lust

When is the last time you wanted sexual contact, right now, with someone? It might have been seeing or relating with an attractive person, before or after a kiss, caress, or lovemaking session, or just a random impulse seemingly arising from nowhere. Write about this in detail in your journal.

This sexual-energy-demanding-erotic-action is *lust*—a powerful and somewhat impersonal drive.

How demanding? Some studies show men in their twenties thinking about sex every five minutes. Romance novels (mostly read by women) are the best-selling fiction genre in the country.

How impersonal? Just the sight of an abstract female figure on a wall can elicit a lust reaction in a man. Almost any woman will feel a physical reaction to a present, powerful, and trustable man focusing on her *right now* with appreciation and desire. That reaction might not subjectively feel like lust—it might feel like discomfort, or lively awareness, or warmth—but lust circuits in her brain and body are activated.

Write about your associations with the word "lust." Are they positive or negative? Does lust feel good or bad? If it varies, when do you believe it to be appropriate and beneficial to feel lust, and when is it inappropriate and harmful? Does how you respond to the experience of lust (approaching another, avoiding another, initiating sex, masturbating, etc.) determine how good or bad the idea of lust feels? Write about this in your journal.

Romanic infatuation

Have you ever been in love with another person—smitten? You probably have! And, as we all know, romantic infatuation rises and falls and hardly ever stays forever. In one study, 90 percent of the respondents had fallen in love, had dumped a lover, and had been dumped by a lover in their lives.[19] Romantic infatuation arises in all cultures. Falling in love, careening through the romantic infatuation joyride, and dealing with its inevitable fading after six months to a few years appears central to the human experience.

EXERCISE: *In love*

Imagine a particularly intense moment when you were looking at someone you were in love with from across a table, on a walk with, talking to on the phone, or in bed with. Write about this in detail.

Read over what you've written. Did you feel energized, sexually charged, focused on this person—even obsessed? Did you want to know about him or her and reveal yourself deeply in turn? Were you jealous thinking that someone else may be interested in your lover? Did you notice his or her faults, but not care that much about them? That's romantic infatuation. It has lust in it, but it is bigger than lust—it involves a particular person that you want to know better, to reveal yourself to, to be as close to as you can.

Lust map plus love map equals romance!

If someone sparks our *lust map*—our personal wiring for what potential lovers are sexually attractive—we want to pursue them or be pursued by them sexually. If someone sparks our *love map*—our personal wiring for who we are in a relationship, and what kind of partner we'd like to be intimately involved with—we can get more interested and involved until romantic infatuation circuits are activated and we fall in love. Romantic infatuation typically lasts anywhere from a few months to a few years and then often transmutes into intimate bonding—less urgent but more reminiscent of family-of-origin closeness.

EXERCISE: *Intimate bonding*

If you've had the experience of falling in love and then having the urgency fade as you became more familiar and habituated to your partner, write about it in detail in your journal. What happened as romantic infatuation ebbed? Did you put more conscious energy into maintaining your friendship and love affair? Did you drift apart or blow apart in conflict? Write about how you and your partner managed the transition out of romantic infatuation.

Most modern people have two or more serious relationships in their lifetime, and romantic infatuation tends to play a serious role for better or worse. Better because of the bliss and magic of erotic love. Worse because of the pains of jealousy, the loss of obsessive romantic feelings, and the challenge of transitioning into a more stable intimate bond.

Intimate bonding

As romantic infatuation progresses, we habituate to our partner and become less obsessed, sexually charged, and urgent. On the other hand, in many ways we are likely to feel deeper intimacy as we become more knowledgeable and familiar with each other—more intimately bonded.

Humans are wired for this. In hunter-gatherer groups it wasn't adaptive to stay maniacally obsessed with a lover for a lifetime—those who did risked missing other important contributions to tribe and family. Feeling identified with and protective of family and direct blood kinship is incredibly adaptive, and translates into the tribal identifications we all experience with families of origin, our nuclear families, our extended families, and sometimes our communities or nations.

As I mentioned earlier, when romantic infatuation progresses to intimate bonding, we often feel levels of closeness similar to the closeness we felt in our family of origin—the mystical blood-kinship bond. Indeed, this is when couples often marry and begin a family. Many times a couple has already had a child by this time (certainly true in all humans groups before the advent of reliable birth control, and unfortunately true today in most teen births).

~~~~~~

EXERCISE: *Significant other*

Have you ever been married or lived with a lover for years past romantic infatuation into intimate bonding—where you loved that person but weren't especially in love? If, like most people, you have been in that situation, then remember a time you were with this person and received some especially good or bad news. You got a big raise! You were diagnosed with something scary! You just had a car accident! Random House wants to publish your book! This news was a big deal to you at the time.

When you got this news, who was the first person you wanted to call and tell? It was probably your intimate partner (but not necessarily—it could have been another family member or important person in your life). After an intense emotional experience, most of us call our life partner—usually our husband or wife—at the first opportunity. Our nervous systems know there is one person in the innermost circle of our social world, our pair bond partner. Write about this in detail in your journal.

Ask your partner whom they would call with good or bad news. Is it you? How does that feel? Is it not you? How does that feel? Write about your conversation.

If you do discuss all this with your husband, wife, or long-time partner, you're describing central elements of your pair bond. Discuss what you both think this means and write about your conversation.

~~~~~~

EXERCISE: *Jealousy and cheating*

Have you ever been out with your partner and someone else starts flirting with him or her? Have you ever watched your partner flirt with another person? How did it feel? Have you ever been cheated on by a partner? How did that feel? Write about this in your journal.

Have you ever cheated on a partner or flirted with someone else in his or her presence? How did it feel? Write about this in your journal. Share what you've written with your current partner and write about your conversation.

Our genes want us to cheat!

Genetically, it makes sense to cheat. Cheating creates genetic diversity—a survival characteristic for a blood line. Additionally, a guy cheating increases the chances of passing on his genes. A woman cheating increases the chances of material and emotional support in the tribe by having another guy (hopefully high status) interested. Studies have found that up to 25 percent of women and 40 percent of men have cheated on a mate. For people under 40, the rates of men and women cheating are about the same (probably partly because women are increasingly joining the work force).[20]

Our genes want us to stop our partner from cheating!

But cheating messes with the pair bond, and so a counteracting force exists to stop cheating in its tracks—jealousy! As I mentioned earlier, over 25 percent of the murders in the U.S. involve love triangles—*25 percent!* Over half of women who are murdered are killed by jealous men. We see a woman hitting on our husband, or some guy hitting on our wife, and we go into full-on mate protection. We become jealous, angry, possessive, and have powerful impulses to drive the other away, claim our mate, and then punish him or her for the whole mess.[21]

Back in the 1970s, many of us thought we could have different sexual partners and still comfortably maintain the pair bond. Polyamory enthusiasts still believe this today. Becky and I tried polyamory back then, and ultimately I hated it! I often say in lectures that I have "earned monogamy." I didn't let the culture decide about me being faithful, I found out that I wanted sexual exclusivity for myself.

When Becky was with another guy, I tried to negotiate away jealousy by reasoning with myself, but such self-talk didn't quell the horrible pangs of possessive anger and despair. I don't personally believe that most modern marriages can sustain infidelity. Polyamory seems to work as a stage that some go through in their late teens or early twenties, and sometimes when recently separated from a long-term relationship, but in my experience, polyamory never helps relationships in the long run, at least for straight people.

Gay couples, especially men, are more likely to negotiate monogamy and sexual adventure, and I've worked occasionally with gay couples who include sex with others. That being said, I've never known a sexually fulfilled couple to be non-monogamous for long, either straight or gay.

EXERCISE: *Stages of sexual bonding*

Read over your journal entries from this chapter with an attitude of acceptance and caring intent toward yourself, your sexuality, your history, and your relationships. Write down any insights you have. Share what you have written and discovered with your partner or someone else you trust.

If this creates problems with your partner, that's fine! Work at repairing the distress through understanding, validation, and warm connection. If that doesn't work, find a good couples therapist and receive influence to resolve the issues that have arisen.

Chapter 12

Arousal Systems

Evolution runs off of three interconnected processes:

* Natural selection—survival of the fittest. You have to survive to pass your genes on.

* Sexual selection—survival of the sexiest. The person who can attract the best mates or claim the best mates is most likely to pass their genes on.

* Kin selection—survival of the blood-kinship group. All animals instinctively want an edge for blood relatives so that their shared gene pool is passed on.[22]

Sexual selection is propelled by our sexual arousal systems, and men's and women's sexual arousal systems are (not surprisingly) quite different in many ways.

In optimizing erotic polarity, understanding your sexual essence and aspects is not the whole story by a long shot. To best support my sexuality and help you best support your sexuality, it really helps to know how we embody the various sexual arousal systems that men and women are born with.

What are these systems? Briefly, male arousal is generally a constant force, primarily driven by "I see her, I want her." It is very visual. Guys have instincts to be lit up by youth, beauty, and a 70/30 hip/waist ratio.[23]

Female arousal is more episodic and contextual. Women can be super into sex in different situations for hours, days, weeks, or months, and then not particularly be interested for periods of time depending on relationship stage and life experiences. Women also seem to have more complicated sexual arousal systems than men. Several core female arousal systems are:

* Sex Goddess: "I am the embodiment of the divine erotic feminine. You see me and desire me."

* Ravish Me: The right guy at the right time *takes me* in exactly the right way.

* Cozy/Cozy: We're close, safe, intimate, warm, and affection leads to sensual pleasure, which leads to arousal.[24]

It's not that guys don't have Sex God, Ravish Me, or Cozy/Cozy arousal systems—they often do. For instance, one third of men say they like to be the submissive in the dominance/submission dynamic that is a sexual universal in men, women, gays, and straights. (You know you're dealing with genetic imperatives when practically *everyone* shares something like a dominance/submission erotic charge.[25])

Women can also be visually erotic—they often are. Most women will occasionally see a particularly beautiful Brad Pitt/Justin Timberlake/pick-your-attractive-archetype guy and feel a tingle.

That being said, men lean toward I see her, I want her, while women lean to Sex Goddess, Ravish Me, and Cozy/Cozy. Perhaps because men have 10 to 50 times as much testosterone (the main lust hormone in both sexes), the powerful "I see her, I want her!" system drowns out the other arousal systems in them.

In women, desire-leads-to-arousal can change to arousal-leads-to-desire in intimate bonding

A complicating factor in understanding arousal systems is that women's arousal profiles tend to change dramatically (often more so than men's) in the shift from romantic infatuation into intimate bonding. During hookups and romantic infatuation, women are primed by testosterone, dopamine, and oxytocin surges to want sex with their guy—like their visually-cued men, they are in desire-leads-to-arousal. This is consistent with the progressive message of many modern mothers to their daughters, "Only do it when you feel like it."

Unfortunately, when women pass into the intimate bonding stage of a relationship, and especially in the years after childbirth, they often shift into an arousal-leads-to-desire system. This means sex isn't particularly appealing *until they begin to do it.*

The consequences of this shift in women from desire-leads-to-arousal to arousal-leads-to-desire in the marital love affair can be staggering, sometimes devastating. Since modern women are generally taught to say "No," when they don't feel like it, and they *naturally* can shift into a mode where they *don't feel like it* unless *they are doing it,* sex can dramatically diminish—even disappear!

I've found that in long-term couples, mutual sexual fulfillment often becomes a matter of sexual knowledge, consciousness, flexibility, and generosity of spirit—all qualities that are generally not adequately taught to children and adolescents in the U.S.

A *further* complication is that women in intimate bonding with one man are *still* primed for lust, flirtation, distracting attractions, and falling in love with *other* men. Without this knowledge and the skill and willingness in her and her partner to maintain their marital love affair, a woman can feel like she's lost her sexuality in the arousal-leads-to-desire system with her husband, and seek sexual validation and reassurance in desire-leads-to-arousal flirtations and/or affairs with other men.

One of my favorite sex researchers is a Canadian professor at Queens University in Ontario by the name of Meredith Chivers. Chivers studied men and women watching sexual scenes of all types. She showed them sexually explicit film clips of heterosexual couples, gay and lesbian couples, individuals masturbating, and individual naked men and women. She even threw in bonobos (a gentler, less aggressive chimpanzee) having sex. I imagine it's a lot of fun to be a sex researcher sometimes!

As men and women watched the videos, Chivers had them rate how turned on they were while she monitored their levels of physiological sexual arousal with vaginal plethysmographs measuring women's levels of lubrication, and penile plethysmographs measuring men's blood flow to their penises. Cameras also recorded where people's eyes tracked on the screens.

Women experienced arousal as their eyes moved from the naked body of the woman—with whom they were presumably identifying—to the eyes of the male partner gazing at his lover with desire. The guys predictably looked mostly at the naked women (though gay males looked primarily at the naked men). When interviewed later, it was further confirmed that women identified with the beautiful naked woman desired by the aroused man.

Also, while the men's self-reported levels of arousal more or less matched the plethysmographs, the women's reporting was often wildly at odds with their plethysmograph readings. For example, women often self-reported more arousal than the instruments showed while watching the heterosexual sex, and less arousal than the instruments showed while watching the lesbian sex. Other research has shown that easily orgasmic women and women who take their time with the ebbs and flows of eroticism in masturbation or lovemaking are more accurate in knowing when they are turned on.

What Chivers' research demonstrates is that we have multiple arousal systems, and women's arousal systems are especially varied, complex, and intertwined with other variables (such as social pressure to not feel arousal at watching lesbian sex).[26]

~~~~~~

EXERCISE: *Arousal*

This week, either have sex with your lover and/or masturbate. Notice what changes as you become sexually aroused in terms of what you do, say, want, and feel. Usually how you feel and behave changes from beginning sex, to middle stages, to pushing for orgasm. Just observe with acceptance and caring intent and write about your observations in detail in your journal.

If you find yourself having critical judgments of you or your partner (guys tend to critique their performance, while women tend to critique their

*bodies), observe your critical judgments with acceptance and caring intent
and write about them in your journal.*

*Notice what imagery, objects, or activities arouse or titillate you. One couple
I worked with had sex on every new piece of furniture they purchased.*

*Some people, more often women than men, are somewhat at a loss about
what turns them on. That's also fine if you find no concrete answers—just
write about that and how having no concrete answers to what turns you
on feels.*

*If there are images, objects, or activities that turn you on, are you accepting
of what erotically energizes you? Are you embarrassed, ashamed, or
anxious? Write about those experiences and share everything with your
partner or someone you love—looking to normalize what turns you on
and create prosocial ways of benefitting from your personal turn-ons.*

*If you do share with your romantic partner, ask them the questions and
listen with interest and acceptance to their insights.*

Normalize your and your partner's arousal systems!

You don't have to get off on what your partner gets off on, and your partner doesn't have to find what turns you on arousing! Just because she likes
having her toes sucked, doesn't mean you have to like it or even do it. Just
because he likes sex outside in nature doesn't mean you have to like it or try
it if you don't want to.

What is important is accepting what excites you and your partner and
looking for intersections in what excites you both. The standard I suggest
is that if there is an activity (like toe licking or semi-public sex) that your
partner likes and is at least mildly pleasurable to you, why not try it sometimes? Don't do stuff that turns you off, but try stuff that is at least mildly fun
for you and might be super fun for your partner.

Sharing all this chapter's materials and exercises with your lover is
going to stir up your sex life! If sex gets more fun, I'm happy for you! If you
discover problems, talk about them, make progress with them, or get help
from a good therapist if you can't resolve issues that arise.

Chapter 13

Love Maps

We are wired by early adolescence to be more drawn to some potential lovers and less to others, to find some activities engaging and some distressing. We also have characteristic patterns of understanding and dealing with the world. John Gottman calls these patterns of attraction and living *love maps*, and has found that the more we understand and respect each other's love maps, the better our relationships tend to be.

My experience over the years, as well as the reports of researchers, practitioners, and writers in the field like Meredith Chivers, Marta Meaney, David Deida, and others, suggest that love maps are largely in place by early adolescence, and then develop as we develop through adulthood. People you're attracted to, comfortable with, and want to create love affairs with are likely to have complementary love maps to your own.

Lust maps are related to, but also different from, love maps. Lust maps are purely what attracts you sexually. For instance, in the classic "Madonna/whore" scenario, guys want their wife to feel socially appropriate and fit into the sacred wife/mother role of a family, while also embodying the sex goddess/porn star/promiscuous-babe archetypes in their marital love affair.

If a guy can't relate to his wife as both archetypes, he can lose erotic polarity as they marry, become parents, and he identifies her progressively more as a non-sexual Madonna. This can lead to affairs.

Sometimes the Madonna/whore scenario is culturally institutionalized. In one beach town in Italy, many of the townsfolk had a spouse and a lover, but it was forbidden to refer to lovers in public discourse—there was a cultural standard of having transgressive sex with a lover, but keeping it secret.[27] Similarly, in the early part of the twentieth century, sex manuals were originally written so wives could have the same pleasures during sex that mistresses did.[28]

Love maps include lust maps, but also involve all the other aspects of another's world that are important to them and affect your relationship with them.

What kind of women or men attract your sexual/relational attention? Personality, shape, posture, clothes, gait, voice tone, references, educational level, professional status, family history, facial features, and expressions (eyes, lips, smile, frown, etc.) all might matter to you.

Love and love maps vary wildly depending on genetic predispositions and cultural contexts, but, as I just mentioned, they are mostly intact by early adolescence (tall/short, dominant/submissive, heavy/slender, dark/light, breasts/ass, nice guys/bad boys, education level, sense of humor, etc.).

~~~~~~

EXERCISE: *Your love map*

Write whatever occurs to you about what kind of person attracts your sexual/relational attention in your journal. Make an effort to be non-judgmental and rigorously honest—remember, fantasies are not reality, real relationships have infinite variations, and all personal work begins with accepting yourself exactly as you are right now.

~~~~~~

EXERCISE: *Your partner's love map*

If you currently have a partner, write a couple of pages in your journal about what is important to him or her. What does that person like and dislike in general? What does he or she find attractive or irritating in you? What are the foundation principles of his or her life?

Share both exercises with your partner, and encourage him or her to make corrections, additions, and acknowledgements to your narrative. Even better, ask your partner to do the exercises about themselves and you. As you explore each other's worlds—likes, dislikes, turn-ons, turn-offs, memories, thoughts, feelings, and dreams—with acceptance and caring intent, you are love mapping each other!

Genes have amazing influences on love and sex.

Genes influence almost every aspect of our sexuality including gender/hetero-sexuality/homosexuality, fidelity, sexual aggression, and sexual development.

Some genetic influences are incredibly precise, as in:

* Women tend to prefer men who are three and a half inches taller than they are, while men tend to prefer women three and a half inches shorter.[29]

* The color red is associated with sexuality in both sexes.[30]

* In the sweaty t-shirt experiment, where women sniffed men's sweaty tees, women were more attracted to men who had the most different immune systems from them.[31]

* In the famous Clark/Hatfield college study where attractive men and women asked strangers for dates or immediate sex, the male/female breakdown on the question, "Do you want to have sex right now?" was 70 percent of men answering "yes" with 0 percent of women answering "yes".[32]

* There is a vasopressin expression gene in men that has different numbers of copies in different men. The more copies of the gene a guy has, the more likely he is to stay faithful to his partner. Two other genes associated with fidelity have been found in men.[33]

* Being especially into sex can be a genetic predisposition in some women, which ironically makes their sons slightly more likely to be gay—their sons inherit the like-to-have-fun-sex-with-guys genes. [34]

✳ Women can develop antibodies to testosterone with progressive pregnancies with boys, making their youngest sons slightly more likely to be gay.[35]

These are a few of hundreds of ways we are genetically programmed to choose and love, with many of them influencing us non-consciously. How can we manage all these Shadow influences? The Five Star questions are designed to help your unconscious connect your programming with another's programming (Shadow to Shadow), which helps you see where you are naturally in harmony and naturally not in harmony.

All that being said, biology is not destiny! If you feel ill-matched with a partner or potential partner in some fashion, talk about it! If your conversation results in progress toward shared understanding and deeper intimacy, you have improved your relationship. If there are problems with your conversation, find a good couples therapist to help you make progress.

〜〜〜〜〜〜〜〜〜〜〜〜〜〜〜〜〜〜〜〜〜〜〜〜〜〜〜〜〜〜〜〜〜〜

EXERCISE: *Love map mind map*

I'd like you to create a mind map of what you believe you like in a potential (or real) mate—a combination of your personal love/lust maps:

✳ *Get a big sheet of paper and some different colored marker pens.*

✳ *Write "**What attracts me**" in a two-inch circle in the center.*

✳ *Draw wavy lines outward from the circle with details of what attracts you in a real or potential partner (size, shape, color, movement, smile, eyes, smell, voice, job, car, clothes, or whatever else you can think of).*

✳ *Draw wavy lines outward from the circle with details of what repels you in a real or potential partner (what you don't like).*

✳ *Use colored pens and illuminate it with photos, flowers, or anything else that captures your love map.*

✳ *Share your mind map with someone you trust—hopefully your partner—and write about your conversation.*

Chapter 14

100 Reasons to Not Have a Secret Affair

This chapter is about unhealthy secret love affairs, where at least one partner is cheating. Some studies show 15 to 25 percent of women and 25 to 40 percent of men cheating on a spouse at some time in their lives.[36] As someone who has had to help hundreds of people deal with secret affairs, I can tell you that secret affairs suck and inevitably cause big problems!

We are fascinated, titillated, and horrified by love affairs overall. Many associate love affairs with infidelity, and secret love affairs are often just that—cheating on a lover. But cheating is just one form of love affair. Most marriages and relationships begin with an open love affair between two available and enthusiastic partners—a healthy and beautiful human capacity, necessary for the pair bond.

Healthy affairs between single or otherwise available people are often wonderful, prosocial, and good for everyone. Healthy affairs are how many relationships begin, and they often provide an erotically charged foundation for great marriages. When a couple comes to me in distress and I ask them, "What was it like in the beginning?" and they respond with some version of, "We were *hot* in the beginning!" I feel a sense of relief and pleasure. That initial love affair can become a touchstone for positive change and healing of whatever relational wounds this couple has come in with.

Enjoyable attractions, distracting attractions, and secret affairs

An *enjoyable attraction* is what you feel when drawn to an appealing other. This can be impersonal, such as observing someone in real life or a movie, or reciprocal, when you feel this appealing other liking you back. When this happens and you feel enlivened but not distracted or obsessed, it's an enjoyable attraction that can be good for everyone. Our responsibilities as self-aware sexual beings is to monitor and adjust our attractions to be enjoyable ones.

A *distracting attraction* is when you (and sometimes the other person) amplify the enjoyable attraction to the point you begin to hunger for the other and be frustrated if you can't be closer. This is delicious if you both are available and interested, but a train wreck if you already are partnered or the other is not available. Unhealthy, distracting attractions often need help and support from others (like a therapist and, often, your partner) to help you deconstruct the obsession and disconnect from the object of your desire.

Secret affairs are when one of you has a primary connection with a partner and you pursue your mutual attraction into romance and sexual activity anyway.

~~~~~~

EXERCISE: *Imagined affair*

Imagine you're a woman in your 40s, and you pick up your husband's phone. There's a message on it from another woman saying, "You were so hot last night! I want your naked body on mine right now!" How do you feel as you imagine this? Write your reactions and associations in detail.

Imagine you're a 39-year-old man, married ten years with a seven-year-old son and a five-year-old daughter. Your wife calls from Cindy's house and says they're having fun and she'll be late. You have a guilty flash of suspicion (you're ashamed of not trusting her, but you sense something is wrong). You think to yourself, "She's been doing this a lot recently," and so you call Cindy and ask for your wife. "She's not here," says Cindy, and it all falls together that your wife is cheating on you. How do you feel about her? About yourself? About the other guy? Write your reactions and associations in detail.

Read everything you've written and see how your reactions square with what you've experienced in your life. Around 90 percent of us have left or been left by a lover[37], and many of those breakups involved cheating. Do you get a taste of the unique pain of being cheated on? Have you had this pain in your life at some point?

Whenever I do this exercise, I am reminded that there are a hundred reasons to not have a secret affair!

That being said, what kinds of secret affairs are there, and what might they mean about us and our relationships?

Exit affairs, opportunistic affairs, and please-can-we-love-again affairs

Affairs have different meanings to everyone involved. Sometimes they are a cry for help. Sometimes they are impulsive mistakes. Sometimes they are attempts to end a relationship. Let's look at three common forms of secret affairs—exit affairs, opportunistic affairs, and please-can-we-love-again affairs.

Exit affairs happen when one partner wants out of a marriage and doesn't know how to do it or can't do it for any number of reasons. Perhaps he or she is in a codependent relationship with an addict, or an emotionally or physically abusive partner, or is too frightened of dealing with the world without the financial or social support of their partner. In these cases an affair can provide a way out of a dissatisfying marriage by forcing everyone to look more deeply at impossible conditions or unacceptable behaviors.

When a couple comes into therapy after the discovery of an affair, and the cheating spouse won't give up the lover, won't work on the relationship, or announces, "I don't love you anymore!", I begin to explore with them the possibility that this affair is an exit affair.

When someone's partner cheats, and he or she immediately files for divorce and refuses any attempts for repair, I explore with them the possibility that they had been hungering for separation and that discovering their partner cheating has somehow liberated that impulse.

Opportunistic affairs happen when we find ourselves with an opportunity to flirt and transgress with an attractive other. The number-one predictor of affairs is opportunity—often at work, on business trips, or with people we might encounter at work, school, church, or in the neighborhood. Seventy percent of people who have affairs describe their marriage and sex life with their spouse as "satisfying,"[38] but they had an opportunity, their genes wanted them to go for it (remember, we all have the instinct to cheat), and they didn't have the clarity of purpose to realize that the pleasure involved was not going to be worth the eventual pain.

It's usually difficult for the cheated-on spouse to understand that the significance of the opportunistic affair is not that their spouse is dissatisfied with them. Often what it *does mean* is that their partner was not prepared to stay resolved in his or her monogamy commitment in the altered state of flirtation/distracting attraction with an available other.

Don't get me wrong; opportunistic affairs are still catastrophic! If anyone who values his or her marriage *knew* how much pain is involved in having and dealing with secret affairs, he or she would *never* say "yes" to an opportunity! No affair is worth the mountains of pain and months of work required to atone, attune, and attach back into your marital friendship and love affair.

That being said, to the 70 percent of people who stay married through one partner cheating, it helps to understand how your partner can value you and your marriage and simultaneously cheat.

Please-can-we-love-again affairs occur when a spouse feels neglected, misunderstood, lonely, unattractive to his or her spouse, or angry about their spouse's affair(s). In these cases the affair is a protest against disconnection and a cry for intimacy in the marriage. When these couples enter treatment, intense yearning for deeper intimacy and passion with their mate emerges quickly from the transgressor as we process the affair.

Secret affairs are almost always catastrophes.

Secret affairs are frequently delicious in the beginning, and then progress into disaster, devastating to marriages and families. Even exit affairs are incredibly messy and destructive ways to end marriages, leaving significant injuries to every family member. It's much better to separate cleanly first and *then* pursue or be pursued by others.

Our lust/romantic-infatuation/desire-new-partners drives influence us to pursue erotic polarities and indulge them into secret affairs. Since we tend to create stories to help us for better or worse, people often come up with rationalizations about why affairs are a good idea.

For example, take Daniel. He came in to see me complaining of being sexually dissatisfied with his wife, Marilyn. He spent the entire session arguing how a secret affair was the answer to his dilemma, until, at the end, he asked, "Why shouldn't I have an affair?" I laughed, as we had been at this for sixty minutes again and again. I responded, "There are a hundred reasons to not have a secret affair!"

Daniel replied, "That's a great title for a book!" He left the session, cheated on Marilyn, and eventually divorced.

I remembered what Daniel said, and wrote the book, *100 Reasons to Not Have a Secret Affair,* but it's never found a publisher. I can see their point. In retrospect, I realized that not many people want to be seen buying or reading a book titled, *"100 Reasons to Not Have a Secret Affair."*

What are some of the hundred reasons? Here is a sampling from my unpublished manuscript:

Reason #1: Affairs hurt everybody.

Reason #2: Affairs distract us from our responsibility to make the relationship we have work better. I believe a great mandate for committed lovers is to support each other's growth as individual souls, lovers, parents, friends, and beings. This is partly a personal moral value that's emerged from my life and work, but science also has something to say. Human psyches and bodies love to help others and be helped by others. Spouses doing this with one another increase immune function, reduce blood pressure, relax into more coherent heartbeats, live longer, boost happiness, and offer more to the world.

Reason #4: Therapy bills skyrocket when you have an affair. I think this is self-explanatory. Sometimes when a partner complains about how long it's taking and how much it's costing to resolve the pain of his or her affair and return to love, I think about someone who drinks and drives complaining about the incredible time, expense, and humiliations involved in getting a DUI. Some mistakes have huge costs.

Reason #8: In the grip of romantic infatuation, you can't trust what you think. This is not just a folk aphorism or new age metaphor. Romantic infatuation literally sedates parts of our brains dedicated to evaluating people and behavior, especially with our lover. If you're married and having an affair, remember that your lover is *deliberately* engaging in behavior that is probably going to be devastating to your husband, wife, or children. Do you really want to be involved with someone who is okay with hurting them?

Reason #14: When we have zero tolerance to cheat, lie, and hide, we become better people generally. Which of your friends do you most admire? Whom do you seek out when you're hurt and need support? I suspect you don't turn to the liars and cheaters in your social circle, but instead to the honorable and caring people whom you trust to have integrity, tell the truth, and support clean love. When your friends need support, which of those two groups do you want to them to consider you a member of? People tend to make general moral judgments about others from one moral failing. Do you want to be characterized as an unfaithful person? Cultivating zero tolerance for cheating, lying, and hiding moves you toward the integrity end of the spectrum.

Reason #16: "Sexy" doesn't equal "sane." Just because a woman is erotically radiant and apparently available, doesn't mean she is stable, faithful, compatible, or honest. Enjoy your see-her-want-sex instincts, but be cautious! Just because a guy is charming, attentive, interested, and handsome doesn't mean he is stable, faithful, compatible, or honest. Enjoy his flattering attention, but be cautious!

Reason #21: Mirror neurons make hiding everything impossible. Looking at your spouse while suffering from the guilt, anger, shame, or fear associated with secret affairs will resonate in his or her brain via mirror neurons—one reason conflicted couples instinctively avoid eye contact, and chronic liars learn to look earnestly into people's eyes. Such avoidance feels threatening to your partner's nervous system, activating defensive systems that judge *you* to be a threat—which feels threatening to you. The healthy repair response of talking about exactly what is going on in the present moment with transparency and acceptance in service of love is not available because of your secrets. Coldness and nastiness often follow, creating downward spirals of bad times.

Reason #29: We can lose favorite places, activities, friends, and outfits because of affairs. Most affairs happen where we live or work. Once transgressive lines have been crossed, it's hard to reestablish comfort and safety in places you associate with trauma. Many couples lose favorite restaurants, vacations, friends, garments, and hangouts associated by one partner or the other with sexual transgressions.

Reason #37: Joyful monogamy helps us age well. Someday—if we're lucky—we'll be old. Which skills are going to serve us best when this happens? Will our capacities to cheat and lie help us have great relationships and great sex through our 50s, 60s, 70s, and 80s? I don't think so. Will the skills generated by a lifetime of development, conscious intimacy/eroticism, and increasing self-knowledge and compassion with a willing and able partner predispose us to a happy life? Of course they will! The time to start practicing joyful, passionate monogamy is now.

Reason #54: Having sex with someone is always a big deal, no matter what you say or believe about it at the time. Research shows that we become more impulsive and reckless when sexually aroused.[39] Letting a distracting attraction blossom into an affair puts two adults into turned-on situations where they unconsciously work to justify consummating their desires. She may say to herself or you, "I just want to have fun without complications," but what happens when she falls in love with you? He may say, "It's fine with me that you'll never leave your husband," but what happens when he says later, "I can't stand it that you go home to him?"

Reason #58: Incredible craziness can be cued by sexual betrayal. Often you don't see your spouse's deepest defenses until they've been evoked by trauma. If you are the source of that trauma, he or she can recalibrate their entire sense of who you are, and sometimes never come back to seeing you as a good person worthy of sharing a life with. Worse, this attitude is transmitted to kids, creating all kinds of conflicts aggravated by mutually despising parents who used to love each other.

Reason #59: If you have an affair, your children will eventually feel betrayed. When you cheat on your spouse, you're also cheating on your children! I've seen it with hundreds of people over the sixty-five thousand therapy sessions I've conducted since 1973. Almost *everyone* whose parents divorced or whose mother or father cheated announces it as a signature event within the first thirty minutes of their first counseling session.

Reason #70: Be a mythological hero, not a mythological jerk. Every myth has good guys and bad guys. What role does cheating give you in your personal myth? Even worse, what role does this give you in your spouse's and children's myths? On the other hand, choosing loving integrity and fighting for a fulfilling marriage is heroic. Even better, it eventually *feels* heroic to you, your spouse, and your family.

Reason #81: Having an affair with someone at work potentially wrecks your job. If you are the boss, you risk censure from management and sexual harassment charges. If your lover is higher on the company power hierarchy than you, you are likely to be sacrificed if the affair causes problems.

Reason #92: Affairs can linger in marriages as signature traumas and then merge into unrelated conflicts. If you want to avoid the, "Well, you cheated!" rejoinder for almost any argument, don't have an affair.

Don't despair if you have an affair!

So far, we've explored an awful lot of information about how we love, cheat, and struggle to love better. Any experience, including secret affairs, can be processed into expansion and growth, and we'll talk more about how to do this in chapters to come. Seventy percent of couples who deal with one partner cheating find their way back to a stable marriage[40] (often with the help of therapists like me). This is one of my favorite miracles of self-aware consciousness and human evolution.

On the other hand, consider this: 30 percent of couples break up over a secret affair—they lose each other *forever!* Be honest with yourself and your spouse. Direct your will and courage toward deeper love and passion within your marriage. If you're having an affair, break up with your lover, come clean with your spouse, and get into therapy! In the long run it's the healthiest for everyone and—believe it or not—the most fun, joy, and passion for you.

~~~~~~

EXERCISE: *Secret affair outcome*

Go back to your answer to my questions in Chapter 11, "Have you ever cheated on a partner or been cheated on by a partner?" In your journal, write about how it turned out for everyone, including those connected to you, your partner, and the third person (your lover or your partner's lover). This includes your spouse, the lover, friends, people at work (many affairs start at work), and everyone's kids. As you got through the various traumas involved, who helped (therapists? ministers? friends? family members? your spouse?) and what forms of support helped the most? Share this with your spouse or someone you trust and write about your conversation.

Chapter 15

How to Deal with Affairs

After reading the previous chapter and doing the exercises, you might be asking, "What do I do if I catch my partner in an affair?" Or, "I'm *having* a secret affair, what should I do? How can I tell if I'm having an exit affair, opportunity affair, or a please-can-we-love-again affair?"

Either way, I'm glad you asked! Secret affairs are confusing and dangerous, but there are effective ways of dealing with them.

Some of my favorite theorists and practitioners in this area are Shirley Glass, who wrote *Not Just Friends,* and John and Julie Gottman who maintain that recovery from affairs involves three stages—atone, attune, and attach. In general, I've found successful approaches to dealing with secret affairs (such as Glass, the Gottmans, and others like Esther Perel and Stan Tatkin) are remarkably consistent.

Imagine you are a therapist and a guy comes in saying, "I just got out of a two-year secret affair. What do I do? I want to feel better, but I refuse to tell my wife." As a therapist hearing this, how do *you* feel? What do you say? Write down how you think you'd respond to him if you were his therapist.

Imagine you're a therapist and a woman comes in saying, "I just got out of a two-year secret affair. What do I do? I want to feel better, but I can't tell my husband." As her therapist, how do you feel? What do you say? Write down how you think you'd respond, and note if it's different from your response to the guy.

Your responses were probably at least somewhat different, reflecting that men and women have similarities and differences in everything, including secret affairs.

The first big questions that I have in these situations are:

* "Do you want your marriage to improve—especially your love affair with your spouse?"

* "Do you want to separate and live independently from your spouse?"

* "Which option feels most attractive and right for you?"

As we explore these questions, I'm beginning to figure out if this is an exit affair, an opportunity affair, or a please-can-we-love-again affair.

People who yearn to live separately from their spouse, who say it doesn't feel right in their hearts to work on their marriage, most often are engaged in exit affairs, or experience their partner's affair as a final straw. I've found these partners more likely to separate eventually.

People who want to heal their relationship, reestablish their spouse as a lover, and feel in their hearts they want to love their husband or wife better are more likely to have had opportunity affairs or please-can-we-love-again affairs, and more often want stay together and work on connection and marital eroticism.

If one partner deeply yearns to live separately and decides that they want separation, I do my best to help them break up as kindly and respectfully as possible. I tell them, "Divorce/separation *always* involves expense and suffering, but you can minimize the pain and expense by being kind, clear, and cooperative."

Couples where both are able to be kind, clear, and cooperative can have a nonviolent, minimally expensive divorce, aided by a therapist who keeps reminding them, "We're not trying to resolve emotional issues anymore. We are working at separating in as fair, kind, and respectful a manner as possible."

A big variable in any conflict, and especially in divorce, is if both of the partners are *normal crazy*, or if one of them is *extra crazy*. Normal crazy is the defensive reactions that all people tend to have in stressful or threatening situations. When we have a normal crazy reaction and someone challenges us kindly, we eventually shift out of the distortions involved and have more compassionate understanding. When we have an extra crazy reaction and someone challenges us kindly, we double down, get more defensive or shut down, and often attack the source of the challenge, refusing to consider changing our angry perspectives.

If one partner is extra crazy, that person can become obsessed with punishing his or her spouse, never trusting or following agreements, and insisting on litigation to unconsciously keep the conflict going until a judge finally forces *his* solution on the couple. These kinds of high-conflict divorces can burn through huge amounts of resources—sometimes hundreds of thousands (or millions) of dollars and years of time. Aggressive and venomous divorces traumatize kids and drain families emotionally and financially.

If both partners want to heal their relationship, therapy can provide a path. The secret affair typically has to be processed through some version of the atone, attune, and attach sequence.

Much more rarely (if the affair is still secret), the partner having the affair, even though they've broken up with their lover, wants to keep it secret and still work on the marriage. I tell individuals who want to do this that they should do marriage counseling to improve their marriage, but not with me. I can't work with a couple if I have a huge secret (like an affair!) that I'm ethically bound to not reveal to the other partner. However an individual or couple want to work on their marriage, the bottom line about what approach works is always *progress*.

Progress toward becoming better friends, better lovers, and more effective healers of marital injuries is the gold standard.

When a couple is able and willing to make progress, they can usually work back to love.

Zack and Jennifer progress through atone, attune, and attach.

All couples are unique, and all affairs involve complex individuals with multiple motivational systems and different life circumstances. That being said, most therapists agree that when you're helping a couple work back to security and love from the devastation of a secret affair, there are stages they go through in recovery that usually involve some version of atone, attune, and attach. The following couple, Zack and Jennifer, illustrate how one couple negotiated those stages.

Atone

The atone stage involves the cheater acknowledging the damage inflicted on his or her partner, and feeling genuine remorse. The cheated upon partner needs to accept that this has happened, decide to stay in the relationship, and gradually learn how to receive the cheater's apologies and help in processing the betrayal.

Zack and Jennifer were in their fifties with two grown children when I met them. They were an attractive couple who exercised, loved to cook and entertain together, did yoga, and generally took care of themselves. Zack was a hard-driving mover and shaker in the music business. Jennifer originally was a successful agent for recording artists, but after she and Zack fell in love, married, and had the kids, she stopped her career to be a stay-at-home mom and run their complicated lives.

Unfortunately, eighteen months previously, Zack fell in love with Karen, his administrative assistant, and continued an affair with her for over a year before Jennifer found out, freaked out, and everything exploded.

They came to me after weeks of bitter fighting. Zack was appalled at his life unraveling and desperate to save his marriage. Jennifer doubted she could ever trust Zack again, but yearned to feel secure and connected as she had for most of their twenty-seven years together.

The first obstacle in therapy was that Zack didn't want to lose super-efficient Karen as his administrative assistant. He told Jennifer, "We've stopped seeing each other socially. I'll never have sex with her again. Why can't we go back to the way it was?"

Jennifer exploded, "How can you possibly expect me to be okay with you going to work with that bitch!"

Zack began explaining how Karen wasn't an evil person, but I interrupted him.

"Jennifer's right, Zack. You've lost Karen as an administrative assistant, a friend, and as a lover."

"But it's over!" he protested, "Why can't Jennifer get that? I'm not even romantically interested anymore!"

I explained, "I'm glad you're not interested—it means your unconscious self is letting you know that you value Jennifer and want to rebuild—but, remember, you and Karen betrayed Jennifer and your kids! Jennifer might learn to trust you again, but she'll never forgive Karen for putting her personal interests over the welfare of your family."

Zack looked down as I said this, hearing the truth and feeling the loss of Karen as his friend and valued collaborator. "All right," he said. "I'll tell her today that I'll help her find another job."

"Finally!" Jennifer exclaimed. "I don't understand how you could be so crazy as to think you could keep working with her! You..."

Now I interrupt Jennifer, "Jennifer! Slow down. Zack just understood that he has to tell Karen to leave. He now realizes he has to lose a valued friend and competent assistant, and risk a sexual harassment suit and incredible embarrassment. I understand your frustration, but in this, the atonement stage of working through the affair, the person who cheated has levels of denial and rationalization they have to work through to fully understand the damage they've done to you and the marriage. Karen leaving is just one step—a really hard one, but necessary—and I'd like you to recognize that Zack is working on getting through this."

Jennifer, who by nature is warmhearted, softened as I spoke, "It's just so hard to hear him defend her!" She turned toward Zack, "Thanks for finally understanding how Karen can't be in our lives anymore."

This is characteristic of the "Atone" part of dealing with affairs. The person who had the affair needs to understand the depth of suffering his or her actions created, communicate that understanding with real remorse, and face the real-world consequences of a secret affair.

Meanwhile, Jennifer, the person cheated on, needs to accept the infuriating reality that, even though she didn't cheat, she now faces an enormous amount of emotional and relational work to heal the marriage that Zack has imperiled.

Attune

In the attune stage, the couple explores the meaning of the affair to each partner individually, and to the relationship itself. They begin to understand that they are now in a new marriage that needs to be understood and honored in new ways.

Three months later, we're having a session and Zack is exasperated. He hasn't seen Karen in two and half months (she's moved on to another job), he has no interest in women other than Jennifer, and he can't understand why Jennifer keeps bringing up the affair. "Why can't you get over it?" he implores. "Why do you have to keep bringing it up and hammering me for it again and again?"

Jennifer, on the other hand, keeps finding herself having moments of enjoying being with Zack, and then remembering the affair and going into a rage. They're progressing—they've even started making love again after a four-month hiatus (because she "couldn't touch him without thinking of Karen!"). She responds angrily, "It's easy for you! You don't have to worry about *me* cheating! I've been busting my ass just to stay with you and give us a chance, and you think I should be over it already!"

I intervene. "Stop for a second, breathe in deeply, and breathe out slowly. You can't successfully relate if your arousal level is too high, and the deep breathing activates your vagus nerve to soothe your heart and your mind." They both visibly calm themselves—we've been here before. "Now, tell the other person what's valid about their point of view."

Zack looks thoughtful. "You're right that I don't worry about you cheating. Also, you've been much warmer these last weeks and I've enjoyed our romantic getaway at Avilla Beach. I know you're working hard."

Jennifer relaxes a little. "I know you're trying hard, and mostly you've been sweet. It's just taking me time to begin to trust again." Zack nods encouragingly at this.

During the attune stage, couples develop skills at hearing non-defensively and sharing their feelings and thoughts nonjudgmentally. They learn each other's love maps in more detail, and hear a fair amount from me about how couples can maintain each other in healthy ways. Gradually they cooperate better at trusting and connecting.

Attach

A marriage includes a friendship, a love affair, the capacity to repair injuries, and a shared future. At the attachment stage of the work, the emphasis is less on the affair and more on the new, post-affair relationship where these components are explicitly examined, negotiated, and reintegrated into the couple's universe.

It's seven months later, and Zack has to take a business trip to Canada to help shoot a music video. Jennifer doesn't want to go—Zack will be working constantly for five or six days—but fears he'll cheat again. She tells him, "I'm worried about you and all the women. You're friendly and attractive and love being social."

Zack is more patient these days. "What can I do while I'm there to help you feel more secure?"

Jennifer thinks about it for a moment. "You can text me during the day and call me after dinner to tell me how everything went."

Zack better understands how connecting with Jennifer in these ways is good for both of them, and responds positively. "You've got it! I'll text during the day, tell you what's up, and we can Skype after dinner." Jennifer smiles appreciatively.

During the attach stage of resolving affairs, couples explicitly learn what each needs to feel secure and *known* by the other when they're together and apart. Zack realizes he needs to stay open and available for Jennifer to trust him. Jennifer gets that she needs to not *pretend* to feel OK, but work with Zack to actually *feel* safe with him traveling and socializing without her.

If couples haven't reestablished their marital love affair by this phase, it becomes a major focus of therapy.

With most couples I've helped through affair aftermaths, we're always working to some extent on atone, attune, and attach, but there is usually more emphasis on one part or another at any given time, and there does tend to be much more need to focus on atonement in the beginning of therapy, attunement in the middle stages, and attachment in the later stages.

What has increasingly stood out over the years through numerous nightmare affairs and recoveries is that *secret affairs are never worth it!* There *really are* a hundred reasons to not have a secret affair!

EXERCISE: *Betrayal processing*

Think back to a time that you cheated or were cheated on. If you or a partner has never cheated, was there another event that wounded trust and connection? Whatever the event, did you resolve back to love and trust or did you separate?

If you separated, was it mostly kind and cooperative, or did you or your spouse keep fighting, never agreeing, till a judge had to make the final decisions? Write about all this in your journal.

If you reconciled, what efforts did you and your partner make to get back to love? Write about this in your journal.

Now, read what you've written and consider what it reveals about who you are and how you've grown or not grown as a person and a partner. Write in your journal any insights, patterns, or awareness you have doing this.

What do your answers reveal about your abilities to be kind and cooperative under stress? What boundaries (if any) are you now better at setting? How did you grow from the process of reconciliation or separation? Write your answers in your journal and share everything with someone you trust—hopefully your spouse.

Chapter 16

Polarity Everywhere!

Erotic polarity is a universal energetic exchange that permeates human existence an all cultures. We do much better being conscious and principled with erotic polarity, and risk hurricanes of social disruption when we are unconscious or unprincipled.

The First Star, "Is there erotic polarity, a spark of attraction, between me and this person," brings these energies into your conscious awareness to help you choose well and maintain an ongoing relationship better.

Imagine you have a married friend named Julie, who comes to you and confesses she has a distracting attraction for Jim at work. She can't stop thinking about him and has been setting up chance encounters.

First, notice the wild difference between you being a woman or a guy! Rarely will a woman seek this kind of support from a male friend. There's too much sexuality and vulnerability involved.

Julie lives with her boyfriend Al, hasn't told Al about Jim, and doesn't know what to do. What do you tell her? Write what you imagine you'd say, especially after reading this last section. Share what you've written with your partner or someone you trust.

Erotic polarities happen regularly in most of our lives. Most of us experience attractions and even occasionally distracting attractions. Julie has a distracting attraction toward Jim, and probably needs to tell Jim she has to back off, and tell Al what happened. If they can't work it out satisfactorily, they probably need to see a therapist to help.

Why tell Al about her distracting attraction? Big secrets separate us and diminish emotional energy between us. Often people describing themselves as "bored" in relationships have significant events, relationships, or experiences they are unwilling to share with their spouse.

Masculine and feminine are metatypes that pervade the human experience. Attunement brought to bear on polarity can lead to enjoyable attractions, sexually satisfying relationships, and enhanced development.

~~~~~~

EXERCISE: *Me as a sexual being*

Read everything you've written on erotic polarities so far in your journal, study your mind map, and then write a description of yourself as a sexual being.

Now, write your answers to the following questions:

✳ *What is your sexual essence and how does it manifest in your manner and relationships? In the sexual occasion, are you more masculine (the leader of the dance, projector of presence and safety), or more feminine (the follower in the dance, projecting love through your body)? Do you switch back and forth, spending more sexual time in one than the other?*

✳ *What are your masculine and feminine sexual aspects? Even if your sexual essence is more masculine or feminine, we all have aspects of both. What are yours?*

✳ *What characterizes your intimate sexual relationships, and what are your strengths and weaknesses in creating and sustaining vibrant sexuality?*

✳ *What skills or principles do you need to focus on to become more confident, fulfilled, and congruent in your unique sexuality?*

* *Is fidelity easy, hard, or impossible for you, and how do you want to be with fidelity?*

Share this with someone you trust, preferably your partner. Read what you've written every day for two weeks. Edit and elaborate as you feel moved. After two weeks, have another talk with your partner or friend about what you've discovered.

Section Endnotes

1 Deida 1997
2 Morano 2016
3 Deida 2004
4 Gilligan 1993
5 Deida 2006
6 Jung 1961
7 Fisher 2004
8 Buss 1997
9 Armstrong 2007
10 Chapman 2015

11 Fisher 2009
12 Cherlin 2009
13 Gottman 2015
14 Bleyer 2015
15 Schreiber 2013
16 Fisher 2004
17 Fisher 2003
18 Cherlan 2009
19 Fisher 2003
20 Cherlan 2009

21 Fisher 2003
22 Darwin 1859
23 Barash 2009
24 Bergner 2009
25 Marano 2016
26 Bergner 2009
27 Evans, 2013
28 Robinson 2009
29 Buss 2003
30 Whitbourne 2012

31 Berreby 1998
32 Clark 1989
33 Shetty 2008
34 Camperio-Ciani 2004
35 Blanchard 1997
36 Cherlin 2009
37 Fisher 2003
38 Cherlan 2009
39 Fisher 2003
40 Cherlan 2009

THE SECOND STAR

· · · · · · · · · · · · · · · · · ·

Does this person maintain their physical and psychological health?

What constitutes physical and psychological health?

When I first read James Masterson's seminal 1981 work on narcissistic and borderline personality disorders,[1] I found it to be like most books by psychoanalysts and object relations theorists—an intricate system of inter-locking perspectives and examples of psychopathology and general crazi-ness. The one enjoyable difference about Masterson's work was a certain hard-nosed practicality he brought to bear. His work has proven to be quite useful to me in understanding and treating extra crazy people and the ones they injure—mostly friends, family, and coworkers.

Like most psychoanalysts, Masterson didn't focus much on health. However, toward the end of his book, he included one sentence about what constitutes a healthy person: "[someone] who takes 100 percent responsi-bility for everything he or she experiences and does."

In the decades since I first read that sentence, I've yet to discover a better definition of health. If we take 100 percent responsibility for everything we experience and do, we are embracing the fact that human life involves constant *choices,* for better or worse. In each moment, we are choosing what to think and how to behave, and these choices are either more healthy or less healthy. Even if we are victims of random events, such as car wrecks, freak injuries, unexpected illnesses, attacks by other people, or natural disasters like earthquakes and floods, as soon as something happens to us, we're responsible for how we respond to the immediate situation and how we continue to process it in our lives.

Admittedly, over 60 percent of our thinking and behaving choices are habitual,[2] and that's one of the reasons I spend so much time on habits in this book. But, unlike all other living creatures, we can *observe* our choices and habits and *choose better* (especially by using the attunement processes discussed in Chapter 3). Choosing *better* is by definition choosing *healthier.*

You can see what a big deal this is in relationships! If I'm making unhealthy physical choices (like engaging in addiction, crime, self-neglect, or unnecessary risks), by definition, I'm a less desirable candidate to you for a relationship as compared to someone who's making healthy physical choices. If I'm making unhealthy psychological choices, like indulging angry, distorted perspectives and defensive states, lying or cheating, self-neglect, resisting caring influence, socially isolating myself, or ignoring emotional pain, you're much more likely to be unhappy and unhealthy in relationship with me.

If *you* are making unhealthy choices, any partner of yours is more likely to be unhealthy and unhappy in relationship with you.

All this has been demonstrated endlessly by research showing how habits are contagious in relationships and social groups—the cultures people exist in. Healthy cultures support healthy habits, and vice versa.[3]

People in the grip of romantic infatuation can see the flaws in their partner, but aren't particularly concerned—medicated as they are by the in-love biochemical joyride.[4] It behooves all of us to be healthy ourselves, and determine *before we fall in love* (if possible) if our partners are healthy.

If we're already in love or in intimate bonding with a partner, it helps to make the relative health of both of our psychological and physical decisions *visible* through self-observation, other-observation, and caring dialogue. Such awareness and conversations influence people to become healthier.

This is one reason married people live longer than singles (with the exception of unhappily married women who tend to not live as long on average as single or happily married women[5]).

How healthy physically and psychologically we and our potential partners are will figure hugely into our relative success and happiness in our lives, and especially our relationships. That's why the second star—"Does this person maintain their physical and psychological health?"—is so important, and why the next eight chapters will explore multiple perspectives and practices supporting those qualities.

Plenitude

In the summer of 2016, I was asked to speak at a unique event being organized in a gorgeous luxury resort called Pena Longa situated near Sintra, Portugal. The event's purpose was to celebrate the 80th birthday of Abilio Diniz, a forward-thinking Brazilian billionaire who had made his fortune bringing supermarkets to Brazil and Portugal. The conference was titled, "Plenitude." It brought together 300 of his friends and family from Brazil, and sixteen speakers from around the world, for a weekend of TEDx-type talks, hour-long workshops, and epic parties. The theme was optimizing a long, healthy, joyful life. My topic was, "Intimacy, Happiness, and Longevity."

Abilio, fascinated with health and longevity for decades, had developed a system of five pillars of body, spirit, mind, purpose, and relationship, which he'd written about in two hugely popular autobiographical books. Each of the speakers was an expert in one of the pillars, and my talk was on the relationship pillar.

Abilio has led an amazing life, rising from immigrant status to national figure, running marathons, being a speed racing champion, and enduring a month of terror after being kidnapped and held for ransom in his 30s. His five pillars approach closely mirrors the Integral principles: that the best understanding of the present moment involves taking into account body/mind/spirit in self/culture/nature.

The speakers were internationally known experts like George Mumford (author of *The Mindful Athlete,* and mindfulness coach to Phil Jackson's championship Bulls and Lakers teams), Dan Buettner (who researched the "blue zones" with the highest percentages of healthy centenarians), and Aubrey de Grey (Chief Science Officer for the SENS foundation on longevity).

I was especially fascinated with Dan Buettner's presentation on those five blue zones. He'd found enclaves in Okinawa, Tunisia, a Greek Island off of Turkey, Costa Rica, and Loma Linda, California with the healthiest longest-lived people on earth. What did these groups have in common?

* They lived in tribal enclaves with shared spiritual beliefs and long-time birth-to-death membership.

* They all had plant-based diets.

* They had lives that kept them moving (often outside in nature), including gardening, food preparation, maintaining their houses and community, walking, fishing, and visiting.

* They regularly took time off for socializing, religious practices, and to be outside.

* They had standards of moderation in eating, drinking, and life in general, and, if they did drink, it was some variant of red wine.

* Each person had a reason to get up and engage the day, often to serve others, whether it was family members, children, or volunteer work.

Apparently health, as measured by number of old, active individuals in a group, is intimately associated with diet, lifestyle, meaning, relationships, shared spirituality, and nature.

All of these blue-zones cultures supported these traits, with members mutually regulating each other to be healthier.

Unfortunately, most cultures—and I'm talking to *you,* America!—don't adequately support these qualities. It leaves us as individuals, married partners, family members, and community members to advocate for healthy living for ourselves and others in the face of cultural pressures to work too hard, sleep too little, eat unhealthy food, excessively indulge in drugs and alcohol, and socially isolate ourselves from caring others. These bad habits begin with *us,* but also extend to *who we choose* to share our lives with—especially our husbands, wives, lovers, life partners, and friends. Why? Because habits are contagious!

Let's just let this sink in for a moment. Decades of research have shown that habits are contagious. Live with non-smokers, you're more likely to be a non-smoker. Live with people who eat healthily, you're more likely to eat healthily, and so on.[6] This is why the Second Star, "Does this person maintain their physical and psychological health?" is such a big deal! We want to choose healthy people who intend to get healthier throughout life, to support us being healthy people who get healthier throughout life.

This section of the book explores what health means in Chapter 17. Chapters 18 and 19 dive more deeply into how we create and change habits (both happy ones and traumatic ones), and which habits are the most central and crucial to a healthy, happy life. In Chapters 21 through 24 we examine defensive states, and states of healthy response to the present moment—the bottom line in psychological health. Finally, Chapter 25 considers the information, insights, and reactions you had to this section in order to shape a personal health program for you.

Chapter 17

Physical and Psychological Health

We all have intuitive knowledge and incredible wisdom about physical and psychological health. I suspect you know more than you think about this subject. How does our intuitive wisdom fit with what science has uncovered in the last hundred years? Mostly, quite well!

EXERCISE: *Assessing the Second Star*

Ask yourself, "Does my partner maintain his or her physical and psychological health?" (If you're single, ask, "Did my last partner maintain his or her physical and psychological health?") What are your first reactions, ideas/thoughts/feelings, as you answer this question? Write these down.

Ask yourself, "Do I maintain my physical and psychological health?" What are your first reactions, ideas/thoughts/feelings, as you answer? Write these down.

Read what you've written and look for patterns—like you and your partner sharing certain good or bad habits. Write about this and share it with your partner, writing afterwards about how the conversation went.

What defines health?

Often the best way to intuitively know if *another* maintains their physical and psychological health is to be dedicated to maintaining *our* physical and psychological health. When we uncover blind spots in understanding ourselves, it often exposes our blind spots in understanding.

Health involves being true to our current understandings of what constitutes a physically/psychologically healthy person, and reaching for better understandings throughout life. This is a growth mindset applied to health—I'm true to my current best health ideas and practices, interested in better ones, and willing to trade old ones for better ones as I encounter them.

Being willing to change your mind in the face of persuasive new data is a big deal! Low-fat diets were recommended in the 1970s, but now we know we want diets high in healthy fats—especially omega 3s. Distance running was a highly touted form of exercise in the 1970s and 1980s, but now many physical trainers know there is an algorithm that tells us that when our acute physical stress load over our chronic load exceeds 1.3, we risk injury. I've changed my mind and adjusted my habits in the face of new data many times in my life, and I expect to do the same more times in the years to come as I learn more about health, love, and happiness.

So, to summarize, health involves being true to our current understandings of what constitutes a physically/psychologically healthy person, and reaching for better understandings throughout life. This covers a lot of territory! Are there ways of breaking this down into more manageable dimensions? Yes!

In Integral studies, health is broadly defined as *horizontal* and *vertical* health.

Horizontal health is being true to the knowledge and values you have in your current worldview about healthy body/mind/spirit relationships.

A college professor named Andy came into a session with extreme anxiety about flying. He would still fly to travel, but was very uncomfortable in planes. As we explored his daily existence, we concluded he lived a generally healthy life. He was true to his values, practiced the golden rule with others, took care of his body, suffered from no addictions, and lived his principles. "I'm all fucked up!" he proclaimed after he explained his fear of flying.

"Andy, I disagree." I responded. "I think you're a healthy guy with a distressing fear of flying—which I'm happy to help you with. Healthy people have problems. They deal with them responsibly like you're doing. They do their best, ask for help when they need it, and receive influence to grow."

I said this to help Andy recognize he was a healthy guy with a problem, and needed to be more true to his current worldview to not let his fears make choices for him. His discomfort with flying was unnecessary suffering, and he had done the responsible thing (the *healthy* thing) to come in to see me to radically diminish his fear.

One unhealthy belief he had was his conviction that one irrational fear meant he was "fucked up." Health is not being perfect, but rather is doing your best to be healthy according to your current standards.

Vertical health is receiving influence to expand knowledge and refine values so that *how you process experience or how you experience yourself and the world expands and changes.*

When I was 35, my son Ethan was born. As a long-time martial artist, I had always loved samurai movies, and one afternoon a week after Ethan's birth, I went and saw the Kurasawa movie, *Ran*. During the first battle scene, as the young men were dying, I couldn't watch. Even though I knew they were actors, I kept thinking, "They were all babies once like Ethan." I walked out of the movie realizing Ethan's birth had influenced how I experienced the world, and it's been the same ever since. Becky's pregnancy and Ethan's birth had created a deeper, felt understanding of the profound sacredness of human life, and the miracle that is every birth. It changed my understanding of martial arts, war, people, and violence in general. This was an upward shift in my moral and interpersonal lines of development (an example of vertical health), as the world I experienced had changed and would never be the same.

Progressive worldviews

Vertical health means you develop through progressive worldviews that become more caring, less distorted, and more whole as you grow, though every worldview has healthy and unhealthy manifestations.

The natural development of worldviews from birth onwards looks something like the following:

* Babies are born without much individual awareness, and then grow to feel psychologically separate from mother and other caregivers.

* At around 14 months of age, children discover that they are a boy or girl.

* At around two years of age, kids can observe themselves and others as thinking beings. Even though they are intensely social human beings, kids tend to be more egocentric in preschool years. For instance, the capacity for co-corrective play, where you and another can share the power in shaping a game, doesn't appear until around three years of age.

* Mostly egocentric preschoolers grow into conformist elementary school children, who are motivated to follow cultural rules and inhabit cultural roles.

* Rule/role grade-schoolers in turn grow into more rational teens, more capable of critical thought and self-reflection, though intensely motivated to be accepted in their preferred social groups.

* Rational teens can grow into more pluralistic and world-centric college students or workers who care about how everyone is treated.

* Non-egalitarian idealists can grow into Integral multidimensional thinkers who have no problem with hierarchies, and can see the strengths and weaknesses of all worldviews.

These worldviews are literally that—the worlds we perceive as we move through our lives—and people stable at egocentric, conformist, rational, pluralistic, and Integral levels of functioning have different *views* of the world.[7]

Any human can lock into a particular worldview in different areas of their lives and resist further development. Selfish narcissists can stay egocentric their whole life. Fundamentalist conformists can ignore even the most blatant facts that challenge their cherished preconceptions and beliefs. Competitive rationalists can focus on profit/loss/winning/losing forever. Self-righteous pluralists can simultaneously take powerful stands for egalitarianism and non-hierarchical social systems, while contemptuously dismissing those who disagree with them, and never discover the irony of their rigid positions.

Vertical development is having a growth mindset toward all aspects of life—social, professional, physical, sexual, artistic, spiritual—so that we stay naturally interested in better perspectives and practices, leading us to progressive awakenings onto new, broader worldviews.

Our views of health often change as we develop.

We all have strong opinions about what is healthy or unhealthy, and these change as we grow. A competitive runner at 25 will push himself with the value of "No pain, no gain." Fifteen years later, he'll likely attend more to the welfare of his body, with values such as, "Don't work out with an injury." A 21-year-old woman might have a value of dating different guys to expand her knowledge of men and relationships, and to be cautious of settling down too soon. A 32-year-old woman might have a value of, "If he's a potential Five Star guy, I will take my time, be patient, and stay committed to progress with him until I find out if he's *really* a Five Star guy."

We grow through different stages of wanting, acting, and thinking. What's most important is to be true to our current values and deep purpose with a growth mindset of, "My ideas and values about physical and psychological health will grow and change, but my desire to be true to my values, to be healthy, to love well and be loved well, will be a constant."

That being said, core values and understandings tend to persist and become more refined rather than replaced as we develop. For instance, we might believe at nine years old that all lies are bad, and at 19 years old that some lies to protect others are good. This is a refinement of the "Be honest" value.

~~~~~~

EXERCISE: *Physically healthy you*

In your journal, make a list of what constitutes a physically healthy you. Sleep, nutrition, exercise, physical environment, risky behavior, relationships, purpose, work, and mindset are good dimensions to explore, all associated with physical health.

EXERCISE: *Psychologically healthy you*

*Now, make a list of what constitutes a psychologically healthy you. You
can include all the above physical dimensions (each relevant to how you
feel/think/function) and add more psychological aspects like mood, relationship skills, mindful awareness, ability to receive and act on caring
influence from others, openness, resilience, stress management, and how
well you down-regulate painful feelings like anxiety, fear, anger, depression, shame, and guilt, and up-regulate pleasurable feelings like joy, love,
gratitude, forgiveness, humor, and compassion.*

*After you make your lists, read and edit them at least three times. What
do you notice? I suspect your lists include the four elements of doing, not
doing, embracing, and resisting.*

Doing, not doing, embracing, and resisting

My physical health list includes doing healthy activities like exercise, eating healthy food, sleep, rest, vitamins/supplements, and practitioner appointments with people like doctors, dentists, chiropractors, therapists, and
teachers. My physical health lists also includes *not doing* unhealthy activities
like smoking, drugs, excessive drinking, reckless risk-taking, and unhealthy
eating and self-neglect.

My psychological list includes *embracing* healthy qualities/actions like
self-acceptance, kindness, compassion, intimacy, generous attitudes and
acts, clean boundaries, and receiving healthy influence. My psychological list
also include *resisting* unhealthy qualities and actions such as self-loathing,
impulsive attacks, unkindness, codependence, disconnecting from others,
and resistance to compassionate influence.

Both embracing and resisting require *affect regulation,* which involves
how well I soothe painful emotions like distress, anger, anxiety, shame,
obsession, or depression, and amplify pleasurable emotions like joy, love,
gratitude, or compassion.

EXERCISE: *Embracing and resisting*

Observe and record in your journal what healthy and unhealthy activities, thoughts, and impulses you embrace, and/or resist each day for two days.

Be especially interested in healthy behaviors that seem easy like brushing your teeth, being loving to your infant daughter, or not screaming at your husband when he leaves his clothes on the floor for the thousandth time. Also, notice which healthy behaviors are hard, like setting boundaries for your intrusive roommate, or not eating the cookies Cindy brings into work.

Share all this material with someone you trust (hopefully your partner), and pay attention to whether the conversation feels healthy or unhealthy to you. Write about what you noticed in the conversation, and then share that with your partner.

Double standards

Do you have the same health standards for others as you have for yourself? Especially, do you have the same standards for your partner? I've found it rare for people to have uniform health standards for themselves and others. Usually we tend to be harder on ourselves or extra hard on others (though some people are extra hard on themselves *and* others). Being extra hard on ourselves or others causes lots of suffering!

Growth mindsets help here. If you are too hard on yourself, observe the hurtful self-talk and hostile, anxious, or despairing feelings with attuned acceptance and caring intent. Over time, we can have compassionate self-understanding even when we make mistakes or feel self-hatred rise from our destructive Shadow selves. Over weeks, months, and years, this accepting/caring attitude becomes more who we feel ourselves to be. Our unconscious Shadow selves grow to identify with acceptance and caring intent of ourselves. This is self-transcendence, a hallmark of vertical health.

EXERCISE: *Unkind habits*

For a few days, observe any unkindness you direct at yourself with as much attuned acceptance and caring intent as you can, and record your observations in your journal.

Similarly, if there is anyone you are unkind to, especially repetitively— like bad drivers or your angry daughter— observe your hurtful or disrespectful tones, references, and actions with attuned acceptance and caring intent. Write about any insights or observations in your journal.

Attribution theory and distortion

We are always instinctively trying to make sense of each moment, and attribution theory is the study of what we add, subtract, or miss in our attributions to ourselves, others, and the world.

Attribution theory is full of studies of how people distort what's happening when not feeling *compassionate understanding*. (This tends to be the most *accurate* understanding, largely free of projections and distortions.)

Attribution research is especially interested in distortions we normalize without reflecting on them. One example is that many people have the attitude, "if you hit me once I believe I should hit you twice," without considering the basic unfairness of the idea. Another example is projecting conscious attack onto innocent mistakes, as when I accidently spill coffee on your dress while we're arguing, and you snap, "You did that on purpose!" without realizing that spilling coffee on your dress on purpose is wildly at odds with my personality. Such distortions are blind spots where we can't see clearly until we bring compassionate understanding to bear on ourselves and others.

Attribution theory is brilliantly illustrated by a principle taught to me by Angus, a successful businessman/athlete I once worked with. Angus called it "the asshole rule."

He and I were talking about a particular guy who was causing him trouble. "You know," he told me. "He fits the asshole rule to a tee!"

I hadn't heard the term, but knew I was going to like it. "Angus, what's the asshole rule?"

He laughed. "You don't know the asshole rule?" I smiled and shook my head. "If you go about your life and every once in a while you run into somebody who seems like an asshole, they probably *are* an asshole. If you go about your life and everybody you meet seems to be an asshole, then *you're* the asshole."

That's attribution theory in a nutshell. There is deep wisdom in this, and paying attention to it can wake you up in unexpected ways, *especially with your partner!*

Never assume a problem is just your partner's! You are responsible for everything you experience and do, so you have agency and input on every interaction and every relationship. You also have healthy and unhealthy responses to problems. There is help you can seek out, decisions you can make, conversations you can start. You have choices!

In general, in relationships, choose love and health! Compassionate understanding of me and you leads to a sense of responsibility to serve the highest good. Love and health are values that lead to the highest good.

Chapter 18

Trauma and Health

Trauma compromises health. It's true that meeting adversity and triumphing can make us stronger and more resilient, but trauma hammers bodies and spirits and makes us more susceptible to almost every form of human malady.

How can I so confidently say this?

Adverse Childhood Experiences (ACE) Study[8]

In the early 1990s, Dr. Vincent Felitti was running a weight-loss program for dangerously obese men and women out of Kaiser Permanente in San Diego. Disturbed at how many of his patients lost hundreds of pounds and then put them back on, he began having participants meet in small groups to discuss what made it so hard to keep the weight off. Astonishingly, almost all participants had an abuse history, with a staggering 50 percent being survivors of sexual abuse.

Robert Anda from the National Institutes of Health saw Felitti present at a conference, and Anda suggested that they use the Kaiser Permanente system to find out the prevalence of childhood abuse in a normal, middle class population.

So, Kaiser Permanente in San Diego asked 17,400 middle class, middle-aged members if they had experienced any of ten different kind of adverse events as children. The categories were:

* Sexual abuse

* Physical abuse—not normal spankings, but beatings that left marks

* Emotional abuse—chronic shaming, raging, or contemptuous dismissals of the child

* Physical neglect

* Emotional neglect

* Observing domestic violence

* Having a family member with mental illness

* Having a family member with alcohol or drug addiction

* Having a family member who was incarcerated

* Not being raised by both biological parents

Scoring was simple—for every kind of adverse experience you experienced, you received one point, so your score could be 0 to 10.

The results were staggering in their implications and forever changed the way trauma was viewed in this country.

Here are some of the findings:

* A third of respondents had scores of 0.

* 11 percent had five or more categories. If you had more than six categories, you lost, on average, twenty years of life compared to someone who scored 0.

* 10 percent of respondents suffered verbal abuse.

* More than 25 percent suffered physical abuse.

* 28 percent of the women and 16 percent of the men were sexually abused by individuals five or more years older than them.

* Over 13 percent witnessed domestic violence against their mothers.

* 25 percent had a family member who was an alcoholic or addict.

* Of those who had adverse childhood experiences, 87 percent had scores of 2 or more.

* 15 percent had scores of 4 or more.

* Of those with scores of 4 or more, over 50 percent had learning or behavior problems at school compared to 3 percent for those who scored 0.66 percent of the 4-or-more women and 35 percent of the 4-or-more men had chronic depression as compared to 12 percent for those who scored 0.

* Those with scores of 6 or more were 4,600 percent more likely to be intravenous drug users than those with scores of 0.

* High ACE scores predicted smoking, obesity, all ten of the leading causes of death in the U.S. multiple sexual partners, unintended pregnancies, STDs, higher workplace absenteeism, financial problems, and lower lifetime income.

* Statistically, no category of adverse event was more predictive than any other of physical or psychological disease.

* The fewer kinds of adverse events people had, the fewer problems they had as adults.

These findings have since been replicated and expanded. Two thirds of adults have had at least one or two traumatic events in their life. We now *know* that adverse childhood events, *as well as adult trauma,* can cause enduring damage, affect gene expression, and rob decades from people's lives.

Adult trauma can hurt as badly as childhood trauma. Soldiers deployed into battle zones developed more trauma disorders (and progressively more compromised brain functioning) the more often they were deployed.[9] For those of us who've never been in combat, one rape, assault, car wreck, episode of domestic violence (which occurs in a third of couples), or any catastrophe can instantly rewire our brain as well.

"Little t" traumas

All of us have had stressful events that didn't rise to the level of catastrophic "big T" traumas, but still affect our sense of self and how we move through the world. These include being bullied at school, having a parent be clueless when we were upset, suffering from a lover deserting us or cheating on us, or our family having to move suddenly, causing us to lose childhood friends. Some call these "little t" traumas.

In some studies, "little t" traumas caused more problems for people—because they *always* occur in normal development—than "big T" traumas. We often discover the effects of "little t" traumas in defensive states where the amplified emotions and distorted perspectives are linked to past events. For example, your daughter uses the same tone that the girls in sixth grade used to humiliate you, and you're shocked at the flood of rage, or weight of shame, you feel when she does it.

What to do?

First of all, statistics reflect trends and tendencies, but we all are unique and mostly resilient. For instance, most adults who experience traumatic events do not develop post-traumatic stress disorders. On the other hand, all of us are influenced by positive and negative events in our development.

Luckily, today we have many proven therapies for both "big T" and "little t" traumas that help us resolve past distress and grow wiser and stronger. Examples are eye movement desensitization and reprocessing (EMDR), somatic experiencing, neurofeedback, yoga, theater groups, sensorimotor psychotherapy, Integrally-informed psychotherapy, martial arts, and countless others. In this era, most competent psychotherapists know how to help people heal from childhood and adult traumas.

If you have psychological or physical health symptoms that are not getting better, get help from therapists and doctors. What conditions might be influenced by traumas? I started to make lists of psychological and physical conditions that could be stress- or trauma-related, and quickly realized they included almost every psychological and physical condition!

Suffice it to say, if you don't experience yourself as maintaining your own physical and psychological health, get help! Nothing is more healing for human beings than loving contact with other caring and knowledgeable human beings, and asking for and receiving helping influence is a human superpower.

Chapter 19

Habits

Brains constantly learn from experience. Our Shadow self—our adaptive unconscious—instinctively guides each of us as best it can, mostly through *habits*.

All life is wired to create habits in one way or another. Humans bring the wild cards of self-aware consciousness and conscious intent into habit creation—yielding advantages and disadvantages.

How do habits form? Evolutionary forces want us to survive and thrive, so our nervous systems constantly program us in response to our experiences. If I frown at you enough at work, you begin to increasingly avoid me. If Becky corrects my grammar enough ("Ethan and me are both..." Becky: "It's Ethan and *I*"), my grammar improves. Starting from before birth, nervous systems respond to the environment to create habitual forms of feelings, impulses, and thoughts.

Forty to sixty percent of everything we do is *habitual*. Our unconscious Shadow selves guide us with instincts, emotions, and impulses. Good habits sustain us; bad habits diminish us.[10]

What were the first five things you did this morning? Write them down, and ask yourself, what choice did I have with each? If there is a sense that a behavior (like brushing your teeth, pouring a cup of coffee, or letting the dog out) isn't a choice, it's just what I do in the morning, it's probably a habit.

Harvey's habits

Check out the following story about man I worked with named Harvey, and see how many of his and others' habits jump out at you.

Harvey was a successful businessman who had built a comfortable living in Santa Barbara (not an easy task in an expensive town; he was a rock-solid consultant for local organizations and individuals). Tall and burly, he struggled with his weight, but daily exercise and organic food kept him in pretty good shape. His wife, Jean, was smart, a good mother, and sexually available, but fierce when challenged, and he had learned to avoid confrontations over their fourteen years of marriage.

Harvey had been born and raised in Boston, and his businessmen friends thought nothing of going to strip bars and occasionally partying with prostitutes while at conferences and business trips. Their collective loophole was, "We work hard, and our wives aren't into sex, so we deserve to party."

Harvey had the additional nuance of how lonely he got when away from Jean and the kids, but, after developing the habit of seeking sexual novelty from prostitutes, he just "couldn't" (didn't want to) give it up when he stopped traveling so intensely. When he moved to Santa Barbara, he quickly figured out the local prostitution scene—"escort services"—and dialed it whenever he felt the hunger for sexual adventure.

Inevitably, Jean caught Harvey in a series of lies leading to the discovery of one liaison with a prostitute, and he ended up in my office, facing possible divorce as the whole scene unfolded. Jean was furious and inconsolable, and Harvey felt his whole life spiraling out of control. When I asked him how it all happened, he responded with his loophole, "I didn't think she'd ever find out, so what was the harm?"

What habits do you see revealed? Here are some that stand out to me:

* Harvey's habit of being a solid consultant with his clients—he always put their welfare first and would have been appalled at the idea of lying to them the way he lied to Jean.

* Harvey's and his friends' habits of rationalizing their solicitation of prostitutes, and reinforcing cheating with each other. Even after Jean caught him, Harvey went back to, "I didn't think she'd ever find out, so what was the harm?"

* Harvey's struggle with destructive eating habits.

* Harvey's increasingly easy transition from sexual unsettledness to calling a hooker in Santa Barbara when he stopped traveling so much. This is how many addictions develop. As you say "yes" to unhealthy impulses that somehow gratify, it gets easier and easier (more *habitual*) to keep saying it.

* Jean's automatic fury at Harvey's infidelity, and her continued attacks as we processed in subsequent session, became a *habit of response*. What Jean wanted was to feel secure and connected to Harvey again, requiring self-reflective and mature communication, but for months any processing of the infidelities resulted in her automatic contempt and fury. Both of these drove Harvey away and inward (his habitual responses to her rage), leaving Jean feeling more frustrated and alone.

* Both Jean's and Harvey's continued participation in therapy reflected their habit of staying married no matter what, even as they hurt and criticized each other.

You can see the power of these habits. It took *years* of therapy for me to help Harvey and Jean change them, and they *still* struggled with them from time to time.

Why aren't habits easier?

The neurobiology of habits explains why good ones can be hard to establish and bad ones hard to break. Habits are mostly contained in the right hemisphere, and associated with survival by the brain, which is primed to learn self-supportive and self-protective habits and not give them up.[11] For example, we get lonely and seek out others (self-supportive), or our husband criticizes us for being late and we offer excuses (self-protective).

The world and our inner experience constantly are flooding us with inputs, which are processed in our unconscious Shadow selves—our adaptive unconscious. Our Shadow has been programmed to send us habitual feelings, impulses, and stories to guide us. At any given moment, our Shadow selves are generating the habits, good or bad, that we've associated with dealing with the current moment. For instance, "It's late," "I'm tired," and "I have to get up early tomorrow to work": A good habit would be telling me, "I'm sleepy. I should go to bed." A bad habit would be to drink coffee and stay up till 3:00 a.m. playing video games.

Habits are based in *implicit* and *explicit* memories.[12] We have lots of different kinds of memory: short term memory, working memory, semantic memory, episodic memory, and consolidated memories, but two general categories that are super-relevant to habits are implicit and explicit memories.

Implicit memories are the programming our brain does automatically from before birth, priming us in certain situations to react in certain ways. They don't *feel* like memories when they show up, but they have images, feelings, and impulses just like memories. Let's say Bob next door yelled at me as 14-month-old for scratching his car and *really scared me,* so my brain encodes a memory saying, "Bob is scary!" I might fear Bob later when I'm older—or even men who *look* or *sound* like Bob—but, if asked why I get so afraid, I answer, "I don't know why. I'm just scared of that guy."

Another example of implicit memory is *semantic memory,* where I know something, but have no idea when I learned it. When did you learn that 2x2=4? Or that Washington D.C. is the capital of the U.S.? It's habitually present in memory with no knowledge of when or how you learned it.

Explicit memories start around 18 months of age, when the brain (especially the hippocampus) matures enough, and explicit memories feel like something is being remembered. If Bob yelled at me when I was four, at seven I'm scared of Bob and know why: "He was mean to me when I scratched his car."

Most habits involve implicit memories—we feel, think, or want to do something, but don't remember how we learned that. This is a significant component of our Shadow selves—our adaptive unconscious—because in many situations we habitually think, feel, and act without consciously knowing *why.*

How do brains learn knowledge and behaviors? The right and left hemispheres learn differently, and in many ways are different brains. The right, non-linear, holistic, emotionally driven, mostly non-verbal hemisphere is where habits are stored and retrieved from.

The right hemisphere usually learns habits *slowly*. You often need to repeat the same habit over and over to make it automatic. John McEnroe, while he was winning major tennis championships, had a little note on his racquet saying, "Keep your eye on the ball!" He wanted to keep reinforcing that particular habit and had to consciously remind himself *thousands* of times to anchor it into his behavior.

The literal, logical, linguistic, and slower-processing left hemisphere learns new routines quickly, but must *consciously decide* to implement them—sometimes like remembering "Keep your eye on the ball!" thousands of times.

For instance, say you wanted to practice being grateful for nature, and I suggest you cultivate a feeling of gratitude in your heart for nature every time you walk outside (actually an excellent practice). You'd need to practice this multiple times before you didn't have to think about it—you just felt grateful for nature every time you walked outside.

Over a hundred years ago, William James, one of the founders of modern psychology, suggested that to learn a new habit, you need to practice it on twenty-one consecutive days. Since then we've discovered that if you activate the same neural networks (by practicing a new habit repetitively) over thirty days, stem cells in our brain can divide, and the daughter cells become integrative neurons that hardwire the new circuits.

Habits are contagious, both good and bad, so social context and who we hang out with really matters

If you eat healthily, your husband is more likely to. If you smoke, your spouse is more likely to smoke. Habits are contagious, for better or worse.

This means if you're asking yourself the Second Star question, "Does this person maintain their physical and psychological health?", you're also checking out what potential influences he or she will have on you if you're in a relationship. Alternately, if you observe how well you maintain your physical and psychological health, you're also observing the influences you are going to have on your partner, family, and friends.

We tend to mirror the habits of the cultures we live in. If we live with smokers, we're more likely to smoke. If we live with meditators, we're more likely to meditate. If our friends are overweight, we're more likely to be overweight ourselves. This is called *social contagion,* and partially explains the phenomenon of culture lifting us up or pulling us down depending on cultural standards.[13] If you think about it, cultural standards are the sum total of cultural *habits.*

EXERCISE: *Healthy and unhealthy habits*

Make a list in your journal of your three healthiest habits, especially with your partner. Are you routinely patient? Kind? Do you easily look for what's valid in points he or she makes, even if you're also feeling criticized? These are all good habits.

Look at your three healthiest habits and cultivate a sense of gratitude in your heart for these life-and-relationship-affirming behaviors. It's useful to notice what you do right and feel pleasure and gratitude. This is a wonderful habit!

Now make a list of your three unhealthiest habits, especially in relationship with your spouse or potential lovers. Maybe you don't apologize easily, or you shut down when you're hurt or angry, or nag your partner when you're frustrated. These are all counterproductive bad habits.

After your three unhealthy ones, write what good habit(s) you'd need to cultivate in order to replace the bad habit, and what would the first thirty seconds of each new good habit look like. For instance, if you habitually don't apologize, you can focus on when your partner is distressed with you, identify what's valid about his or her complaint, and apologize without defending or explaining.

For the next several days, replace a bad habit with a good habit at least 50 percent of the time. Write in your journal how this went and share it with someone you trust—hopefully with your partner.

The first thirty seconds are the key!

A study of smoking cessation found that people who had a plan of what to do when they felt like smoking were twenty-three times less likely to smoke. Other studies have demonstrated that the first thirty seconds of a new habit are the most difficult and necessary seconds of new learning.[14] It's better to start and quit than not to start. Overwhelmingly, if we get good at starting a new habit we are predisposed to keep strengthening it.

If you can consistently engage in the first thirty seconds of a new habit, you are home free. Even if you start and stop, consistently doing the first thirty seconds will eventually transform you in any area you wish to grow. Creativity has been studied endlessly, and every expert I've encountered says that starting, even if you start and then walk away, is the key to creative output and establishing new habits.

I suggest you apply this to the previous exercise. Whatever good habits you intend to learn, make sure you *at least* do the first thirty seconds of each one regularly.

Habits and optimal stress

Most of us have a fair amount of habitual stress. Modern life often presents us with more demands than we have time to address, and the rushed out-of-control feelings associated with this can lead to a habitual background hum of anxiety and frustration in our lives—a recipe for becoming stressed out! This is clearly one of the reasons why 70 percent of the problems brought to doctors end up being stress-related,[15] 10 percent of the population is on some form of psychotropic medication,[16] and relationships falter when couples have small children (the first parental casualties of family demands tend to be self-care and maintaining the couple relationship).[17]

But don't despair! Stress can make us weaker, but also stronger! A life with *no* stress is a life without challenge, and that can lead us to fixed mindsets where we'd rather stagnate than risk change, growth, and the inevitable mistakes and failures associated with progress. Life and love involve many individual and interpersonal processes where we either grow or become stuck and stale.

Maintaining the marital love affair and friendship within a lifetime of growth means embracing some stressors like travel, difficult conversations, necessary assertions with each other and others, sexual expansion and experimentation, and new perspectives in general. In other words, creating new good habits and supplanting old bad habits with new good habits is a lifelong practice that makes us wiser, stronger, and healthier.

Hormesis is optimal stress for growth and health

Hormesis is the study of optimal stress to promote health and happiness. We want habits of maintaining optimal intensity and quality of stressors at the right intervals, so our body and consciousness keeps disintegrating partially with challenge, and reintegrating to greater complexity, functionality, and strength with adequate rest, processing, and help. With exercise, this is balancing the stress of exercise with rest and recuperation to get stronger rather than weaker. This balancing act is how we can tune our physical and psychological/relational lives to maximize happiness and growth, while minimizing disease or unnecessary suffering.

This is challenging because *the same activity* can be healthy or unhealthy, depending upon the dose. (Paracelsus said in the sixteenth century that the difference between medicine and poison is the dosage.) One great example of this is the finding that people who exercise too much have about the same life expectancy of people who don't exercise at all! Another relational example is that an occasional argument with your wife can clear the air if you argue respectfully, but daily arguments can ruin your marriage.

Your life and your relationships will have their own carrying capacities for stress, and no two people or relationships are exactly the same. Hormesis says we want the optimal amount of stress in our relationships and personal lives to maximize health, growth, and love for us and our partners.

So, we want the *right amount* of stress to maximize health and love, and we want to make maintaining that right amount as *habitual* as possible.

How can we do this?

EXERCISE: *Hormesis*

Observe and record as many healthy and unhealthy physical, psychological, or relational habits you exhibit throughout your typical day as you can. Examples of healthy habits could be flossing your teeth, kissing your husband goodbye and hello, exercising, eating a healthy lunch, listening to your son talk about his day, or resting for an hour in the afternoon. Unhealthy habits could be smoking cigarettes, eating doughnuts for breakfast, drinking coffee instead of resting, or flirting with the waitress while eating dinner with your wife at the diner. Write about these habits in your journal.

* *Go back over previous journal entries and use what you observe and insights you generate to expand this list of healthy habits and unhealthy habits.*

* *As you write each unhealthy habit, be alert for healthy alternative habits and write them down. If you're usually late, you could learn to be five minutes early. If you ignore your partner often, you could look at him and smile every time you see him. If you smoke cigarettes, you could have a cup of tea instead of a smoke.*

* *"Keystone habits" are habits that have many unexpected positive consequences, like regular exercise, food journaling, receiving caring influence, or lovingkindness practice. (We'll be talking much more about keystone habits in the next chapter.) Any new good habit you experiment with might turn out to be a keystone habit with unexpected benefits.*

* *Almost any attuned, healthy discipline could become a healthy new habit for you! Remember your human superpower of focused intent and action, in service of principle, and driven by resolve. Left hemisphere keeps deciding and enacting until right hemisphere takes over and the new behavior becomes habitual.*

* *Choose one new habit you'd especially love to eventually practice automatically and effortlessly—a potential game changer in an important*

area, like healthy exercise, or being significantly more kind or affectionate with your partner—and practice it every day for a week, with special emphasis on the first thirty seconds.

✳ *After a week, write about your experiences and tell someone you trust about the experiment. According to William James, you only have fourteen more days to go before this new strength becomes a habit!*

Relational habits

Let's dig deeper into habits and relationships. How do you habitually relate to your partner? Are you loving, dismissive, friendly, warm, cold, attentive, appreciative, critical? You probably have a mixture of responses, with an emphasis on one or the other in certain situations. Many people feel loving and connected right after making love. Alternately, couples often can get stressed and irritated with each other discussing finances or a child's misbehavior.

How do your habitual responses change when you are happy, unhappy, rested, tired, irritated, threatened, or secure (not to mention PMSing, or pissed off that your football team lost today)? As detailed in Chapter 11, it's easier to be attentive and supportive in the romantic infatuation stage of relationship, and harder in intimate bonding when we habituate to each other and our old family-of-origin habits of defense become more urgent.

~~~~~~

EXERCISE: *Relational habits*

Write in your journal when it is easier to be positive and loving with your partner, and when it is hardest. Share what you've written with your partner, and talk about what you are willing to do to be better during the hard times. Respectfully ask him or her to do the same, and then write about your conversation.

Practice good habits in relationships!

Habitual *appreciative* attention is good for relationships! Habitual *critical* attention degrades relationships. Couples who mutually celebrate either partner's victories stay together longer and report more relational satisfaction.[18] Newlywed couples who only turned *toward* the other's bids for attention a third of the time (they ignored or dismissed the other's smiles, requests, or questions two thirds of the time) were likely to be divorced six years later.[19] Newlyweds who turned *toward* bids for attention 86 percent of the time (they responded positively to smiles, requests, or questions) were more likely to be together and happy with each other six years later.

Do you smile at your partner when you first see him or her entering a room? Do you ask about his or her day and listen with interest? Do you stay attuned to him or her in a social situation? If your partner makes an irritating error, do you jump to conclusions and criticize, or do you remain supportive and talk it out back to mutual satisfaction?

Notice how it's easy to see the difference between the healthy and unhealthy habits I just mentioned? As I suggested at the beginning of this book, we all have incredible intuitive wisdom about how to love that can guide us *if we access it.*

~~~~~~

EXERCISE: *Use your partner as a guide*

Make a list of all the good habits you want your partner/spouse, or potential partner/spouse to have. Use as much detail as possible. He puts all his dirty clothes in the laundry hamper, she doesn't interrupt my stories at parties, he always smiles at me when I come into a room, or she is consistently patient with our son.

Now look at that list and put a star by the ones you practice with your partner. Consider cultivating the ones you have trouble with, and choose a couple to experiment with for the next three days. Write about your experiences each day, and then on the fourth day talk with your partner or someone else you trust about what you discovered.

Chapter 20

Keystone Habits

Some good habits create cascading positive effects—often unexpectedly. These are called *keystone habits,* and are particularly potent in creating and maintaining physical and psychological health. Two of the most widely researched keystone habits are exercise and food journaling.[20]

Regular exercise leads to being on time more, less depressed, and less vulnerable to multiple illnesses and disorders (leading one doctor to say that exercise was the closest we've come to a panacea, a cure for all ills!).

Food journaling, writing down the kinds and amounts of everything you eat, leads to healthier eating, planning wiser meals, and losing twice as much weight as people who don't food journal.

Here's a list of keystone habits that researcher Charles Duhigg included in his 2012 book, *The Power of Habit:*

* Having family dinners
* Making your bed every morning
* Exercising regularly

* Keeping a food journal

* Developing daily routines

* Meditating

* Planning out your days

* Practicing self discipline daily to increase your willpower (turning away from unhealthy foods, stopping videogames in time to get enough sleep, coming to a complete stop at every stop sign—any activity that is beneficial and requires effort increases your willpower)

In my practice over the last forty-plus years, I've found *lovingkindness meditation* and receiving caring influence to be keystone habits that enhance health and love in multiple areas. They are especially effective in intimate relationships. Let's dive into them more deeply.

EXERCISE: *Lovingkindness meditation*

Lovingkindness meditation is easy to learn and practice. It is a great way to improve how you naturally relate to your partner and others. All meditation enhances aspects of bodily health including increased heart rate variability, reduced blood pressure, better moods, clearer thinking, and many others. In two studies, lovingkindness meditation additionally deactivated inflammation genes and activated antiviral genes in people who engaged in the practice.[21] Apparently, wishing well to others is healthy for us.

Do the lovingkindness meditation right now. Breathe deeply and attune to yourself. Imagine your partner, or someone else you love, and focus on directing the following statements and attitudes into their body, heart, and mind, wherever they are.

* *"May you be safe. May you be healthy. May you be happy. May you have an easeful life."*

* *Try saying these statements in your mind like a mantra for a few minutes as you focus on this other person. Write what you experience in your journal including your sensations, emotions, and thoughts.*

* *Now do the same with these statements about yourself. "May I be safe. May I be healthy. May I be happy. May I have an easeful life." Write what you experience in your journal.*

* *Practice lovingkindness meditation toward your partner and then yourself a few minutes daily for two weeks. Write down your experiences in your journal and share them with your partner.*

At this moment I am doing lovingkindness meditation toward you, the reader of these words. I am imagining you and directing at you, "May you be safe. May you be happy. May you be healthy. May you have an easeful life." How do you feel reading this? Even more, how do you think your spouse/partner would feel knowing you were practicing this with him or her? How would you feel knowing that your partner was periodically directing this intentionality at you? Write about this in your journal and share it with your partner.

Receiving caring influence

John Gottman is my favorite couples researcher and the author of *Principia Amores,* the most rigorous scientific analysis of healthy/unhealthy couples ever written. Gottman was asked by an interviewer to choose one central characteristic of happy marriages, and he responded, "The man's willingness to receive influence from his wife."

In my work I've found this to be generally true. I suspect there are evolutionary reasons for this, since women tend to have more social circuits in their brains, and are also programmed to be more frightened of male anger than men are programmed to be frightened of female anger. When stressed and angered, men are more drawn to solitude, while women are more drawn to affiliation with other women.

In other words, social solutions to distress come more easily to women, and so men who can regulate their own distress and receive influence from their female partners will have an edge in regulating unhealthy states of anger, frustration, fear, jealousy, shame, anxiety, depression, and disgust.

With everyone I've worked with including men, women, teens, kids, and families, the ability to receive and act on caring influence from *anyone* predicts health and success. *Resisting* caring influence diminishes health and success, and is a central aspect of defensive states, which we'll explore in detail in Chapter 21.

I suspect that the effectiveness of psychotherapy rests on the therapist's ability to generate a safe enough intersubjective container with his client(s) so that that the client *receives* caring influence—hears it, internalizes it, and acts on it. This has certainly been true in the more than sixty-five thousand plus sessions I've conducted over the years.

Remember Harvey and Jean from Chapter 19? Jean caught Harvey soliciting prostitutes and the ensuing storm drove them into treatment with me. Here's an exchange we had dealing with establishing trust. Watch how receiving caring influence is central to the process.

Jean: "I don't see how I can ever trust you again!"

Harvey: "I don't know what to tell you! I'm not cheating! I'm sorry! How many times to I have to say it?"

Not much caring influence is going on at this moment! I interrupt, "What do each of you want right now?"

Jean: "I want to trust my husband again."

Harvey: "I want Jean to realize that I get it and will never cheat again!"

Keith: "Look into each other's eyes. What do you feel?" They calm down as they look into each other's eyes. Due to mirror neurons recapitulating states of consciousness when we look into another's eyes, couples will often look away from their partner when either are being mean or cruel, and calm down when directed to look at each other.

Harvey, warming up a bit looking at Jean: "I love Jean and want her to trust me."

Jean, wants to trust, but is understandably gun-shy: "I want to believe Harvey, but look what happened the last time!"

Keith: "Notice how you warm up a little doing this?" They nod. "To trust again you need to provide caring influence, not angry attacks."

Harvey, in a softer tone: "What can I do to help you trust me more?"

Jean: "Let me look at your phone and computer when I'm anxious and be nice when I do."

Harvey: "That's fine, but could you do your best to believe that I'm trying to tell you the exact truth when you ask me questions? It's hard when I answer and you don't believe me." Jean nods.

Keith: "Now you're receiving caring influence from each other! Harvey, I think it's wise to make your phone and computer available to Jean, and Jean, I think Harvey has a point about believing he's doing his best to tell the truth."

Jean: "I'm glad I can reassure myself looking at his electronics when I'm worried, but how am I supposed to believe him when I don't sometimes? I can't just pretend!"

Keith: "Excellent point! When you don't believe Harvey is doing his best to tell the truth, you need to stop the conversation or talk about something else where you do believe him. No couple can have a productive talk if one partner believes the other is currently lying. Save those talks for sessions like these." Both nod thoughtfully. This is frequently a soothing idea to couples—that the price of admission to a productive conflict conversation is that they have to believe they both are doing their best to tell the truth.

The shift into receiving caring influence

You'll notice how the dialogue became less violent and more productive as we all began receiving caring influence. I was influenced by their goals of trusting more, they were influenced by me to soothe themselves and self-reflect, and they in turn influenced each other to soften and listen.

~~~~~~

EXERCISE: *Receiving caring influence*

I suggest you receive caring influence from me by doing the following exercise.

✳ *Who in your life generally has your best interests at heart? Often this is your husband/wife/lover. Sometimes a child, parent, or friend consistently has your best interests at heart. Write about this person, and which influences they offer that are easy to receive and which are hard to receive. Influences could be to clean up after yourself, to be more affectionate, to be less defensive, to be more patient with your kids, to not dominate conversations, to contribute your opinions to conversations, to live a healthier lifestyle, or to go to bed earlier so you get better sleep.*

* *In the areas where it is hard to receive caring influence, write why this is. What about the input in these areas do you resist?*

* *Decide to focus on receiving caring influence in one particular area, like cleaning up, affection, listening, being kind, or using a friendly tone, for the next week. Tell your partner you're doing this.*

* *After a week, talk to your partner about how this went, and write about your conversation in your journal.*

* *Ask your partner whom they rely on for caring influence, and how you could offer caring influence to them in ways they could embrace. Listen with interest and acceptance. Write about your conversation.*

I'm always on the lookout for new keystone habits, and I suggest you be too. Especially notice what habits you admire in others. If you are super-impressed with how Sally goes to yoga three times a week, try doing that. If you admire Jim playing math games with his eight-year-old, play some math or reading games with one of your kids. If it touches your heart how loving Hank and Jennifer are toward each other at social events, try being more loving with your spouse at parties. This is how we use admiration and envy to become better people!

You'll notice I'm not suggesting you complain to your spouse about what you'd like him or her to change! Such conversations are important, but dangerous, and require lots of care and positive framing to go well. We'll discuss this in much greater length in future chapters.

Chapter 21

Defensive States

We are *so* social! Over fifty-five million years of mammalian evolution to give kin groups the best chances of survival have culminated in you and me, the most social mammals ever. Most of the human brain is dedicated to helping us relate in groups, and some argue that the size and power of the human brain evolved *in response* to social demands.[22]

That being said, the biggest threats to humans for millions of years haven't been saber-toothed tigers or hurricanes. Rather, they have been other humans! So we all have *instinctual wiring* to protect ourselves from other people when we feel threatened.

When we feel safe, we're more likely to be socially engaged in healthy response to the present moment. That's why eight billion powerful individuals get along more or less cooperatively on this planet. This is especially true if we are attuned to ourselves and each other.

When we feel threatened, our Shadow selves, our adaptive unconscious selves, generate habitual defensive states to protect us.[23] Our emotions become amplified or numbed, our stories about the current moment become distorted toward the negative, we lose capacities for empathy and self-reflection, and we have destructive impulses to attack or flee. This is our nervous system hijacking our consciousness to protect us *right now* from a threat. Unfortunately, defensive states can lead us into crazy, and can ruin relationships if we can't learn to notice them and regulate them into states of healthy response to the present moment.

Matt and Barbara

Matt and Barbara come into their seventh therapy session with unhappy looks on their faces. As soon as they're seated, Matt starts right in.

"Barbara has been on my case for days!"

Barbara rolls her eyes: "Really? You've been nothing but critical and nasty since your brother left. All you two did was drink and get stoned all weekend!"

Matt fires back: "You were rude to go to bed at eight on Saturday night. Everyone knew you were pissed off!"

Barbara: "Excuse me for not wanting to get drunk and wasted and be all hung over on Easter Sunday when we're hosting your entire family!"

Matt: "We didn't get drunk! We were drinking!"

Barbara, sarcastically: "Oh, yeah. Tell me about it."

In situations like this, the fight often escalates without either partner recognizing the toxic pattern. You can see the amplified emotions, distorted perspectives, destructive impulses to keep attacking, and the lack of empathy and self-reflection. Even worse, since communication is *complementary,* these two states are self-amplifying in an escalating conflict. Barbara and Matt are *cooperating* in creating this horrible bad time!

In situations like these, I often interrupt and ask the question that each should be asking him- or herself. "Wait just a second! What is each one of you doing right now to keep this fight going?"

Both look confused. I've distracted them enough to disrupt their defensive states, and this leaves them caught between wanting to feel better and the urgent demands of their destructive Shadow selves to protect themselves from this aggressive other by *attacking* or *disengaging*. Our unconscious does not care whether whoever is threatening us is three years old, 40 years old, big, small, an intimate, or a stranger. If our adaptive unconscious reads "threat!", it will create the protective defensive state and resist self-reflection and attunement with this dangerous other. I continue: "What you really want to do is work this problem out and feel loving toward each other. What your defensive states are doing is trying to get relief by attacking each other."

Barbara: "Well, what should we do?" Matt nods.

Keith: "You're beginning to make it better right now. You're reaching for something other than indulging your defensive impulses to see the other as bad and attack them to try to get relief." Both look a little embarrassed as they realize this is exactly what they've been doing.

EXERCISE: *Defensive states*

Remember the last time you felt angry or afraid in dialogue with another person—especially your partner—as if it's happening right now. What are you thinking about your partner and yourself? What are you feeling in your body? What kind of person do you think they are, and what judgments are you making about them and yourself? Nice, not nice, reasonable, irrational, a jerk, a bitch? Write all this in your journal.

Now, go back and see how accurate you were in your evaluations, and how proportional you were in your emotional reactions. Did you give in to your destructive impulses? Did you resist them? Write down your answers.

If you were inaccurate and disproportional at all, are these familiar reactions to you? Have you had these reactions before? In what contexts with which people? Write this down.

You probably just explored one of your characteristic defensive states!

Defensive states happen *all the time.*

When our nervous systems read "safety," we usually naturally enter states of healthy response to the present moment *where* we're empathically attuned with others and ourselves and taking care of personal and social business.

Our brain is determining we are safe and can relax into our vast programming for relaxed living and social engagement. For instance, I feel comfortably socially engaged with you right now as you read this, and with myself, since I'm considering myself a secure, worthwhile human being trying to help you love better.

When we feel threatened, we often enter defensive states of amped-up and/or numbed emotions, distorted perspectives, destructive impulses, and diminished empathy and self-reflection. We begin developing these states at birth and continue programming them the rest of our lives.

For instance, imagine you're a seven-year-old kid, sitting at the dinner table with your parents and your four-year-old sister, and your father looks at your mother and says, "You always cook the chicken too long. You're a terrible cook!" Your mother's face tightens, she looks away, and, frightened of your father's anger, says. "I'm sorry; I didn't mean to do it again."

Mom is feeling a surge of anger and fear, quickly suppressed by looking away and changing her breathing (both amplified and numbed emotions in this case). She is thinking, "He is such a mean man!" (a distorted perspective since he's okay most of the time, but occasionally is a hostile bully). She's also feeling destructive impulses (suppressing her feelings and adapting to the bullying) and diminished capacities for empathy (disconnected from you, your sister, and your father) and self-reflection (unaware she's caught in a codependent loop at this moment). She is unaware of the traumatic effects of her codependence on you and your sister.

Dad is unaware of how his bullying of your mother reduces him in everyone's eyes and makes everyone fear and resent him. His statement, "You always cook the chicken too long. You are a terrible cook!" arises from a defensive state in him. It is amplified anger over the chicken being a little dry, and a distorted perspective of your mom being a bad cook (she's actually quite a good cook and, even if she wasn't, she just cooked dinner for everybody and is getting no recognition or gratitude whatsoever!). He has little capacity for empathy and self-reflection, and is surrendering to a destructive impulse to publicly humiliate your mother.

You feel a surge of anger and fear and literally shrink into your chair and try to disappear. You don't want to get caught in the crossfire and are organized not to be their target. Humans, when threatened, go into fight/ flight where they want to dominate (your Dad's bullying), disengage (you look down and start strategizing how to get away from the table), or submit (your mom's codependent apology).

Your sister, on the other hand, is more immature and impulsive than you are and starts to loudly cry and fidget around, knocking over her milk and distracting your parents from their argument.

Everybody is generating a defensive state, and nobody is taking care of emotional business ("instantiating" a state is what our nervous system automatically does in response to different stimuli).

Neither Mom nor Dad is aware of their distorted defensive state (no capacity for self-reflection). They're actually *pretending to themselves* that they are acting reasonably (distorted perspectives), and believe it is exclusively the other who is acting badly, is responsible for the scene, and deserves attack or passive-aggressive compliance (destructive impulses).

Normal crazy

All of us have tendencies to fall into defensive states periodically, and we can deal with them for better or worse. In fact, most of us enter and shift out of defensive states *every day* without even noticing. For example, my wife, Becky, asks if I know where the paint primer is, and I feel an irrational flash of defensive anger, thinking, *"She thinks I lost the primer. I didn't."* I catch the thought and tell myself, *"Lighten up. She just wants to find the primer!"*, and I feel affection for her and relief at my anger subsiding. I just regulated myself out of a defensive state.

If we can adjust out of defensive states on our own or with a little direction from someone else, we're what I call *normal crazy.*

If the imagined family above enters therapy with me, I might work with Dad's cluelessness about the pain he's causing to these three people he loves so much, and Mom's reluctance to be assertive when he's mad.

If Dad is normal crazy, he'll probably get it and say something like, "I see how I'm being a jerk, ruining dinner and distressing everyone. I need to be more positive and supportive when I get irritated like that."

If Mom is normal crazy, she'll probably get it and say something like, "I need to speak up when I think the conversation is unhealthy."

Catching yourself being unpleasant and domineering, apologizing, and making amends usually reflects a state of healthy response to the present moment. Catching yourself being silently passive-aggressive and standing up for yourself assertively usually reflects a state of healthy response to the present moment.

This is normal crazy and, if people receive caring influence, will lead to such scenes happening less, self-regulation happening more, and people becoming progressively more effectively self-reflective.

Extra crazy

When we can't regulate out of a defensive state into a state of healthy response even with help, we become *extra crazy*, which can be extra problematic.

For instance, if the above Mom is extra crazy, I explain to her what's happening, and she might say, "I can't disagree with my husband. I don't have the right to talk back. I'm not worth it because he's always right and I'm wrong in those arguments. And besides, he might yell at me."

If the above Dad is extra crazy, I explain to him what's happening and he might say, "She deserves it! Should I just sit there like a wimp and take it when she wrecks dinner?"

This is extra crazy, possibly reflecting personality disorders or trauma conditioning of some sort—defensive programming so deep and distorted that it doesn't become visible even when pointed out, and he or she might actually feel more depressed, angry, or worthless and get more distorted and destructive as we discuss it.

We can get stuck by being clueless and by indulging defensive states.

Why do we get distorted like this? Why do we get stuck, even when we consciously want to create good habits of noticing defensive states and regulating to states of healthy response? Often we get stuck by being *clueless* about defensive states, and/or by *indulging* defensive states.

EXERCISE: *Catching a defensive reaction*

Keep attuned to yourself for the next two days and notice when you're afraid, ashamed, guilty, irritated, angry, prideful, anxious, jealous, envious, contemptuous, sad, or depressed. Write in your journal what you feel in your body, what your beliefs are, and what impulses you have while you're experiencing the distressing emotion.

If another person is involved, what are your feelings toward and beliefs about him or her? What impulses do you have while feeling this way, and do you indulge and act on your impulses or pause and question them? Write about this in your journal.

After you write all this in your journal, share it with your partner or someone you trust, with the goals of finding some cues that trigger you into a defensive state and what some of your personal defensive responses might be.

As you do this, be aware that you are observing your defenses from an attuned viewpoint of acceptance and caring intent, and notice how good it feels to have this flavor of awareness. Compassionate self-observation, even of our mistakes and destructive Shadow, almost always feels clean and satisfying in a mature kind of way.

Chapter 22

How Defensive States Develop

Defensive tendencies are a normal and necessary part of being human. We all have to deal with them, and most of us know how to regulate defensive states to some extent—meaning we can at least occasionally observe, moderate, or transmute them into deeper understanding and more caring actions.

Think of a time you got pissed off at someone and felt like snapping something hostile at them, but got hold of yourself and said or did something constructive instead. You might even have started to be mean and then caught yourself. This was you self-regulating out of a defensive state toward a state of healthy response to the present moment, and reflects your personal growth in identifying and regulating defensive states.

When your nervous system reads *threat,* it often instantly (eight to sixty milliseconds) instantiates a defensive state that involves amplified or numbed emotions, distorted perspectives, diminished capacities for empathy and self-reflection, and destructive impulses.

These defensive states are learned from birth onward and are necessary parts of human development, because danger needs an *immediate* response to protect us.[24]

This is great if we really are in danger! It's fast, automatic, and gives us impulses to fight or flee without us having to figure anything out. You see the snake, you instantly jump backwards. (Or, in Ronald Reagan's case, when he saw a rattlesnake next to his boot while dismounting from his horse on his Santa Barbara ranch, you stomp the snake to death. This completely freaked out Soviet psychologists at the time who advised the Kremlin to not antagonize this guy!) These two examples reflect instinctive fight/flight defensive impulses.

Since we're so relational, we are always socially referencing the people around us. We usually register "safety," and create cultures where we can cooperate, self-regulate, and get along comfortably. Our human bias is to get along and help each other.

Defensive states begin to be programmed when our nervous system reads "Threat!" We develop our defenses in progressive include and transcend waves beginning *before conception!* Each wave builds on the frameworks that preceded it. Let's do a quick progression of defensive programming from before conception until death:

* Defensive capacities begin with our genetic endowment and our parents' physical states when we were conceived, both of which influence temperament and brain development. Some of us are destined to be mellower, some of us more anxious, some of us more depressed, some of us more sexually urgent, and so on.

* In utero, mom's nutrition, general emotional and psychological health, and especially her relative ability to regulate stress, influence her baby's self-regulatory capacities after birth. Mothers who emotionally regulate well during their last trimester tend to have babies who are better at self-soothing.[25]

* After birth, how attuned mother is largely determines how secure baby feels. Neglected or abused infants tend to have stunted social development and more capacities for dissociation (like spacing out, losing touch with bodily experience, or disconnecting from the world). These deficits tend to intensify defensive states as the child develops.

* Parents' disapprovals create shame reactions in toddlers (aged 10 to 20 months) that result in social learning, but also in program-

ming defensive states to defend from shame and fear. Our nervous systems don't like the shame response to disapproval, so, in addition to moral and behavioral compliance ("Put that knife down now! Don't play with knives!"), we develop defenses. We get mad at Mom for reproving us—projection. We go kick our cat—scapegoating. We pretend we did nothing wrong—denial. At 16 months, kids can suppress emotions—can hide them from parents—and that capacity can lead to private emotional/behavioral processes that can turn into habitual defensive states.[26]

* At two years old, when a child develops awareness of self as a thinking being (what developmentalists call a *theory of mind*), he or she can observe him- or herself approvingly or disapprovingly. Self-disapproval generates shame, which activates defensive states that are either indulged or regulated by parents and other caregivers. This dynamic continues through childhood. For instance, kind but firm boundaries when kids are aggressive or destructive help children regulate defensive states and set the stage for self-awareness of defenses later. Authoritative (not authoritarian!) parents tend to attune to kids, name and explain emotions, give permission to have feelings/impulses/and experiences, and set firm/fair boundaries. This is called *emotional coaching*, and is super-good for kids.[27] On the other hand, kids who have blanket approval and are indulged indiscriminately with very little attunement tend to become more entitled and narcissistic as they develop. In authoritarian families, one or both parents bully other family members and are emotionally dismissive, predisposing the kinds to be insecure, and more likely to be victims or bullies themselves in social relationships.

* Since neuro- and social development involve progressive abilities to be aware of and self-regulate defensive states, by early adolescence we have the neuro-architecture to become aware of and challenge amped/numbed emotions, distorted perspectives, and destructive impulses. We also can potentially better observe ourselves losing our capacities for empathy and self-reflection. We can occasionally see ourselves denying responsibility, taking distress out on others, or

generating lame rationalizations for unhealthy behaviors. Of course, by adolescence we have been practicing and strengthening defensive habits for many years, and so we all have deep defensive programming we need to keep untangling as part of healthy development. I call our progressive understandings of defenses combined with our increasing abilities to regulate defenses the integration-of-defenses line of development.[28]

✳ As our brains and bodies mature (and as we become more socially aware), we can get progressively more awake to our own and others' states of healthy response and defensive states. Awareness itself regulates to some extent, but simple awareness is not enough to consistently grow on the integration-of-defenses line. We also need abilities to self-soothe, receive caring influence, and reach for better states. Mechanisms for self-soothing and receiving caring influence have permeated customs and social structures of human societies forever. Every religious/therapy/growth/spirituality system has methods for receiving caring influence, waking up, and self-regulating defensive states.

Choose it and you'll keep losing it!

Indulging defensive states by normalizing amped/numbed emotions, rationalizing distorted perspectives, ignoring diminished empathy/self-reflection, and indulging destructive impulses is doing violence to ourselves and others and creates horrible habits that can lead us into extra crazy. Think of any three ugly scenes that you may have observed or participated in, and you can identify people indulging defensive states.

Catch it and you won't regret it!

Noticing defensive states, while adjusting to proportionate emotions, compassionate perspectives, healthy behaviors, and increased empathy and self-reflection guides us toward states of healthy response and moves us from extra crazy toward normal crazy, and from normal crazy toward being mindful and dialed-in.

A classic case of indulging defensive states occurred in 2014 on the freeway just south of Santa Barbara. Two trucks were being driven by a clueless 23-year-old hothead and a clueless 52-year-old owner of a body shop—also a hothead. After tailgating and posturing, the young driver threw a Big Gulp-type drink through the open window of the body-shop owner's truck—perfectly hitting him in the face. Enraged, the body-shop owner swerved to the right, running the young warrior off the freeway. Meanwhile, several cars behind, a plainclothes policeman observed the whole thing and arrested them, resulting in jail for both.

EXERCISE: *Observing your own and others' defensive states, and states of healthy response*

Over the next two days, observe yourself and others in states of healthy response, normal crazy states, and extra crazy states. Write what happens when you or someone else indulges defensive states or struggles to adjust to states of healthy response. Share what you've written with a partner.

If you're in an intimate relationship, pay special attention to you and your partner, with an emphasis on your defensive states. When you notice your partner's defenses, are you also noticing your complementary defensive patterns? Write in your journal what your part is or might be and share what you've written with your partner.

EXERCISE: *Receiving regulatory influence*

At least once, when you're in a defensive state, ask someone to help in adjusting to a state of healthy response—something like, "I have this crazy idea that you were late on purpose. Please reassure me that it was just a mistake," and then monitor your feelings as they respond. Are you feeling much better when you're reassured or helped? Feeling better means you've received their feedback. Are you still just as irritated, ashamed, or shut down? This means you haven't received their help. Write down what happens and share it with your partner, looking for better ways to receive caring influence.

Chapter 23

Brain and Heart Intimacy Intelligence

Take a deep breath and exhale for ten to fourteen seconds.

Now do it again—a deep breath and slow exhale.

How do you feel? Probably a little more relaxed and centered. That's because you just activated your tenth cranial (vagus) nerve to tell your heart everything is fine, and then your heart sent messages back up your vagus to your throat, face, and brain to calm down, soften your expression, and feel safe.

Now imagine your spouse just started complaining about how you bring up old problems during arguments. Feel the stress of your partner's imagined hostile tones and references, and then take two deep breaths with slow exhales. Try it right now. You probably calm down and lighten up at least a little bit with the deep breathing.

Remember the last time you were happy, face-to-face with your spouse or lover, looking into his or her eyes. How do you feel? Probably pretty good! If you were within three feet of each other, your heart rhythms were harmonizing. Mirror neurons in your brains were recapitulating your states of consciousness. Your and your partner's happiness were resonating, making both of you feel safe and loved. Your positive social engagement was activating your vagus nerves to tell your hearts everything was fine, which caused your hearts to tell your faces to smile and your ears to hear the pleasant tones.

Our hearts actually process information—there are tens of thousands of integrative neurons in the heart—and are intimately connected to our brains, moods, and attitudes. We *literally* have heart intelligence! We can harness this intelligence with our human superpowers of focused intent and action, in service of principle, and driven by resolve.

EXERCISE: *It works both ways*

Try saying the words, "I hate you!" and "f#*k you!" five or six times. Pay attention to sensations in your heart area and solar plexus as you do this, and write down what you feel.

Now say the words, "Don't hurt me" and "I'm so sorry!" five or six times and pay attention to sensations in your heart area and solar plexus as you do this, and write down what you feel.

Now say the words, "I love you!" and "You are wonderful!" five or six times and pay attention to sensations in your heart area and solar plexus as you do this, and write down what you feel.

Your heart isn't just responding to these statements; it's actually weighing in and informing your brain about its opinions.

EXERCISE: *Helping your vagas concentrate*

Conscious intent can amplify and clarify your heart's processing. You can turn the experiment I just described into a practice where you breathe deeply when stressed by another, look into your partner's eyes with love to create attunement, and interrupt yourself when you are on a negative track and repeat positive mantras to calm down.

When it comes to just being at peace with yourself (often a necessary first step in dealing with others), there are lots of exercises to activate your heart intelligence to help you feel better. The HeartMath Institute in Walnut Creek, California has spent decades developing superb techniques and publishing them in books like Transforming Anxiety.[29]

Like most therapists, I've gathered together multiple practices over the years to support heart intelligence. Here's one of my favorites:

* *Ask yourself this question while paying attention to your heart and solar plexus area, "Am I willing to love and accept myself at this moment no matter what?"*

* *If you feel a pleasurable loosening in your chest, the answer is "yes," and you and your heart are cooperating in positive self-attunement.*

* *If you feel a tightening in your chest area, the answer is "no," and you and your heart are in conflict.*

* *If the answer is the tightening "no," ask yourself, "Why am I not willing to love and accept myself at this moment?" Pay attention to whatever answer comes, no matter how bizarre or unfair (like, "I can't love myself because I made a mistake," or "I can't love myself because I'm not perfect").*

* *After you've answered the question (not argued with yourself about it, just answered it), ask yourself again, "Am I willing to love and accept myself at this moment no matter what?", paying attention to whether your chest feels tighter, looser, or the same. If you're still tight, do the rest of the steps one more time.*

* *Repeat this five times a day, writing about your experiences in your journal.*

As the days and weeks pass, you will feel more loosening in your chest as you enjoy this practice. That's because this exercise builds Shadow affect regulation tendencies in your adaptive unconscious, creating attractor states of "I am willing to love and accept myself at this moment no matter what."

As the days and weeks pass, you'll probably find yourself more patient, warm, and clear with your partner as you enjoy this practice, which will help him or her feel calmer and more socially engaged. In this way this exercise can become a keystone habit.

Stephen Porges' gorgeous polyvagal theory

Stephen Porges is a professor of medicine in Chicago and the originator of the *Polyvagal Theory*, which describes how brains constantly scan the external/internal environment for safety and send signals of safety/danger (both physical and social) through the parasympathetic vagus nerve to the heart.

The heart (surrounded by integrative neurons) processes this information and communicates back up the vagus to the brain stem (80 percent of nerves to the brain stem are *afferent*—from the body to the brain).

The brainstem sends these messages to the throat, face, and limbic areas (involved in emotions, relationship, expression, and motivation), which results in facial expressions and states of consciousness that protect/inform/guide us and others (through our non-verbal and verbal communications and mirror neuron circuits).[30]

Heart rate variability (HRV) and health

When we breathe in, our heart rate goes up, and when we breathe out, it goes down. If we are fully present, our heart rate perfectly matches our current needs. If we're safe, we have slow steady heart rate—around sixty to a hundred beats per minute (though super-fit people like marathoners can have resting heart rates as low as forty). If we need to move fast in response to threat (like a car screaming around the corner) or the demands of the situation (like running a race), our heart rate instantly goes up, perfectly in tune with the demands of the moment. This is called high *heart rate variability (HRV)* and it is a very good thing!

HRV is considered perhaps the best single measure of overall health, and it is mediated by the polyvagal system. Calming ourselves and attuning to ourselves and others tunes us into the present moment and results in high HRV, where our brain/heart systems give us just the amount and quality of arousal we need.

Getting lost in anxiety, depression, or trauma disconnects us from the present moment and our heart rate can be all over the place, jagged, uneven, or unnaturally slow or fast. Even though we might be in a safe situation (as most of us are most of the time!), in distress our brain/heart *polyvagal system* tells us we're in danger and reacts accordingly. It sends stress chemicals through our bodies, creating hostile, frightened, or blank expressions on our faces, which in turn tell our heart that the world is getting even more threatening. Our heart then agrees and sends more stress signals to our face and brain, keeping us in unhealthy arousal or numbness. This is low HRV— it makes us sick, and it can go on for *years.*

Our expressions, attitudes, beliefs, and behaviors resonate with others in self-reinforcing patterns, usually positive if in states of healthy response, or destructive if in defensive states. Since communication is *reflexively reciprocal and self-reinforcing,* it is both difficult and extremely important to interrupt our own defensive states when we're threatened, and reach for states of healthy response with ourselves and others. We need to not indulge reflexive defensive states when confronted with perceived threat or attack from another. Indulged defensive states invariably make things much worse for everyone and severely mess with our HRV.

Consciously adjusting *from defensive states toward states of healthy response* soothes us and influences pissed off or frightened others to calm down. This leads to new prosocial experiences, which generate more accurate decisions of safety or dangerousness, which broadcast more prosocial signals from the brain to the vagus, which soothes the heart, which communicates back via the brain stem to the brain and face, which sends prosocial facial expressions to others, which helps them calm down, which feels better to us, and that's a miracle of evolution. Hallelujah!

All the exercises in this chapter (and most of the others throughout *Loving Completely*) harness the polyvagal system and neuroception to promote individual and relational health.

How does all this show up in intimacy? Henry and Anna have a fight

Here's an example of a couple, Henry and Anna, having an escalating conflict, unconsciously jacking up their polyvagal systems to create more suffering and confusion.

Henry gets a call right before quitting time and has to deal with a demanding client. He hurries home, is a half-hour late, but feels a warm sense of relief as he walks in the door to Anna and their teenage son, Henry, Jr.

Meanwhile, Anna was okay for the first ten minutes of Henry being late, irritated the next ten minutes, and pissed off the last ten minutes. As Henry walks in the door, she greets him with, "You're never home on time!" It accelerates from there.

As soon as Anna was critical, Henry's brain registered threat, activated a defensive state via the polyvagal circuit, causing his heart to say, "You're in danger! Protect yourself!" This caused his anger to rise, his face to frown, his beliefs about Anna to become insulting, and his responses to get nasty (amplified emotions, distorted perspectives, and hostile impulses). Anna in turn had her hostile story of Henry being an uncaring jerk reinforced by his defensive response, leading her expression to become contemptuous, and her tone to become insulting. You can see why we call this an escalating conflict! Partners keep upping the ante until someone blows up or breaks down.

Henry and Anna kept accelerating until Henry told Anna to "Shut the f@#* up!", which activated a defensive state in Henry, Jr., who told Henry to his face, "You're being an ass!" At this point Henry stormed into his study and everyone felt horrible the rest of the night. These states were indulged and reinforced in an escalating conflict that resulted in less and less HRV and more and more negative arousal.

Yuck!

We can develop habits of soothing ourselves that utilize the polyvagal system to calm us down, or we can be hijacked by defensive states that harness this system to keep us normal crazy or extra crazy. Henry, Anna, and Henry, Jr. all entered defensive states that coordinated to form escalating relational defensive patterns—bad news for the family!

When we soothe this system, we create higher HRV and greater vagal tone: the reflexive capacity for the vagus to soothe the heart.

Mostly we want to keep breathing deeply while telling our nervous systems we are safe. This can guide us to prosocial states of healthy response to the present moment. Either Henry or Anna in the above example could initiate this in themselves, and thus encourage it in the other. Attunement increases vagal tone. For example:

* Anna could have attuned to herself and Henry and said, "I realize you're trying to be home more on time and I appreciate it."

* Henry could have attuned to himself and Anna and said, "I get it that you're distressed when I'm late, and I will get better at calling and being on time."

* Even after the episode, Henry could have come out of his study, apologized to Henry, Jr. and Anna, and they could have all gotten back to love.

***

EXERCISE: *Increase our HRV*

Think about someone/something for which you are grateful, and pay attention to the sensations in your chest area. Keep focusing until you have the sensation of gratitude (it's good for your relationship to include feeling gratitude for some aspect[s] of your partner). This increases HRV/ vagal tone. Practice this five times a day. Write about your experiences and share them with a partner.

After two weeks, continue the exercise and start prolonging the sensation of gratitude for two or three minutes each time. Do this five times a day for two weeks.

After two more weeks of prolonging the gratitude, start noticing when you're not feeling grateful and then generate and sustain gratitude. This is a keystone habit that really delivers if you can practice it enough for gratitude to become an unconscious attractor state!

Chapter 24

Complexity Theory
and Defensive States

What do you want to create or improve in your life? Do you want more intimate connections with your partner? Better sex? A dominating serve in tennis? The ability to paint a beautiful sunset? Perhaps you want to write poetry or record some original music. All these desires reflect evolution working through your desire to create a bias to greater complexity that came into existence with the Big Bang.

The bias toward more complexity is a force in the universe as primal and powerful as gravity. It is a force that longs for more coherence, greater energy efficiency, and more functional interconnections. *Complexity theory* is the bias of everything in the universe to reach for, and stabilize at, more coherent forms.

I discuss chaos theory, or complexity theory, in Chapter 4, but let's briefly review it before we see how it applies to defensive states and the Second Star, "Does this person maintain their physical and psychological health?"

Complexity theory, or *chaos theory,* was discovered by Ilya Prigogine, a chemist famous for thinking outside of the box (he actually proved that time moves in one direction, which was a big deal in the latter part of the twentieth century). He discovered that a system of linked differentiated parts, arranged hierarchically, energized from the outside, and not lost in chaos (such as a cloud of smoke disappearing in the wind) or rigidity (like a diamond), naturally self-organizes to greater complexity. Greater complexity, since it is more energy efficient and has more functionality, actually looks simpler—just like your iPhone looks simpler than the huge computers that sent people to the moon, but is actually more powerful and way more complex.[31]

Human brains are complex systems, relationships are complex systems, ecosystems are complex systems—all biased to seek greater complexity.[32] *This is a tendency that infuses every atom in the universe!*

Linked differentiated parts

In consciousness, our different parts include our memories, states, ideas, and beliefs. Most psychological problems involve disconnections of memories, states, ideas, and beliefs. You get stage fright as you approach the podium and forget the opening to your speech. You get angry at your boss for insisting you stay late to finish a project and lose your sense of him generally being a good guy who doesn't like people to stay late. Your husband stares at a bikini babe at the beach, you feel outraged, and you have no sense of how loyal and attracted to you he is.

Connecting—linking—different parts of ourselves usually results in enhanced health, because these parts then integrate to help us become smarter and healthier. You can check your notes and connect with the beginning of your speech. You can remember how your boss has worked hard to not keep people late. You can tell your husband to stop ogling, but stay in contact with how much he loves and is attracted to you. Make these connections and your consciousness tends to integrate to deeper understanding and more compassion—hallmarks of greater complexity in humans.

What blocks intrapsychic linkage? Sometimes it's just simple ignorance. Anna, from our previous example with Henry, came into an individual therapy session with me saying, "I acted just like my father with Henry that day. I was mean and bullying! I hate my abusive father! I want to kill him! I feel so ashamed and small. He was always criticizing, and part of me hates him and wants to hurt him! I have a critical angry part of me that's just like him and I hate it! I want to erase that angry part of me!"

I tell her, "First of all, I'm glad you noticed that Henry was getting some of your anger at your father. When Henry started getting mean like your dad, you got angrier and instinctively attacked back! We always want to bully the bullies. I get it that you hate seeing yourself bullying like your dad, but killing or eliminating this part of you is not the answer!"

Anna gets this, but still protests, "I don't want to be a bully!"

I continue, "Of course not, but we can't erase parts of ourselves. We *can* heal them. You need to accept your angry and violent self, while feeling secure you're not going to kill or badly hurt anyone—especially Henry." Anna's face and body relax as I say this. The message feels soothing to her, because it links her angry/violent self with her more mature self—she's connecting her differentiated parts with attuned acceptance and caring intent.

Sometimes linking our mature and immature selves is all we need. Simply the knowledge that her angry, bullying self is normal and needs to be accepted and integrated might be enough to resolve Anna's distress and lead her to apologize to Henry for not getting the whole story before attacking him.

This linkage allows her brain to integrate the angry and wise parts to greater complexity. Greater complexity in human consciousness often shows up in more compassion and deeper consciousness.

Sometimes lack of linkage is just ignorance, but mostly disruption of linkage of different parts of ourselves is caused by our habitual defensive states. Defensive states are based on dissociation—automatic disconnections we first developed as infants and children (often in response to threat and shame reactions) that become habits of disconnection.

Attuned self-awareness of distortions—bringing acceptance and caring intent to the flavor of defensive states in their anger, fear, anxiety, contempt, or blank dissociation—is a crucial step in linking the immature selves embedded in defensive states to our more mature "acceptance-and-caring-intent" selves. This empowers our brains to integrate toward greater complexity, which shows up as deeper consciousness and more compassion.

As we more consistently connect all the different parts of ourselves in the past/present/future with acceptance and caring intent, we help our brains integrate to greater complexity. Greater complexity in human consciousness is usually characterized by a wider view from more contexts including the personal, social, cultural, developmental, past/present/future, etc. In general, this makes us more caring.

We usually block awareness of what we are ashamed of, thus preventing linkage through acceptance and caring intent with our more mature/wise/caring selves. As discussed in Chapter 21, this is based on social conditioning beginning around 10 months of age and extending throughout life. These shame dynamics are necessary for social learning, but are also the source of many psychological defenses like denial, projection, scapegoating, and rationalization.

~~~~~~

EXERCISE: *Shame into complexity*

Observe and record in your journal over the next three days when you feel guilty, ashamed, or embarrassed, and each time ask yourself, "What value did I just violate to lead my brain to generate this shame emotion?" We tend to feel shame emotions when our unconscious Shadow self has determined we've broken a rule or violated a value. If I feel crippling regret and shame at making a scheduling error with a client, the rule I'm breaking is that I should never make such mistakes.

Cultivate acceptance and caring intent to either refine the rule/value or follow it better in the future, and write how this feels. Do this for at least three days and then share it with a partner. The rule I prefer for scheduling errors is to keep getting better at not making them, and quickly forgiving myself when they occasionally occur.

You'll probably find yourself feeling better about your mistakes. Often, all you have to do to grow is link interior aspects by observing them with acceptance and caring intent. This is complexity theory in action—you consciously contributing to your personal evolution.

Chapter 25

Health Is Managing Processes

In reading this section about the Second Star, you might have noticed that all health involves managing *processes*.

How we eat, sleep, exercise, work, love, relate, think, and deal with all sorts of life demands involves processes we manage, either for better or worse.

Health is then less *about* our current states of being, and more about *how well we're managing* our current states of being. One woman I worked with exercised intensely until she was in her thirties, and then just stopped. When I met her in her mid-forties, she was obese, had high blood pressure, and was at risk to develop diabetes. She stopped exercising and attending to her body, and she physically deteriorated. Another woman I worked with never started exercising until she was 38, but discovered she loved it and religiously went to her Pilates and Jazzercise classes each week. When I began working with her in her late forties, she was one of my healthiest clients physically.

Many people I've known and worked with over the years have had horrible physical, psychological, and relational habits that they've struggled with. Addiction, jealousy, cheating, bullying, victimizing, abusive parenting, horrible dietary habits, self-loathing, inactivity, isolating, procrastinating, and generating chronic stress are all common examples. With each of these examples, when someone took on the responsibility to maintain healthier processes in whatever toxic habit they chose to address, wonderful things happened.

So, physical/psychological health is being aware of healthy and unhealthy dimensions, and doing our best to establish and maintain processes to be healthier and less unhealthy.

Relationships matter!

There are always relational aspects of healthy and unhealthy behavior. We are the sum total of our intra- and intersubjective relationships with ourselves, people, and the world, and so physical and psychological health processes will always involve relationships.

We want all those relationships to harmonize, to be coherent in the complexity theory sense. More coherent is better habits, better adjustments from defensive states to states of healthy response, better vagal tone, and increased HRV.

As we become more aware and accomplished in these areas, we become better able to see defensive states and states of healthy response in others, and get much better at adjusting back to attunement.

We are responsible for everything we experience and do, and so are responsible to manage all the physical and psychological processes in our lives. As we choose and engage in healthy processes, we not only get healthier ourselves, but we become more discerning about how others are handling *their* processes. This helps us accurately answer the Second Star question, "Does this person maintain their physical and psychological health?"

~~~~~~

EXERCISE: *Integration*

Explore what ideas and aspects of physical and psychological health were most useful to you personally in this section.

As you review your reading and journal entries from this section, what is one aspect of physical health and one aspect of psychological health that stood out to you? Write these down in your journal.

After each aspect, write a new habit you could cultivate to enhance or grow these aspects of physical and psychological health.

Try doing at least the first thirty seconds of at least one of these habits every day for the next three weeks, remembering that the first thirty seconds are the most crucial in learning new habits. Write your experiences and, after three weeks, share what you've written with your partner or someone else you trust.

EXERCISE: *Reviewing what you liked*

Go back again over what you've written about in this section—definitions of health, habits, defensive states, the polyvagal theory, and applying complexity to shame emotions—and notice what you especially liked and what was especially useful to you. Write these down and read them every day for three weeks. Try talking about your insights and experiences with your partner or someone else you trust.

Who knows, this last practice of reading useful insights and discussing them might turn out to be a major keystone habit in itself!

Section Endnotes

1 Masterson 1981	10 Duhigg 2012	19 Gottman 2015	27 Gottman 2007
2 Schore 2015	11 Goldberg 2009	20 Baumeister 2011,	28 Witt 2015
3 Duhigg 2012	12 Siegel 1999	Duhigg 2012	29 Childre 2006
4 Fisher 2003	13 Wilber 2000	21 Pace 2009	30 Porges 2011
5 Cherlin 2009	14 Achor 2011	22 van der Kolk 2015	31 Prigogene 1996
6 Duhigg 2012	15 Davidson 2012	23 Porges 2011	32 Siegel 1999
7 Wilber 2000	16 Brogan 2016	24 Witt 2006	
8 Felitti 1998	17 Gottman 2015	25 Schore 2003	
9 van der Kolk 2016	18 Gable 2006	26 Schore 1994	

In conflict, would this person be able and willing to do what it takes to get back to love?

You'll notice how most of the physical and psychological health examples in the Second Star section of the book involve relationship problems. Whether it's social isolation or repetitive conflict with people we love, most of human suffering involves other people—relationships.

All relationships, if they're intimate enough and last long enough, will eventually have conflict, and then you and the other person are on the spot to handle it for better or worse.

If two people are able to consistently do what it takes to get back to love from conflict, relationships tend to thrive and grow. Unfortunately, this is a lot harder than it sounds. I've lost good friends over the years from conflicts where one or both of us were either unable (didn't have the skills) or unwilling (didn't have the resolve) to get back to love. I imagine you've had that experience yourself, probably more than once.

As the years have passed, my goal has been to do what it takes to be available to resolve conflict back to love with *everyone*. This doesn't always mean happy resolution happens, but at least my standard is to not lose relationships because I was unable or unwilling to do what it took to resolve conflict. If others are unable or unwilling, I've learned to accept their capacities and decisions as gracefully as possible, though the losses have occasionally hurt and confused me.

As you read the material and do the exercises involving the Third Star, consider making a decision to be able and willing to do what it takes to get back to love from conflict with anyone you care about. If you and another can't do it just by yourselves, there are always therapists and coaches to help. Remember, receiving caring influence is a human superpower!

The pages that follow explore some basic truths about relationships, and then move on to receiving influence, regulating conflict and pleasure, and maintaining the marital friendship and marital love affair through conflict, all the time exploring the styles of relating that are most useful to getting back to love.

Chapter 26

Bids for Attention, and
All Love Involves Suffering

Let's explore some basic truths about relationships. We regularly want attention from others and they regularly want attention from us. Also, all love involves suffering of some sort.

Yes! Love *always involves suffering!* In an inspiring lecture at UCLA sponsored by the Lifespan Learning Institute in 2003, anthropologist Helen Fisher quoted a study where college students were asked if they'd ever broken someone's heart or had their heart broken by another. *Ninety percent* answered "yes" to both questions. In other studies, self-described long-term happy couples routinely said that they had experienced dark times, conflicts, and troubles in the course of their marriages. People in long-term marriages almost universally said that those unions were the best thing that ever happened to them, but that they were hard.

So, in addition to *how satisfying our friendship and love affair is, how well we repair injuries and how effectively we accept and manage the suffering of intimacy* is a big determinant of how satisfying our relationships are.

This is the importance of, "In conflict, would this person be able and willing to do what it takes to get back to love?"

Bids for attention

Do you remember the last time you wanted attention from your partner? (Or, if you're currently single, do you remember a time you were in relationship and wanted attention?) How did you try to elicit attention? Did you hug or kiss your partner, ask for sex, or initiate a conversation?

Couples researcher John Gottman calls these "bids" for attention, and couples who have high frequency of "Yes!" in response tend to have *much* better relationships. Bids and responses often don't involve words; more likely, they're nonverbal actions like reaching out, holding a hand, or offering a warm smile when you catch your partner's eye.

Gottman filmed newlyweds for a weekend in his couples lab, and found that when one partner made a bid—looked at, talked to, touched, asked for something, or suggested interaction, the other generally responded in one of three ways:

* The partner *turned toward* his or her spouse in a positive way, validating the bid and attempting to provide positive attention.

* The partner *turned away from* his or her spouse by ignoring or missing the signal.

* The partner *turned against* his or her spouse by attacking, arguing, or dismissing them in their bid.

I often make bids to Becky by smiling at her and hugging her. She almost always smiles or hugs back. She "turns toward" me. If she turned away, she might ignore me. If she turned against, she might ridicule me for wanting attention. You can feel the difference between the three modes—toward, away, and against—and how central the make-a-bid/turn-toward circuit is for happy relating.

This is especially important in conflict, and some research has suggested significant differences between husbands and wives in bids for resolving problems. Gottman found that women initiated 80 percent of conflict conversations, and that marital happiness was heavily dependent on how effectively the husband turned toward those particular bids. Interestingly, another study found that men's satisfaction in long-term relationships was in direct proportion to how much physical affection they experienced with their wives (physically turning toward them with caresses, hugs, and other affectionate touches).

~~~~~~

EXERCISE: *Bids for attention*

Explore how you and your partner navigate bids for attention.

* *Write down your typical bids for attention and your partner's typical responses. Do you smile, point interesting things out, reach out for your partner's hand, or bring up events and ideas that are emotionally significant to you? How do you attempt contact?*

* *Write down your partner's typical bids for attention and your typical responses. Does he or she smile, point interesting things out, reach out for your hand, or bring up events and ideas that are emotionally significant to him or her?*

* *When was the last specific time your partner (or a past partner if you're currently single) made a bid for positive attention? This could be a smile, hug, sexual overture, request to talk or take a walk, or anything else involving them wanting your attention. How did you respond? Write this down.*

* *When was the last specific time you or your partner made a bid to address a problem? How did either of you respond? Write this down.*

* *Share what you've written with your partner and discuss turning toward each other more consistently both for positive attention and to resolve problems. Write about this conversation in your journal.*

Able and willing

"In conflict, would this person be *able and willing* to do what it takes to get back to love?"

As I described in Chapter 1, "able" asks if this person has the depth, knowledge, skills, and maturity to deal productively with conflict. "Willing" asks if this person can manage their own fears, resentments, and impulses to attack and flee enough to hang in *with you* in conflict and work their way back to understanding and affection.

Of course, if *you're* not able and willing to do what it takes, then it's not going to work even if your partner is.

We can grow to be more able and willing.

Don't panic if you don't turn toward your partner most of the time in conflict to do what it takes to get back to love, or if they don't turn toward you much. Remember that growth mindsets create huge progress over time with effort and progress orientations. We don't have to be perfect at resolving conflict back to love, but we want to do better each time. We want to keep making progress.

Central to growth mindsets is the understanding that we can only grow so fast. What we want is to maximize our development and help our partner do the same, without demanding from ourselves or our partner that we grow faster than we are able. A beautiful approach to optimal development is offered in the late George Leonard's wonderful book, *Mastery*.

Leonard, an Aikido master, first observed the mastery pattern of development in his martial arts classes, and found it was widely applicable to most human learning. Briefly, this pattern is:

* Enthusiastic effort initially producing rapid progress, which is followed by a plateau where effort doesn't seem to deliver much.

* If the student perseveres though the plateau, and continues to learn and practice, there will be another spike, and so on.

This is the rhythm we seek when learning how to love each other better, and especially how to resolve conflict more effectively. We can relax into this mastery process with the warm understanding that we can keep growing throughout our entire lifetime, and, even better, help the people we love keep growing.

Rob and Leticia and Pricilla and Ryan

Rob and Leticia chronically criticized one another, and often turned against bids for attention with more criticism. They couldn't sign on to growth mindset effort-and-progress orientations, and insisted on blaming one another. In therapy, each kept beseeching me to change the other to solve their shared problems. Feeling how gridlocked they were in conflict, I suggested they both be in individual therapy and couples therapy simultaneously to maximize positive change, but they refused and finally left therapy in frustration. Eventually they divorced.

A second couple, Pricilla and Ryan, suffered chronic disinterest in each other's lives, routinely turning away from bids for attention. This led to Pricilla's two-year secret affair, which Ryan discovered and demanded she immediately end. After struggling with the decision, Pricilla concluded she wanted to share her life with Ryan and not leave him. Ryan was devastated, but committed to working on growing himself and his marriage.

Each therapy session involved current conflicts influenced by past traumas and mutual distrust, but Pricilla and Ryan were committed to improvement. Both received influence from me to learn to offer *clean bids* (meaning asking respectfully or playfully rather than complaining or criticizing) and turn toward each other consistently, even in conflict discussions. Now, fifteen years later, they're living happily together with their three sons. To be able and willing to get back to love from conflict, you need to catch yourself turning away or against and gradually get better at turning toward.

Defensive states and relational defensive patterns

Everything is relationships!—We can't *not* relate when we're in the presence of another. As discussed in Chapter 21, when one of us feels threatened, we're likely to enter a defensive state of amplified or numbed emotions, distorted perspectives, destructive impulses, and diminished capacities for empathy and self-reflection. Defensive states in one partner evoke defensive states in the other partner, which aggravate and intensify the other's defensive states, thus creating relational defensive patterns. Such patterns, if unchecked, can lead to escalating conflict (lots of turning away and against) and/or progressive emotional separation and avoidance, both of which predict dissatisfaction, low intimacy, and eventual divorce. Chronic escalating conflict additionally increases the likelihood of situational domestic violence.

These reciprocating relational defensive patterns get us stuck in conflict with diminished emotional, communication, or caring recourses. To be able to get back to love, we need to have abilities to observe and regulate these states. We need to *notice* turning away and against and be able to turn toward instead.

Most of us could use better skills at communication and problem-solving, and I've encountered many people eager to resolve problems to get back to love, but lacking the skills to do so. These skills are *learnable*.

If we are *willing to receive caring influence,* we can acquire the skills necessary for us to be *able* to resolve conflict back to love. Even more, if our partner is willing to receive caring influence from us and others, our partner can learn the skills necessary to resolve conflict back to love.

When a couple first comes into my office with problems, often after years of unresolved conflicts and nasty interpersonal relational defensive patterns, I am intensely curious about whether each partner is *willing* to receive caring influence to learn the skills necessary to be able to repair injuries back to love. Everyone *says* they are initially, but we find out in the sessions ahead if they *really* are.

The following chapters look at practices that help us be able and willing. Let's end this chapter with attunement, the most basic self-observational tool to help us grow.

Attunement is often the answer to replace escalating *conflict* with escalating *contact*.

The attunement exercises we practiced in Chapter 3 are ideal for noticing and soothing defensive states into states of healthy response. If I'm struggling to observe what you and I are sensing, feeling, thinking, judging, and wanting *with acceptance and caring intent,* I am regulating myself out of my defensive state, and influencing *you* to do the same via my expressions, tones, and more compassionate attitudes. This harnesses our mirror neuron systems to replace escalating *conflict* with escalating *contact*.

To be *willing* to self-observe turning away and against, and to consistently keep turning toward, we need to harness our human superpowers of focused intent and action, in service of principle, and driven by resolve.

To use this superpower to get back to love, we need to use these aware-ness/regulation attunement skills when *we don't feel like it.*

~~~~~~

EXERCISE: *Attuned when you don't feel like it*

Remember your last argument with your lover or spouse—not an animated discussion, but a real argument where you were angry and hurt. See if you can feel some of the amplified or numbed feelings, the hostile story you had about him or her, and your impulses to argue, flee, shut down, or fight back. Notice how little empathy you had for his or her suffering, and how invisible your suffering seemed to be to your partner. Write about all this in your journal.

Imagine yourself back in the argument, and stopping the attack and defense, while attuning to your sensations, feelings, thoughts, judgments, and impulses. Additionally, imagine yourself attuning to your partner's sensations, feelings, thoughts, judgments, and impulses, with acceptance and caring intent. Write about this in your journal, and how the argu-ment might have gone differently if you starting speaking exclusively from your attuned awareness of yourself and your partner.

Can you feel how hard it is to not defend against his or her unfair accu-sations? Can you sense how hard it is to not tell him or her how wrong they are? Your Shadow self, your adaptive unconscious, does not want you to be vulnerable under threat, and will resist such efforts until you have practiced the new attunement alternatives successfully so many times that your unconscious fully integrates how superior they can be.

I've found reflexive attuned awareness to be a keystone habit. When someone naturally goes to attunement in the face of conflict, they often experience unexpected benefits in physical health, social effectiveness, and general joy in living.

Talk to your partner about attunement and the possibilities of mutual prac-tice to resolve conflict. Write in your journal how your conversation went.

Chapter 27

Positive Mutual Influence

We can influence and be influenced in healthy or unhealthy ways, and the more we can tell the differences and choose healthy influence, the better!

I've found that a person's willingness to receive caring influence accelerates their growth on every developmental line. Conversely, resisting caring influence blocks growth on every developmental line and eventually ruins relationships.

Receiving influence can be tricky!

Receiving influence can be trickier than it sounds. Imagine you and I are in relationship. Listen to the following two messages from me while paying attention to how you feel in your body as I speak. Write down how you feel imagining me saying this to you, and how you think you might respond to each statement:

* I say contemptuously, "You don't contribute enough around here! How selfish do you have to be to just take, take, take and never give?!"

* I say kindly, "I often feel disconnected because it seems I'm doing more for us than you are. I think I'd feel closer and more appreciative

of you if you helped more with the dishes, the kids, or cleaning up. However you'd like to contribute, I'd appreciate it."

I'll bet you had radically different reactions! The second message is probably easier to hear and consider than the first.

Whether you felt more or less defensive hearing these messages, you could respond more positively or negatively to either. For example,

* You could respond positively to the first statement by saying, "I get than you're angry and hurt and believe I don't contribute enough. I don't want our life to feel unfair, so let's talk about me doing more."

* You could respond negatively to the second statement by saying, "You're always whining and complaining about how much work you do!"

The difficulty in always responding positively.

It's certainly *easier* to respond kindly to kind messages, and harder to be kind in the face of nasty or demeaning messages, but *we can always choose to respond kindly to distressed people, and it is always a good idea!*

The reason it's difficult to respond kindly to a hostile message is our genetic social programming. Most of our brains are dedicated to getting along with others, and in the ancestral tribes if someone threatened us our instincts were to fight back, take off, or submit. These instincts maintained social order and protected the group from losing members to escalating physical violence. We can still see these tendencies in primate groups today.

For instance, you try to grab my papaya, and I growl and make an angry gesture to back you off with a larger threat of my violence. You try to grab my papaya, and I turn and run like hell. You try to grab my papaya and I meekly look down and let you have it. Check out any primate group and you'll see this played out endlessly—aggression is met with more aggression, flight, or submission. All these approaches are instincts to maintain social coherence in blood-kinship groups or tribes.

In the modern age, where human consciousness routinely develops deeper and farther than at any time in human history, the *more adaptive response* is to respond to anger with kindness. This "turn the other cheek and deal in a mature fashion with the situation" approach works best in our current modern and post-modern world, and to learn it, we have to self-observe and manage our innate predispositions to respond to hostility with hostility or submission. As I taught my karate students many years ago, the only time it makes sense not to be respectful of another person is when you're backed into a kill-or-be-killed situation like an unavoidable street fight. *Every other* situation does better with respectful assertion.

Even though the more primitive part of our Shadow selves (our destructive Shadow) says, "That's not fair! You're bad!" when someone threatens us, the more mature parts of our Shadow selves (our constructive Shadow) knows that meeting hostility and contempt with kindness is almost always the more effective response. That's why we tend to feel good hearing stories of people acting with empathy and care in the face of hostility and contempt. Our adaptive unconscious knows that these responses are more beautiful, good, and true. Especially in intimate relationships, kindness is more likely to get us back to love.

Contempt is the great intimacy killer; kindness is the great intimacy balm.

It's hard to remember when we're mad or hurt, but contempt is the great intimacy killer. Kindness is the great intimacy balm.

We always influence, but if we allow ourselves to contemptuously try to influence we'll destroy intimacy and have bad influence. If we insist on kindness, even in the face of hostile and contemptuous impulses, we tend to deepen intimacy and have good influence. Numerous studies have shown that contempt wrecks relationships, and you can see from many of the examples presented in this book how contempt refuses positive influence and offers negative influence.

Relational ruptures need repair.

Here's a complementary dialog of escalating conflict extending from our previous example. It's complementary because contempt is being met with more contempt:

Me: "You don't contribute enough around here! How selfish do you have to be to just take, take, take and never give?!"

You: "F#*k you! I never asked you to do half the stuff, and most of the time you do a crappy job anyway!"

Me: "Well f#*k you, too! That's the last time I'm doing the dishes in the morning."

You: "I couldn't care less about you, you doing the dishes, or anything else!"

Escalating conflicts predict marital discord and eventual divorce. Complementary contempt and hostility drive and inflame escalating conflict.

Now look at an alternative dialogue, where you make the effort to respond to my hostility with kindness, seeking to repair our relational rupture.

Me: "You don't contribute enough around here! How selfish do you have to be to just take, take, take and never give?!"

You: "I'm sorry that you think it's unfair. What do you want to change so it feels better?"

Me, still angry and not receiving your caring influence: "You have eyes! You can see how much I do and how little you contribute! Don't tell me you don't! That's just dishonest!"

You: "I'm sorry! I really don't. Again, what could I contribute that would make a difference to you?"

Me: "You could do the dishes once in a while!"

You: "Sure! How about I start tonight?"

Me: "Really? You'd do that for me?"

You: "Yes! I love you! I don't want you thinking it's unfair around here."

Your insistence on kindness was *not* complementary to my hostility because it kept interrupting my unconscious attempts to bully you. Eventually your kindness enabled me to self-soothe, attune to you, and have a *positive complementary dialogue.* This positive complementary dialogue repaired the rupture in our intimacy.

If I'm contemptuous toward you, I'll naturally dismiss anything you say, no matter how valid, well-reasoned, or potentially productive your points, and I'll be a negative influence on you. If you respond with your own contempt, there will be a lot of words and energy but not much communication and no positive contact.

If you and I consciously can be kind enough to open to mutual positive influence, we'll tend to make sure we each feel heard, and tend to tell each other what we believe is valid about each other's points of view. This needs to start with *at least one of us* choosing kindness over defensive impulses to attack, flee, or submit.

To do this, *we must be willing to be wrong!* In my opinion, by definition if I am angry, frightened, or contemptuous, my perspectives are going to be distorted somehow. In conflict, the more I focus on my distortions (and apologize for them when I find them) and the less I focus on yours, the easier it is for me to take a stand for kindness.

A central feature of repair is to keep it simple. How can we both be right?

In conflict dialogue, it's usually best to make only one or two points at a time, and then respect and consider your partner's points and reactions. Fewer words lead to more understanding. Look for what's valid in *their* complaints and tell them! Admit your own mistakes, apologize, and commit to improvement. In this sense it's best to always keep looking for how you both can be right.

The shared standard is for us both to be heard and validated (authentically, which usually means we agree with some points and disagree with others), with the purpose of finding deeper truths. This engagement to influence each other to find deeper truths is called *dialectic,* first popularized by Socrates in ancient Athens. It is completely different from an *argument* where I want to prove myself right and you wrong.

Alice, Tony, and Alex

Alice and Tony have a nine-year-old son, Alex, who has a lot of anxiety, but doesn't like to talk about problems. One night, Alex is willing to talk with his mom about a friend problem, and Alice spends an extra fifteen minutes at bedtime discussing his social issues.

After she comes out of Alex's room, Tony is irritated. (He wanted some private time with Alice, and she tends to crash quickly after Alex goes down.) He tells Alice, "I think you're indulging the boy." They have a kind conversation about their different points of view.

Alice begins by validating Tony's points, "You're right that sometimes I say 'Yes,' when I should say, 'It's time to go to bed now.' But this time I think it was super-productive to have the talk."

Since he's not in an activated defensive state, this makes sense to Tony, "Thanks for recognizing that it's a problem sometimes, and I get that you figured it was different tonight."

Repair is central to getting back to love in conflict.

The scene above illustrates a growth mindset model of repair, usually a necessity in getting back to love in conflict. Here are the typical stages of many effective repairs:

* Recognize there is a problem that requires repair. Amazingly, I've often seen people begin fights without even being aware they are being provocative or defensive.

* Calm yourself down. You won't be able to give or receive influence if you are surrendering to a defensive state. Attunement is a wonderful way to calm down.

* Listen. Get what the other is saying to *his or her satisfaction*.

* Validate. Say what you agree is true and right about the other's points.

* Look for shared understanding. Combine your truths with his or hers in a way that feels right to you both.

* Make some progress. We rarely solve a problem completely with one conversation. Studies show that 69 percent of all marital problems are perpetual problems that never get fully resolved! What couples can do is make some progress so you both feel heard and responded to.

* Create warm contact. You've never completely repaired until you feel warmly toward each other.

In general we want to be scanning our partner's points, tones, expressions, and behaviors *for what we appreciate and admire,* rather than scanning for what we despise and disagree with. This requires *conscious effort* when we're upset.

Effective repair is one way discussions stay dialectics and don't become arguments. It works because couples go back and forth mostly from what they find valid rather than the typical back and forth of disagreement and attack. Alice telling Tony he's selfish to not let her spend an extra fifteen minutes talking to Alex, or Tony telling Alice she's coddling Alex for letting him extend bedtime, would be going back and forth with what they disagree with, and would create a non-productive argument.

Kindness, emotional stability, and receiving influence are (not surprisingly) the most important predictors of satisfaction and stability in a marriage.

EXERCISE: *Relational assumptions*

Attune to yourself and observe yourself when you are in the presence of an intimate other—a spouse, lover, family member, or good friend. Notice if you are mostly noticing aspects of him or her you like and appreciate, or aspects you dislike and critically judge. Interestingly, people tend to be more consistently positive with friends than with spouses. (This probably explains why people tend to be over 30 percent happier when a friend lives next door, and only about 8 percent happier living with a spouse.) Write about your observations in your journal.

Do you assume positive intent when your partner irritates you (you believe they mean well), or negative intent (you think they are deliberatively or thoughtlessly irritating you). Write about this.

Notice what style of communication you use, what tones you use (kind or dismissive), and what expressions you have on your face. Are there moments where you are positive, interested, attentive, or kind? What characterizes those moments? Are there moments when you are critical, frightened, disinterested, dismissive, or contemptuous? What characterizes those moments? Write down what you discover and share everything with someone you trust, hopefully the person with whom you observed these moments.

Chapter 28

Regulating Conflict and Pleasure

Down-regulating conflict (soothing yourself and your partner during conflict) and *up-regulating* pleasure (finding and creating shared fun, love, play, support, and passion) are critical capacities in happy long-term couples.

The bottom line? Down-regulate conflict when somebody feels angry, hurt, and/or disconnected, and up-regulate pleasure whenever possible!

Down-regulate conflict

When Becky and I were 25, we started living together in a big house we rented near the mountains. It was a measure of how scared we were of living together that it was a four-bedroom house just for the two of us. One night we had a big argument about something (sex probably). I was using nasty tones and references and Becky was fighting back. Finally she said, "I've had it!" and went to the closet to get her coat.

"Where are you going?" I asked, beginning to feel anxious and abandoned rather than self-righteous and pissed. "I don't know!" she said, with a hurt and suspicious look on her face. I burst into tears and apologized. She softened almost immediately, and we had some productive talk, ending up comforting each other that night.

How do you feel reading about that fight? Does it remind you of any similar situations between you and your current partner or past partners? Write about this in your journal.

One way we down-regulate conflict is with repair of such ruptures (rips in the intersubjective fabric of a relationship). They are injuries that shift us from trust and affection toward distrust and anger. Relationship ruptures usually involve issues, arguments, perceived slights or betrayals, and painful emotions like hurt, anger, fear, anxiety, shame, contempt, disgust, or disconnection. They usually are at least partially fueled by past traumas that add intensity and distortion to the present moment, often with us having no idea that the past is intruding into the present moment.

Repair is essential

The previous chapter looked at the steps of repair. They were: recognize there is a problem, calm yourself, listen, validate, look for shared understanding, make progress, and create warm contact.

You know you've repaired a particular conflict (for now) when you both feel respectfully heard and understood, there is a sense that some progress was made, and you have made affectionate connection. In the above example, Becky and I stopped attacking and defending, and instead listened to each other and validated some of the other's points. We expressed our intent to be better in the future, and felt close again by the end of the talk.

In repair, it often helps to speculate how past distressing experiences might be influencing you to react extra intensely. Correspondingly, it usually makes things worse for you to speculate how your partner's past traumas might be influencing him or her right now. In a fight, such speculation about the other person comes off as hostile analysis.

The power of apology

Repair doesn't always have to be so extensive. Sometimes all that's required is an apology. Apologizing for hurting your partner while reaching for shared understanding is sometimes all you both need to feel better. I can't tell you how many times I've heard the words, "He or she never apologizes!" as a fundamental complaint of unfairness in some relationships. "My father/mother/sister/brother/husband/wife/son/daughter/boss/employee *never* apologizes!" Usually that "never" part is an exaggeration, but occasionally it's true because some people literally never apologize. Let's face it: Never apologizing is an indefensible bad habit in intimacy!

Apologize any chance you get! Help other people feel better when you make a mistake, or they feel injured. One study showed that physicians who apologized to their patients for making mistakes got sued significantly less for malpractice.

Stages of repair: time matters

Injuries, ruptures, problems, and fights always happen in intimate relationships and need repair.

Quick repair (as soon as possible) is preferable because the longer you feel injured, the more of a negative load you accumulate. You want to spend as few minutes/hours/days as possible feeling bad about your partner and (usually) ruminating about and amplifying your negative, contemptuous, defensive stories. The last thing you want in an argument is to go your separate ways and continue to expand and elaborate your injuries and complaints. The more amplification and expansion of angry narratives, the harder it becomes to attune and repair.

If Becky would have gotten into her '62 VW bug and left that night, we would both have spent that evening feeling bad, blaming the other, remembering similar past injuries, and thus accumulating distress and pain.

Instead we repaired and got back to love.

What are the typical stages of repair? As we detailed earlier, repair usually involves some variant of the following steps:

* Recognize there is a problem that requires repair.

* Calm yourself down.

* Listen. Get what the other is saying to *his or her satisfaction.*

* Validate. Say what you agree is true and right about the other's points.

✳ Look for shared understanding. Combine your truths with his or hers in a way that feels right to you both.

✳ Make some progress.

✳ Create warm contact.

~~~~~~

EXERCISE: *Previous repair*

Write in your journal about a painful argument with an intimate. Where, when, and how did it start?

Conflict is cooperative, in that it takes two to keep an argument going. What was your contribution to the argument? How much time did you spend unnecessarily holding on to negative stories and feelings about your partner before you felt better about him or her again? What could you have done to repair sooner and more effectively? Write about this in your journal.

How did this argument work out? Satisfactorily for you, your partner, or both of you? Write about this, remembering that repair is usually some version of, "I feel heard, you feel heard, we both believe we made some progress, we make affectionate connection?"

Share this with the person you had the conflict with and write about your conversation.

~~~~~~

EXERCISE: *Couples repair*

Discuss some current conflict with each other, deliberating going through the five steps of repair. Notice what is easy and hard for you. Acknowledge to your partner what's difficult for you, apologize to your partner for your parts of the problem, and make a decision to improve those areas, telling your partner how they might be able to help you improve. Write about your conversation, looking for insight in how you help or get in the way of repair when conflict arises.

Up-regulating pleasure to get back to love

We don't have to always talk things out to get back to love. Sometimes we can just go have a good time! For example:

* ✶ "Let's stop arguing and take a walk."
* ✶ "Why don't we just get naked, take a shower, and lie down?"
* ✶ "We're both tired. Let's hold each other for a while, go to sleep, and see how we feel in the morning."
* ✶ "I'm sorry I hurt you. Let's go out to dinner!"

All these involve up-regulating shared pleasure—an often underused resource in intimate relationships. For instance, when couples have painful discussions about one partner's complaints about lack of sex, I suggest they make love and talk about the issue afterwards.

Like in the above sex example, we often up-regulate pleasurable contact and shared pleasures with intentionality and prioritizing fun and intimate contact. William Doherty in *The Intentional Family* talks about how conscious family traditions strengthen family bonds and support development, and his work has been validated by countless others.

You can do this in so many ways. Have daily, weekly, yearly rituals of pleasurable connection like hugs, walks, vacations, visits, sex, and affection. Turn everyday activities into intimate time with each other including eating, sleeping, recreating, working together, cleaning, parenting, watching favorite shows, socializing, or engaging in spiritual practices and community ceremonies (good habits all).

~~~~~~

EXERCISE: *Pleasure rituals for couples*

In your journal, make a list of all the rituals you and your partner have, or have had, of up-regulating positive, pleasurable feelings. Now add some items you'd like to have, or you believe your partner would enjoy, and show the list to your partner. Write about your conversation.

Ask your partner to do the same exercise and write about what ensues.

The more good times couples have on a daily, weekly, and yearly basis, the easier it tends to be to get back to love from conflict.

Responding to good news

How couples respond to each other's good news is crucial. In a 2006 study, Shelly Gable found that couples typically responded in four ways to their partner's good news:

* Passive destructive—"Oh. I don't know if it will really work out."

* Active destructive—"You think you're so hot? Even a blind batter hits a home run every once in a while!"

* Passive constructive—"Oh. That's nice."

* Active constructive—"That's fantastic! You deserve it, and we should go out and celebrate!"

By far the best predictor of happy couples was active constructive ("That's great!", I'm happy for you!", "Let's celebrate!") Enjoying and celebrating good news up-regulated pleasurable contact and was a particularly potent form of turning toward bids for attention. Couples that did it reported being happier and were less likely to break up.

～～～～～～～～～～～～～～～～～～～～～～～～～～～～～～

EXERCISE: *Shared pleasure #2*

Write in your journal about the last time you shared fun, pleasure, or sweet intimacy with an intimate. What did he or she do, and what did you do, to make the fun happen and keep it happening?

Have you complimented this person on their contributions (active constructive)? If not, why not?

If you were complimentary, how did they respond to your praise and appreciation and how did it feel to you? Write all this down.

Share your entries with your partner, and see if your conversation is a fun time or leads to conflict. If it's fun—celebrate! If it's conflict—repair and then celebrate!

Chapter 29

Great Sex Makes
Conflict Easier

How many fights have you had right after you and your partner enjoyed sex?

I didn't think so!

Beyond the immediate hormone-fueled bliss, two recent studies found couples on average tend to feel happier with each other for *forty-eight hours* after sex.

I think you get my point. In general, the more sex you have, the less conflict you have, and the better disposed you're likely to be in a conflict.

Couples who report mutually satisfying sex have fewer problems than couples where one partner feels unfulfilled sexually.

Of course, there are exceptions. I've occasionally worked with a couple where sex stayed hot while the friendship languished and conflict went unrepaired.

That being said, let's face it! Regular, fun sex bonds us together in special ways.

EXERCISE: *Fun sex*

When was the last time you had fun sex? How did it start? Did you initiate, or did your partner? Did you plan to have sex, or did it just happen spontaneously? Write about all this in your journal. Share what you've written with your partner, and discuss everything, focusing consciously on acceptance without criticism, defensiveness, or advice.

EXERCISE: *Initiating sex*

Remember the last time you wanted to initiate sex, or wished your partner would initiate, and it didn't happen. If you're in a long-term, committed relationship, there's a good chance this happened in the last couple of months. You might not remember a recent time, or it might have happened this morning. Write about this episode in detail, including how you felt and what you thought about your partner.

Since men are more visual-erotic, and have ten to a hundred times more testosterone (the let's-get-frisky hormone) than women, they are more often conscious of wanting sex. Women are more contextual and relational sexually, so many women in the intimate bonding stages of a relationship don't realize sex is a good idea until they're having it.

In this case of wanting sex and sex not happening, after you write about what you did and how you felt about yourself and your partner, share what you've written without blame or advice.

American Tantra

After romantic infatuation fades (in six months to two years generally), sexual urgency associated with the elevated dopamine and testosterone levels of romantic infatuation diminishes as these levels go down. At the same time, couples are feeling more familiar and like family as they enter the intimate bonding stage of relationship.

Sexually, men tend to be more visual and testosterone-driven, which results in still seeing and desiring their feminine partners, even without the hormonal boost of romantic infatuation. Often women, not as visually oriented sexually as men, can lose sexual urgency and gradually be distracted away from *beginning* sex. Once sex starts they still enjoy it, but are not cued into it as much by lust (associated with novelty) and romantic ardor (associated with romantic infatuation). This can leave women shifting sexually from *desire leads to arousal* to *arousal leads to desire.*

Modern sex education rarely prepares men and women for the shift from desire-leads-to-arousal to arousal-leads-to-desire, which is a big deal! In intimate bonding, *consciously* organizing sex to be mutually fulfilling often requires transitions into sex based on consciousness rather than visceral drives.

In addition, during intimate bonding there are other challenges to the marital love affair, such as having kids, progressing in your career, new financial responsibilities, and physical challenges. Responsible, stressed parents tend to sacrifice self-care and couples' time as they have increasing demands of work, family, school, and life.

Self-care and couples' time often requires intentionality after the romantic infatuation period.

Intentionality in service of a couple's love affair is what I call *American Tantra.*

Sex is good for couples. As I mentioned earlier, sex often leads to a two-day glow of warmth for your partner, probably driven by sex-generated elevated levels of oxytocin in women and vasopressin in men. This makes us more kind and generous, and I think we all agree that more kind and generous is good for relationships!

Good news about American sexuality

A Kinsey study found couples aged 25 to 59 were five times more likely to have sex two to three times a week than singles, and that long-term couples tended to get better at sex, and get more pleasure out of it, as they aged together. Another study found that two thirds of women and one third of men in committed relationships reported beginning sex when they didn't feel like it (which means they *consciously* chose to have sex).

Here's some more good news if you are an American or Austrian. In one study of twenty-nine countries, the U.S. was second to Austria in sexual satisfaction for couples between the ages of 40 and 80 (Japan and Taiwan were last, so I hope this book is translated into Japanese and Chinese as soon as possible!) Premeditated sex and not letting conflict interfere with connection for very long are important traits in happy relationships and are central to American Tantra.

EXERCISE: *Sexual satisfaction for couples*

Ask yourself, "Do I feel satisfied with my sex life?" and write your answer in your journal. It the answer is "yes," write what characteristics of you and your lover you believe contribute to your satisfaction. If the answer is "no," write what's missing, what you and your partner could add to become fulfilled, and what's stopping you right now from working with your partner to add those elements.

Share what you've written with your partner, focusing on understanding and validating.

If the conversation feels pleasurable and intimate, are you letting your partner know with words, tone, expression, movement, or touch?

If the conversation generates tension or conflict, do you and your partner shift to repair and get back to love? If not, I suggest you discuss finding a therapist to help you talk more productively.

Write in your journal about this after your conversation.

Chapter 30

Marriage Problems Are Primarily *How* We Relate

Common problems in marriages, like sex, money, time, work, children, in-laws, or chores, are secondary to *how* we deal with them. Process—how we relate—is usually a much more powerful influence than content—what we're talking about. This is true for small problems such as parking too close to the trash cans, and major problems such as secret affairs.

There is a common illusion that problems can often, even always, be solved, but, as I mentioned earlier, researchers John Gottman and Neil Jacobson found that 69 percent of couples' problems are never completely solved. Instead, they are *perpetual problems*.

A realistic goal for dealing with problems is to keep getting better at acceptance, repair, and effort-and-progress growth mindsets.

The pattern of relating *beneath* the issues, awareness of our habitual beliefs about ourselves and our partners, and especially awareness of our defensive states, is where the real action is.

Negative relational patterns

I've found countless varieties of negative defensive patterns in couples. Some common negative relational patterns that show up frequently include:

* Attack/withdraw—where one partner pursues for time, sex, talk, or intimacy, while the other obviously or subtly resists.

* Distress/avoid/endure—where conflict leads to separation and tension, which is tolerated in an atmosphere of passive-aggressive indirect expressions of hurt or anger.

* Offering resentment and refusing influence, which activates your partner's defenses to do the same. When you won't receive influence to repair, you tend to either amplify negative emotional intensity to protect yourself and coerce your partner, becoming more out of control and scary, or you dissociate from the conversation (spacing out, stonewalling, changing the subject, remembering an errand), creating frustration in your partner and thus passively escalating the conflict.

None of these negative patterns help us get back to love.

EXERCISE: *Your relational conflict patterns*

What are your most common relationship conflict patterns? Are they variants of the ones I just described, or different ones? Write your answers in your journal with as many details of how they occur as possible.

As you describe the patterns, try to start when you are not consciously involved in a conflict, proceed to where you become aware of conflict, and then detail the patterned responses you and your partner habitually go to in defensive states.

When you've had successful repairs from these conflict patterns, what did your partner and you do right to get back to love? Write about this in detail.

Talk about this with your partner, and offer him or her at least one commitment for you to be different the next time a negative pattern begins.

EXERCISE: *Repair strength*

As you did the previous exercise, what do you notice is your most effective approach to repair? It could be the steps I shared earlier, or some other method that works fairly consistently for you and your partner. Write about this strength in detail, putting special emphasis on what you both do right. Discuss this with your partner and offer one commitment for you to do it even better and quicker.

Receive influence!

For many years, researchers have observed what they call the *Michelangelo Phenomenon,* which involves couples influencing each other over time to be happier and healthier (contrasted with the *Blueberry Phenomenon* which is couples shaping each other to be *less* happy and healthy).

When your partner has a need or resentment, do you look for what is valid in his or her position and make efforts to improve? That's receiving influence, and is one of the main predictors of happy marriages. When you often find *nothing* valid in your partner's resentment or need, it's a good idea to go to a therapist, because somebody, probably both of you, has a blind spot!

Trying to point out your partner's blind spot in an argument is like trying to offer a contrasting point of view at a political rally—it's just going to get you in trouble! One of the beauties of therapy is that it is a safe container for couples to explore and illuminate blind spots, with *someone else* responsible for helping your partner see his or hers.

Michelle and Gabe

Michelle is married to Gabe and shops at Trader Joe's each week. As she stands in the checkout one day, a cute guy flirts with her and she flirts back, even going so far as telling him her name, smiling coyly, and letting him know, "I shop here every Friday morning." Cute guy says, "My name's Daniel," and smiles happily at her attention. As she walks out she feels uncomfortable, partially realizing she went too far, but—instead of consciously exploring the shame emotion and considering what this episode might mean about her life and marriage—she tells herself, "Nothing happened, so what's the harm? Gabe's too critical to understand; he'll just get mad if tell him."

Michelle conveniently forgets the whole encounter until next Friday when she finds herself eagerly looking for Daniel as she enters the store wearing a particularly revealing top.

Two weeks later Michelle and Gabe walk into Trader Joe's, and Michelle and Daniel happily greet each other by name. "Who's that?" says Gabe in a hostile tone, and the fight is on.

Five days later they enter my office.

Gabe: "You were fully flirting with that guy!"

Michelle: "He's just a nice guy! You're making way too big a deal about it."

Keith: "Have you two been arguing about this?"

Michelle: "We had a big fight and decided to wait to talk about it till we got here." Michael nods.

Keith: "Deciding to postpone the talk till now required some cooperative activity. How did that happen?

Michelle: "Gabe suggested it and I agreed it was a good idea."

Keith: "Good job to you Gabe for offering positive influence, and good job to you Michelle for receiving it!"

Gabe: "But nothing is resolved!"

Keith: "Receiving positive influence is often the hardest step in repair. For instance, Michelle, with the benefit of 20/20 hindsight, what is valid about what Gabe said in the argument?"

Michelle (looking thoughtful): "I was flirting with Daniel, and I guess I was embarrassed to admit it."

Gabe (looking surprised): "That's really nice of you to say! I admit I was somewhat of dick while we were talking about it. I guess I got jealous."

Michelle: "I like it that you're protective of us."

Keith: "You both are receiving positive influence from me and each other right now. How does it feel?"

Gabe: "Pretty good!"

Michelle: "I think we need to get better at it!"

Keith: "Getting better at receiving positive influence is a lifelong process. See if you can slow down, listen better, and validate more when something like this happens again."

Reaching a more or less not-conflicted-with-each-other state, sooner or later, is a big deal, and sooner is *way* better than later.

Chapter 31

Getting Back to Love

Getting back to love is central to successful relationships and healthy living.

There are extraordinary pressures and demands in modern egalitarian relationships and the life stages of bonding. Each new life stage—lust to romance, to commitment, to marriage, to transition into parenthood, to aging—brings new challenges, and all are informed by our drives to love, have sex, be secure, grow, and feel known and supported by our partners and others.

We've talked about turning toward and turning against, receiving influence, up-regulating pleasures and down-regulating conflicts, American Tantra, and common relationship patterns.

Able and willing to get back to love can be keystone habits we cultivate and improve throughout life.

EXERCISE: *Getting back to love daily*

Each morning, write answers to the following questions in your journal:

* *Do I feel connected with and grateful for my partner at this moment?*

* *Does he or she feel connected to and grateful for me?*

* *If not, or if we're dissatisfied, disconnected, or restless, there's probably some conflict between us. What can I do right now to make this a little better?*

* *Am I able and willing to make an effort? When today will I make this effort?*

* *Is my partner able and willing? How can I help my partner be able and willing, and when today will I make this effort?*

At least once a week, talk to your partner about your answers. Remind him or her of your commitment to getting better at being able and willing to get back to love, and what first steps you're intending to take, starting now. If you get stuck or don't become progressively more confident of your abilities to get back to love, go talk about all this with a therapist.

~~~~~~

EXERCISE: *Getting back to love integration*

Look back over everything you've written in this get-back-to-love part of the book. Write what strengths you have in repair and what your typical problems are.

After each problem write what you should do to improve, and then write if you are able to improve, and willing to improve.

Share this with your partner, and listen with acceptance and caring intent to his or her responses. How do you feel as you do this? Write about your conversation, and then later show your partner what you've written and have a productive conversation. If conflict arises, do the repair process we discussed earlier.

If you both don't feel a comfortable sense of making progress or being able and willing to get back to love, go have a session (or two or twenty) with a therapist until you are comfortable with your growing abilities to get back to love from conflict.

Remember growth mindsets! We can continue to grow in most ways throughout our entire lives, and the Michelangelo Phenomenon means our primary relationship can be an ever-expanding crucible for positive change and increasing love.

THE FOURTH STAR
· · · · · · · · · · · · · · · · ·

Would this person show up appropriately as a parent or family member?

Whether we're actively in a family or not, we interface with children and families directly and indirectly throughout life, and someone who *doesn't* show up as a parent or family member when it is appropriate to do so is not likely to consistently show up for *us* in clutch situations. Someone who *does* show up as a parent or family member is more likely to have that mature quality of care we associate with healthy family members of all ages, and is more likely to show up for *us* when needed.

Over the last hundred years, thousands of studies have been done on healthy and unhealthy family systems. From all this research has emerged much consensus on what helps children thrive, families prosper, and individuals live and love well.

This section examines many of these key factors in healthy families and child-rearing, and what to do if some aspect of the family is not optimal.

Don't despair if you or your partner has problems showing up as parent or family member! Just because someone has trouble doesn't mean he or she can't learn to show up better. No matter what our mastery level is of any relationship skill, part of our responsibility as partners and parents is to keep growing and to help our loved ones keep growing.

This reflects the fact that the Five Star questions are not primarily Yes/No evaluations. The Five Stars are questions to help us evaluate ourselves and our partner (or potential partner) in core areas over time—they represent dimensions that we monitor, adjust, and improve throughout a lifetime.

The impact of trauma

When someone *feels* traumatized they need connection and help from others, and everyone experiences "small t" traumas (everyday hurts and humiliations like a critical sibling, or occasional teasing on the playground) and often "big T" traumas (shocking assaults, betrayals, catastrophes, or abuse) in life. Children are especially vulnerable to trauma because their nervous systems and self-systems are immature and forming constantly, needing external regulation and explanations about the world. This makes them particularly vulnerable to adults and other kids abusing, neglecting, or exploiting them, and the worst thing for a kid feeling traumatized is *to have no one show up for them.*

As I've discussed earlier, in their famous Adverse Childhood Experiences (ACE) Study, Vincent Felitti and Robert Anda asked 17,400 San Diego adults if they had experienced any of ten categories of trauma as children. Each "yes" answer was recorded, giving possible scores of 0 to 10. The number of categories was correlated with symptoms in later life. The ten categories they asked about were:

* Physical abuse

* Sexual abuse

* Emotional abuse

* Physical neglect

* Emotional neglect

* Having a drug addict or alcoholic in the family

* Having someone with mental illness in the family

* Have a family member incarcerated

✳ Not being raised by both biological parents

✳ Observing domestic violence[1]

This is by no means a comprehensive list. Bullying, physical injury or sickness, learning disabilities, physical disabilities, developmental delays, shaming, loss of friends or homes, social humiliations, or everyday frustrations can all be experienced as traumatic by children (and later by adults). Traumas *hurt* and they *shape us* and *sensitize us*. Most of the time when one of my clients enters a defensive state, we can trace the amplified or numbed emotions, distorted perspectives, and destructive impulses back to traumatic events or situations.

Anda and Felitti were shocked at the prevalence of trauma in ordinary middle-class American life. Two thirds reported at least one "yes." Twenty-six percent of the women and 16 percent of the men had been sexually abused by someone five or more years older. One in eight people had seen their mother assaulted by a partner, 28 percent reported physical abuse, 40 percent of the group had scores of two or more, and 12.5 percent scored four or more.

As I noted previously, higher ACE scores were consistently correlated with later problems in life, more physical and emotional disorders, and reduced lifespan.

In other words, trauma is ubiquitous in childhood, and we have responsibilities to help, starting with the children and family members closest to us. The biggest help we can provide is *showing up* when a child or family member needs us!

Showing up is protecting, listening, accepting, believing, appropriately responding, loving, and supporting health and growth as best we can. Showing up is dedicating ourselves to a growth mindset lifetime commitment to keep getting better at showing up.

To show up for children and family members, we need to be aware of the existence of "big T" and "little t" traumas, be willing to discuss them and process them with those we care about, and create family systems where everything is "talkaboutable." A story I've heard a hundred times from adults is, "I didn't talk about my sexual abuse (physical abuse, bullying, fears, isolation, humiliations, etc.) with anyone."

When I ask, "Why not?", the answer usually is some version of, "We just didn't talk about those things."

Parents and other family members often don't want to either believe or talk about painful or difficult topics, and children are easily shut down in such areas, often merely by the attitudes of family or community members. This is why most states had to pass mandatory reporting laws for therapists, teachers, and medical professionals for potential physical or sexual abuse with children and the elderly. Even therapists and doctors were avoiding asking about, processing, reporting, and dealing with traumas.

Part of showing up for a child and family member is creating systems that reference sex, sexual abuse, violence, bullying, humiliations, and subjective distress in *normal conversations,* starting as soon as possible in a child's life.

I have two grown children, Zoe and Ethan, and all these dimensions were discussed and referenced with them all their lives. When they had the subjective experiences of "little t" or "big T" traumas, they talked about them with Becky and me (and still do, even in their 30s), and we all processed them—sometimes with the help of therapists—until everyone felt resolved and comfortable moving forward. Showing up for a child or family member often means parents seeking and receiving caring influence from others like therapists, teachers, and doctors to help kids or other family members resolve distressing incidents.

This book is not primarily about what trauma is and how to resolve it, but it is about creating relational systems where trauma is acknowledged and addressed in caring ways. This always starts, for better or worse, with family.

This part of the book illustrates the multiple dimensions of healthy families, which are organized to help everyone with development, including dealing with trauma, *but we have to hear about events to help with them.* I've found the best way to help kids discuss what's important to them is to begin the conversations early in life and keep them going, while always being open to caring input from outside the *family.*

These conversations are facilitated by open family systems, emotional coaching attitudes, and authoritative parenting styles (all of which we'll discuss), but also by having *no forbidden subjects,* and talking about everyone's inner and outer experiences. Inner experiences are what we feel, think, crave, remember, dream, and fantasize. Outer experiences are what we see and hear as well as do and have done to us. To help support development, prevent traumas, and help resolve traumas when they happen, everything needs to be "talkaboutable" in families in attuned contexts of acceptance and caring intent.

Refusing to have forbidden subjects and talking with attuned interest about anything and everything, wonderful or horrible, helps us show up for children and other family members.

Chapter 32

What Is an Attuned Family?

Remember the attunement exercise we practiced in Chapter 3? Breathe in deeply and breathe out slowly, paying attention with acceptance and caring intent to breath, sensations, emotions, thoughts, judgments, and desires. This is attuning to yourself, and is an excellent tool for meditation, self-soothing, and for cultivating the compassionate witness. Observing yourself and others with compassion is central to all contemplative practices and psychotherapies.

Attuning to your partner is imagining, with acceptance and caring intent, your partner's current breath, sensations, emotions, thoughts, judgments, and desires.

Attuning to your children is imagining, with acceptance and caring intent, your child's current breath, sensations, emotions, thoughts, judgments, and desires.

An attuned family has a parent who attunes to him or herself and other family members, does his or her best to protect and support children, and is dedicated to a lifetime of growth as a parent. This helps create healthy open family systems (which we'll discuss in a little bit).[2]

EXERCISE: *Couples' attunement*

At this moment, attune first to yourself and then to your partner. Write about how this feels and what you discover, and then share it with your partner. If they sense/feel/think/judge/want differently than what you imagined, receive their influence and assume they are right about them-selves. Whether they are or not, it is generally a bad idea to disagree with someone's experience of themselves!

EXERCISE: *Attuned family*

At this moment, do an attunement first with yourself and then with your child (or a child you know if you don't have kids). Always attune to your-self first, then your child. You put your own oxygen mask on first! Do this exercise at least once a day for the next week and write what happens and what you learned from these conscious attunements. Share this with your spouse or another parent.

EXERCISE: *Attuned self-soothing*

Notice when you are impatient, irritated, or critical of your partner or your child (or any child in a movie, a book, on the street, or at a party), and do the attunement exercises. Write what happens and if/how your experience is different from when you don't consciously attune. Be aware of how different the world is from inside your partner's or child's perspec-tives. Share this with your spouse or another parent.

Open and closed systems

A family system is the sum total of all the people, relationships, feelings, memories, attitudes, beliefs, and habits in everyone in the immediate fam-ily, and everyone deeply connected to parents and children. The most sig-nificant family systems developmentally are the one you grew up in (your nuclear family) and the one you're currently living in.

Families can be more healthy or less healthy, but it's generally better to grow up in a stable parent/child system. Half of all people incarcerated in this country grew up in foster care, which is where children go when parents are absent, dysfunctional, abusive, or can't maintain even a marginal family culture.[3]

Family systems can be open or closed. An open system welcomes knowledge and people from outside the family, and encourages family members to engage with the world in any healthy way they want.

Open systems tend to create healthier children.[4] "I love my teacher," says fifth grader, Jenny.

Mom replies, "Let's invite her and her family to dinner!"

Open-system parents are less likely to be threatened by other people, and more likely to include other people and perspectives in the family.

Closed systems are often characterized by dark secrets like alcoholism, drug addiction, neglect, or physical, sexual, or emotional abuse. Closed systems resist knowledge and people from the outside. An 11-year-old says at the dinner table, "I heard from my teacher that pumpkin seeds have antioxidants and anticancer substances in them." Dad replies dismissively, "Your teacher is so full of herself. Pumpkins are no big deal!" Closed-system parents are more likely to be authoritarian and fearful of challenges to their authority.

People who are able to show up as a parent or family member tend to generate open systems, and are much more likely to create happy, healthy relationships. That's why showing up as a parent or family member is super-important whether or not you have kids.

Interdependence, codependence, and counterdependence

Everything is relationships and no man or woman is an island. The central social question is never, "Do I need others?", because we all do! The central social question is, "Am I relating optimally to others?"

Three major *styles* of relating are *interdependence, codependence,* and *counterdependence* (spoiler alert: interdependence is healthy, and codependence/counterdependence are unhealthy):[5]

    ✳ **Interdependence** is appropriately relying on others and serving others in ways that make everyone healthier. An attuned family is about all members growing and working on their individual challenges, helping others with their issues, and supporting the whole family, with each member having different responsibilities. For instance, it's unhealthy for children to experience themselves as entitled service receivers in a family. They are much happier feeling like citizens of a family with responsibilities to the group. Values of mutual respect, non-violence, and receiving caring influence, compassionately championed by attuned parents, lead family members to support each other in being healthy, happy, and growing.

* **Codependence** is helping another person in ways that compromise health. The most classic examples of this are families with alcoholism, addiction, or domestic violence present, where non-addict members *adapt* and *enable* rather than set boundaries and seek help.

* **Counterdependence** is pretending you are so independent you need no one. Particularly in the 1950s and 1960s when I was growing up, there was a John Wayne standard of "rugged individualism" where "I don't need anyone!" was considered admirable. Not surprisingly, pretending you need no one, and not seeking help and contact when you crave it, makes you sick and prone to all kinds of stress illnesses, addictions, and social problems.

We all have dependent and counterdependent moments, so don't get worried that your family is unhealthy! Healthy families learn to distinguish interdependence from dependence and counterdependence, and have the family value of adjusting to interdependence.

Jimmy is 10 years old and has trouble with writing reports. His book report on *The Lion, the Witch, and the Wardrobe* is due tomorrow and he panics and runs to his mother, Marie. "You have to write if for me! I can't do it!"

A codependent response might be Marie saying, "I understand it's hard for you, so I'll write the report for you this time."

A counterdependent response might be, "It's not my problem. You got yourself into this mess, so you can get yourself out of it. I'm going to watch TV and you can do whatever you want!"

An interdependent response might be, "Let's sit down and I'll help you outline your paper. You can write a draft and then I'll go over it with you and help you edit it."

Interdependent is always the gold standard in healthy relationships.

Child-centric families are not good for kids.

Currently America is a child-centered culture in many ways. This means that many consider it moral to attend to their kids at the cost of self-care or maintaining their marital friendship and love affair.[6]

This is a disaster, because study after study has shown that the best parents are those who take care of their love for each other and don't focus all their attention on work, tasks, and children.

If you have kids, have you ever gone camping with another family? When our kids were small, we home-schooled them with a bunch of other families for several years, and the homeschoolers (as we called ourselves) frequently camped together in some of the numerous beautiful camp-grounds in California.

Everyone always commented on how restful it was. The kids would play with each other, sometimes joined by adults. Couples would have time with each other and others doing shared camping tasks. After dinner, I'd take the children to a separate campfire and tell them stories while the adults hung out together at the adult fire.

We were not kid-centered as much as *family* centered, and there was an assumption that each couple's relationship was an important part of the mix.

Most couples I've worked with who've camped with other families have reported similar experiences. I believe that such multi-family camping events recapitulate our ancestral hunter-gatherer tribes, and everybody's genes tell them, "Yes! This is what feels most natural to us!"

If you want to improve your children's lives, focus on being a happy couple first. That's almost certainly better for them than more ballet lessons, or dutiful parents watching every game, practice, or lesson, while neglecting the parental friendship and love affair.

Do you like kids? How can you enjoy them more?

In one study by Daniel Gilbert, people generally preferred shopping, watching TV, playing sports, or reading to being with their children.[7] If this is you, it doesn't mean you're a bad parent! It just means you don't particularly like hanging out with your kid right now. Development is complex. The delightful infant can become the exhausting toddler. The angelic nine-year-old can become the moody pre-teen. The successful high school student can become the out-of-control party animal college student. We always love our children, but we don't always enjoy them.

That being said, parent participation in children's lives where we are interested in their inner experience, their emergent worldviews, and their own passionate concerns is *very* good for children. This doesn't mean you go to every practice and game, or take your kid to every museum and event. Hanging out, being *interested* and *accepting* of your child's feelings, thoughts, experiences, judgments, and desires, is super good for children (and everybody else too, if you think about it).

I encourage parents to find shared activities that everyone enjoys, and during those events have conversations about what interests their children. Ask them their thoughts, feelings, opinions, and moral distinctions rather than lecture them about your own.

For instance, I liked reading to our son and daughter, Ethan and Zoe, and telling them stories. I read to them or told them a story most nights until Ethan went away to college. When they were little, we'd play puppets, marbles, ping pong, or other games that were fun for everyone. Both kids enjoyed cooking with Becky. After dinner, we'd put on loud rock music and sing along as we all did the dishes together. We had family meetings when issues arose, and special family dinners for birthdays and other occasions.

Intimate conversations tended to happen during these events. When Ethan was four, he'd take his scooter and I'd take my skateboard down to the street, we'd ride a little, and then Ethan would say, "Daddy, let's talk about things." I'd always sit down on my skateboard and respond, "Sure, Ethan. What do you want to talk about?"

That year Ethan almost always answered, "Let's talk about rattlesnakes," because he and I often hiked in the hills and he had just learned how to watch out for them. "What about rattlesnakes?" I'd ask, and we would talk about what they were and how we felt about them.

As William Doherty maintains in his book, *The Intentional Family,* such activities form rituals of bonding and connection that sustain families, and they come in many combinations, like the family dinner, date night for

Mom and Dad, private time for individuals, and different combinations of family members.[8] To this day, Ethan or Zoe will call and say, "I'd like to talk to Daddy," or, "I'd like to talk with Mom," and we're all fine with that.

How about you?

What is your relationship with children? Do you have kids? Nieces or nephews? Godchildren? Friends or family members with kids? We all have relationships with kids to some extent.

When someone says, "I don't like kids," they often *really mean,* "I fear kids." Adults can fear the demands and challenges of being responsible for a developing young being, or being injured by child's thoughtlessness or impulsivity.

Most of us, when responsible for a child, begin to find ways to understand and care for that child. It's in our genes to care for children. Like everything, we can keep getting better at this forever.

~~~~~~

EXERCISE: *The wonderful parent*

Who do you know that you think is a wonderful parent? It could be you, your spouse, your mother or father, a mentor, or someone else. Write what you believe makes them a wonderful parent.

In your opinion, is this a Five Star person? The erotic polarity would be with his or her partner. Specifically, what are their strengths and weaknesses with each Star? Write this down, and then read what you've written. What stands out to you about this person's parenting and parenting in general? This person probably instinctively creates and maintains an attuned family. Share what you've written with your partner, and with your kids to the extent they can understand. Ask your partner whom they consider a wonderful parent and why. Listen with interest and respect to their thoughts. Write about your conversation afterwards.

A good parent keeps developing.

A good parent does his or her best to protect their children and help them thrive, and is dedicated to a lifetime of receiving influence in improving in the role. We can keep getting better at attuning to ourselves and our children our whole lives. I believe that *all of us* have a responsibility to be good parents to our own kids and other kids we encounter.

This is relevant to your relationships, whether you have children or not, for a number of reasons. Most of us will hang out with kids or teens at some point. If someone can't show up as a parent or family member *when it is appropriate to do so,* they very likely won't show up for *you* some time when you really need them. We're not talking codependence here, where you care for someone in ways that make things worse. We're talking about caring for another in healthy ways when it is serves the highest good to do so.

Children grow through different worldviews and adults see through different worldviews.

One aspect of Integral psychology that most excited me was Ken Wilber's heavy emphasis on how we all develop through different worldviews, and that all of us see the world differently through our different combinations of worldviews.

We also have many lines of development on which we progress, all characterized by stages that progressively include and transcend previous stages. These include moral development, the development of skills like dancing or playing an instrument, to psychosexual and psychosocial development, and so on. Some developmental lines are heavily determined by biological maturation. For instance, cognition (how we think) progresses through:

* Sensorimotor in infants who literally think with their bodies and senses.

* To pre-operational where two- to five-year-old kids have language and concepts, but tend to think magically and non-linearly.

* To concrete-operational where kids can do if-then logic and understand the world in concrete, black and white terms.

* To formal-operational where teens can self-reflect on inner experience and understand the world in more shades-of-gray terms.

* To post-formal-operational where people can harness reason and intuition to solve problems to make their way through the world.

We also grow through progressive worldviews (which also include and transcend each other). These are true in developing children and also characterize adults. The progression is:

* Egocentric from birth to kindergarten where the focus is more on self and self-gratification.
* To conformist during grade school where we want to conform to family and school cultural norms.
* To rational in high school where we want to do well on merit-based hierarchies and achieve individual success.
* To pluralistic where we are attracted to egalitarian, non-hierarchical ideas of everyone being equal and deserving.
* To Integral where we have a felt sense of appreciation for all points of view, and can see the healthy and unhealthy aspects of all worldviews.

As you can see, adults come primarily from one of these in different situations, and the worlds that people see through egocentric, conformist, rational, pluralistic, and Integral eyes are very different worlds.

All this being said, every child does better when parents can understand his or her current worldview, meaning *right now* when you're relating with him or her.

As a parent, whatever your worldview is in a certain situation, there will be a healthier and less healthy way of enacting it. In this way, all the *Loving Completely* practices and principles are designed to apply to the healthy version of any worldview.

EXERCISE: *Inside every worldview*

Find a relaxed place to sit with your journal. Take a few deep breaths and attune to yourself. This exercise is for getting a sense of how you might experience each of these major worldviews.

Egocentric: *Remember two times—one healthy and one not—you were just focusing on your gratification.*

* *Healthy versions might be getting a massage, taking a relaxing nap, or enjoying a bite of chocolate. Try to feel the sensations in your body and*

the beliefs about yourself ("I'm doing a pleasurable good thing for me," is one example) that you felt and believed then. Describe this healthy egocentric moment in your journal.

* An unhealthy version might be gratifying yourself to the detriment of you or someone else. Examples could be not paying attention to your engine light until your engine blows up, continuing to drink wine at the party when you know you need to get up early for work tomorrow, or being nasty to a waiter because the chef overcooked your steak. Try to feel the sensations in your body and the beliefs about yourself ("I shouldn't do this, but I'm going to anyway," is one example) that you felt and believed then. Write your unhealthy egocentric moment in your journal.

Conformist: Remember two times—one healthy and one not—you wanted to fit in with a like-minded community.

* A healthy version is respectfully going through a sacred ceremony with other people whose opinions about how you look, act, and believe matters to you. Church services, weddings, traditional martial arts classes, are all examples. Try to feel the sensations in your body and the beliefs about yourself ("I value being a member of this group," is one example) that you felt and believed then. Describe this healthy conformist moment in your journal.

* An unhealthy version is going along with a group belief or behavior that you don't personally believe to the detriment of you or someone else. Examples might be standing idly by while someone is mistreated in your presence, or pretending to agree with someone just to fit into the group at that moment. Try to feel the sensations in your body and the beliefs about yourself ("I shouldn't do this, but I don't want the group turn against me," is one example) that you felt and believed then. Write your unhealthy conformist moment in your journal.

Rationalist: Remember a healthy time and an unhealthy time you wanted to compete, succeed at business, win position on a merit-based hierarchy (like a pool league, poker game, or a corporate ladder), or felt science and rational analysis to be superior to biases, intuitions, or faith-based beliefs.

* *A healthy version is committing yourself to healthy success like training to advance on the school tennis ladder, or developing skills to make you more competitive at work. Being interested in how scientific data says about how the world works is another example. Try to feel the sensations in your body and the beliefs about yourself (like "I compete well" or "I am successful" or "I change my mind if given observably verifiable evidence of a better understanding") that you felt and believed then. Describe this healthy rationalist moment in your journal.*

* *An unhealthy version is pursuing success and rational analysis to the detriment of you or someone else. Training so hard on an injury that you aggravate it, or taking away pension benefits from workers at your company because you legally can are examples. Try to feel the sensations in your body and the beliefs about yourself (like "I shouldn't do this, but I can't NOT compete" or "I have to hurt these people because it will give me more profit or advantage") that you felt and believed then. Write your unhealthy rationalist moment in your journal.*

Pluralist: *Remember two times—one healthy and one not—you took stands for equality, equal say, mutual care, and treating everyone with the same standards.*

* *A healthy version might be insisting everyone have a say in a family meeting or advocating equal respect and dignity in an organization or group. Try to feel the sensations in your body and the beliefs about yourself (like "I stand for love and care for everyone" or "I am more into service than personal profit") that you felt and believed then. Describe this healthy pluralist moment in your journal.*

* *An unhealthy version is not recognizing subtle contempt for profit seekers or fundamentalists, or refusing to accept that sometimes hierarchy and dealing differently with various types of people is legitimate. An example might be feeling contemptuous toward a businessman friend excited about increasing profits at his company. Try to feel the sensations in your body and the beliefs about yourself (like "I am morally superior" or "I see no differences between men and women") that you felt and believed then. Write your unhealthy pluralist moment in your journal.*

Integral: Remember two times—one healthy and one not—where you had the sense that every point of view had a valid side and invalid side, and where you believed that different situations warranted different reactions and different power hierarchies (with the most able person having the most influence).

* *A healthy version might be participating in a conversation where others keep arguing (not communicating) from different worldviews (say an angry fundamentalist denying human-caused global warming and a rationalist angrily quoting study after study), and looking for what is valid in each person's perspective. Try to feel the sensations in your body and the beliefs about yourself (for example, "I am about letting people know I hear them and agree with some of what they believe" or "I see their obvious biases and they don't, and I strive for compassionate understanding,") that you felt and believed then. Describe this healthy Integral moment in your journal.*

* *An unhealthy version might be feeling superior as you walk through the world, believing that your expanded vision entitles you to not consider your own destructive Shadow material that regularly arises from your adaptive unconscious. Try to feel the sensations in your body and the beliefs about yourself (like "This person is so clueless about biases that are so obvious to me" or "I can dismiss your distress with me because I have wider understanding") that you felt and believed then. Write your unhealthy Integral moment in your journal.*

Discuss your experiences with your partner and ask them to consider their own moments of healthy and unhealthy expressions of these worldviews. Write about your conversation.

Include and transcend

As you do the above exercise, you might notice that you never lose any worldview that you've lived through. Our previous worldviews show up when appropriate (or sometimes not!) while our main sense of the world is what feels most natural to us most of the time. Healthy conformists allow cultural norms to supersede unhealthy egocentric impulses, but still allow egocentric feeling and thought in the right circumstances (like taking the rides you want at Disneyland). Healthy rationalists can allow science to change their opinions over sacred texts (like evolution over creationism), while still feeling faith and connection with God by receiving communion on Sunday. This reflects the "include and transcend" Integral principle of development on specific developmental lines or through worldviews, giving us progressively more complex understandings of the universe as we grow.

What's especially significant about the Integral worldview is that the healthy and unhealthy versions of all previous worldviews are visible in us and others, and we understand that even more complex worldviews lie ahead if we keep growing.

Integral perspectives are especially useful in parenting, because we can identify our child's current most natural worldview (called "center of gravity" in Integral language), knowing that our job is to help that child live a healthy version of that worldview while preparing him or her for the next one to come, and that *everyone in the family* has a growth edge, beyond which lie better perspectives.

Goodness of fit

Over fifty years ago, Stella Chess and Alexander Thomas decided to study families to see how well parents and children fit together psychologically. They figured that since everyone has unique personalities, there would be combinations of personality types that would work better or worse for parents and children. They called the combinations of personalities *goodness of fit.*[9]

There have been great cultural changes from the Chess and Thomas goodness of fit model to modern attachment theory and Integral psychology, but their findings still hold true. Chess and Thomas found that when parents' temperaments and a child's temperaments matched, the child, not surprisingly, did better. Novelty-seeking parents did better with novelty-seeking kids, and worse with harm-avoidant kids. Extroverted parents did better with extroverted kids, and worse with those who were introverted.

Today most of us understand that we and our kids are different types of people, so the new standard is to start over with each child, interested in *who* this unique child is, and what this child needs from me and the environment to thrive.

For instance, shyness. Shyness has a heavy genetic involvement, in that some kids are born more shy than others. If I am an extroverted, easily socially engaged parent I might be impatient, mis-attuned, and coercive with my child's shyness. If I am accommodating (or perhaps a little codependent), I might indulge shyness, which amplifies it and causes social problems for my kid. If I'm impatient and demanding, I might attack my child's shyness, which leaves emotional scars and may potentially inflict "small t" traumas.

How do I create a goodness of fit with my shy child? Research has shown that if we accept the shy child for who he or she is, and encourage appropriate social risks, by 11, this child is indistinguishable from socially assertive children. Statements like, "That's what courage is, doing what you believe is right, even though you're scared", over time help the shy child become socially more brave and competent.

This reflects the modern standard of being curious about who our child is, and then adjusting our approach to create a goodness of fit with that particular boy or girl.

~~~~~~

EXERCISE: *Goodness of fit*

Make three columns on a sheet of paper. In one column write down descriptors of you, using words such as friendly, happy, shy, stern, anxious, relaxed, adventurous, risk-adverse, etc. In the second column write descriptors of your spouse, and any other co-parents of your children (for instance, if you're divorced, your ex-spouse and his or her current partner). Now in the third column, if you're currently parenting children (if you're a parent you never stop parenting!), write descriptors of each of your children. After you're done, study the page and look for connections that make parenting easier or harder for you and each child. Share this with your partner or another parent, and write about your conversation. If your child is 12 or older, share what you've discovered with your child and write about your conversation.

EXERCISE: *Couples' parenting*

Couples fight about parenting frequently, and this isn't good for anyone. Here's an exercise to improve your parenting processing skills:

* *Sit down with your co-parent and make a list of everything you agree about in parenting.*

* *Then tell the other three things you appreciate and admire most about him or her as a parent, and write these down.*

* *Find one area of disagreement and discuss it until you begin to argue (this might not happen, but it often does!).*

* *When the argument starts, do the repair process detailed in Chapter 27.*

* *For the next week, make an effort to notice anything positive your partner does as a parent and acknowledge and appreciate it!*

* *For the next week, make an effort to notice any parenting argument that starts, and immediately switch into the repair process.*

Chapter 33

Authoritative Parenting Is Best

With couples, we know there are productive ways of relating and destructive ways of relating. In our first thirty-one chapters, we've established that productive ways of relating are:

* Monitoring the Five Stars in yourself and with your partner and staying in positive dialogue with each other about keeping the answers to the five questions always adjusting toward, "Yes!" for both of you.

* Connecting regularly in positive ways. Especially turn toward your partner with interest when they indicate in any way they want contact.

* Honoring and regularly nourishing the marital friendship and love affair.

* Receiving caring influence from your spouse and others.

* Practicing quick repair of problems and injuries.

* Being positive about each other rather than negative.

* Examining *my* defensive states, and *my* contributions to problems, acknowledging them, and gradually improving, rather than attacking *you.*

* Pointing out specific irritations with, "I feel...(a feeling/sensation) when you...(do a specific behavior)", rather than criticizing a person's character or questioning the relationship.

* Having daily, weekly, and yearly rituals of connection and shared appreciation and pleasure with one another.

Non-productive ways of relating are:

* Lying, cheating, or withholding important personal experiences or information from your partner.

* Criticizing your partner's character, questioning the relationship, or habitually making general complaints and negative attributions.

* Being contemptuous or dismissive (in any circumstance—contempt is never the best response).

* Being non-responsive and emotionally disconnected (what John and Julie Gottman call "stonewalling").

* Surrendering to defensive states by not identifying and soothing amplified/numbed emotions, by believing and expressing distorted perspectives, by indulging destructive impulses, and by not reaching for compassionate empathy and self-reflection.

* Refusing caring influence from your spouse and others.

When you add kids to the mix, families become even more complicated and challenging. For instance, disagreements about childrearing are common and can lead to divorce if parents persist in conflicting parenting strategies.

Back in the 1960s and 1970s, there was golden age of family therapy in the United States. Gifted clinicians, drawn to what then was a new field, accurately evaluated how families functioned and generated forms of therapy that were extremely effective at helping distressed families love better.

In the 1970s, I and a variety of colleagues created several family therapy centers and programs in Goleta and Santa Barbara, offering services to couples and families, and training and supervising clinicians. It was fun times! We studied with family therapy luminaries like Virginia Satir, Walter Kempler, Martin Rosenbaum, Shirley Luftman, and Denton Roberts. We learned systems, taught systems, and generated our own systems.

One clinician, Salvador Minuchin, had special interest to me, and still does to this day. Born and raised in Argentina, he became a famous therapist and theorist in the U.S., creating an approach called *Structural Family Therapy*.[10]

Minuchin found that power hierarchies, along with the rules and standards they generated and maintained, largely determined the health and distress of everyone in the family. Parents in charge in fair and kind ways, appropriately receiving caring influence from each other and others, tended to create systems where people agreed the rules were fair, where everyone was treated with respect, and where Mom and Dad functioned as the good king and queen of the family system—a system dedicated to help each member grow and thrive in their own ways.

These principles were largely supported by Berkeley researcher Diana Baumrind, beginning with studies she conducted in the 1960s on parenting styles. Baumrind discovered that most parents used combinations of four different styles—authoritative, authoritarian, uninvolved, and permissive—and that only authoritative was consistently good for children. Briefly:

* **Authoritative parenting** is being in charge, but fair and open to influence.

* **Authoritarian parenting** is using coercion and bullying routinely to control your children.

* **Uninvolved parenting** is not being involved or interested in your child's emotions, thoughts, behaviors, or life.

* **Permissive parenting** is indiscriminately saying "yes" to children's desires or demands without setting boundaries on healthy or unhealthy behaviors.[11]

Subsequent research has found that:

* Authoritarian parenting predisposes children to be more violent, more likely to be the victims of bullying, and less socially effective.

* Permissive parenting plus parental noninvolvement and coldness predisposes kids to narcissism.

* Uninvolved parents tend to produce emotionally avoidant children who are more likely to have social problems, academic problems, and problems with the law as teens.[12]

Authoritative parenting is best.

If you're a parent, you know that parenting involves aspects of all four different styles—permissive, authoritarian, uninvolved, and authoritative—and each can show up at different moments. Sometimes, like at Disneyland, you want to be permissive. Sometimes, like when your kid is scratching your car with a rock, you end up being authoritarian. Occasionally, like when your daughter is totally into Justin Beiber, you find yourself uninvolved. In general, though, authoritative parenting is much better for children and families.

Here's an authoritarian parenting example: I once worked with a man named Barry whose father regularly disapproved of him, discounted his feelings, and tried to coerce him to fulfill *his* vision of how Barry should be, with no interest in *Barry's* vision of how he should be. Barry rebelled by chronically failing at everything his father tried to coerce him to do, with his father generally responding with contemptuous attacks and dismissals. These wounds continued through subsequent disasters in Barry's life, and, sixty years later, he was still furious and wounded when discussing his family relationships. Authoritarian parenting sucks!

Here's a permissive parenting example: A woman I worked with named Carrie was never disciplined by her parents, and everything she did was "the best!" Her mom and dad essentially let her do what she wanted and ignored bad behavior. Fifty years later, she can't hear the slightest criticism without breaking down, and she can empty rooms with her boring, self-referential stories. This is permissive parenting and it sucks!

Here's an uninvolved parenting example: I had client named Cindy whose father left when she was two and didn't bother to stay consistently connected with her or her sister. He wrote just enough cards, and sent just enough presents for her to feel constantly deprived of his presence. Forty years later, she still can't trust a man and flies regularly into extreme rages at her husband, never trusting him to show up when needed. This is uninvolved parenting and it sucks!

Here's an authoritative example: I worked with a mother named Jennifer who adored her two sons and supported their feelings, ideas, and activities, but set firm, fair boundaries when they broke rules or acted badly. She's currently happily married to a fellow authoritative parenting guy, and her two sons are thriving in different universities. This is authoritative parenting and it is the best!

Intersubjective fields are created when two or more are gathered together and we all have influence on the fields we generate. Good parents want their contributions to be wise, strong, and accepting, as well as loving, connected, and grateful. They establish firm family rules for respectful behavior, non-violent communication, and support for everyone's development. These rules generate intersubjective states of trust and affection in the family. Reaching for these states guides us toward more compassion and depth of consciousness—more complexity and coherence—and research has demonstrated unequivocally that authoritative parenting is superior for generating and maintaining such states.

EXERCISE: *Parenting style*

If you're a parent, write moments when you have been authoritarian, permissive, uninvolved, or authoritative with each of your children (or, if you're not a parent, with people or children you've encountered). Include how you felt at the time, what story you were telling yourself about the kid, and how he or she responded.

Now write whether you were raised in a mostly open or mostly closed family system and how you experienced it—especially notice how you experienced it from before you were eight, and from eight to 20. We often change our understanding of our family as our brains mature into deeper capacities, and we tend to get more involved with the worlds outside our families as we age.

Share this with your spouse or another parent, and discuss how you can help each other be better parents. If either of you feels injured doing this, go back to our repair process until you both feel understood, have made a bit of progress, and have affectionate connection.

Chapter 34

Emotional Coaching and Dismissing

I was raised in the 1950s and 1960s. I heard the words "crybaby" and "crying like a girl" applied to boys at school (but girls were supposed to be tough, too). My parents, both public school teachers, told me if a kid hit me or bullied me, I should strike back harder. My mom, who taught kindergarten and first grade, and my dad, a biology teacher, were progressive thinkers by the standards of the day, and considered this suck-it-up philosophy best for me and my brothers.

I don't remember crying from the ages of seven or eight until my 20s. I guess I internalized suck-it-up-and-carry-on, and certainly this approach contributed to my major depression and hospitalization at 15.

Countless studies over the last sixty years have demonstrated overwhelmingly that emotions and emotional regulation are central to development, and that there are profound negative consequences to being raised in families and cultures where feelings are ignored, attacked, or trivialized.[13]

So, given that how we conceptualize and process emotions profoundly impacts on our lives, our relationships, and our children, what are the best ways of understanding and managing emotions in families? Two broad categories of dealing with emotions are *emotionally dismissing* and *emotionally coaching*.

Back in the 1970s, John Gottman and his colleague, marital researcher Neil Jacobson, were interested in how parents understood and communicated emotion, so they studied families to see how that played out. They coined the term *meta-emotion* to indicate people's attitudes toward emotions, as well as how they processed them. They found that there were two main styles of dealing with emotion—*emotional dismissing* and *emotional coaching*.[14]

Emotional dismissing parents are suspicious of emotions, especially negative emotions. They think feelings are a choice; we need to *choose* feeling good, and when we feel bad, we should simply ignore it and take care of business. Emotionally dismissing parents generally are uncomfortable and judgmental of their children's painful emotions. Their philosophy with emotions seems to be "suck it up and carry on."

Emotional coaching parents think emotions are guides and messages from our unconscious selves. When their kids have an emotion, they see it as a learning opportunity, wait until the child is able to talk comfortably, label the feeling ("You're angry," "You're anxious," "You're happy," "You're sad"), and accept it while not necessarily approving destructive behaviors like rule-breaking or selfish acts. The emotional coaching approach generally is:

* Identify a charged situation as a learning opportunity that involves strong feelings.

* Wait until the child can talk coherently. If the child is too upset to think and express collaboratively, the parents contain them respectfully until they can.

* Identify, name, and accept the emotion without endorsing destructive behaviors.

* Engage in problem-solving or limit setting.

Emotional coaching parents and families do much better!

Kids of emotional coaching parents tend to have better math and reading scores, better attentions skills, better self-soothing when they're upset, and more mature play and prosocial habits with friends. In one study, these effects persisted until age 14.[15]

This is not to say that emotionally dismissing is bad! Everyone needs to be able to suck it up and carry on occasionally—your nine-year-old skins his knee in his soccer game, so you reassure him, but then encourage him to get back into the game. Your daughter is terrified to get on stage for her dance performance, but you gently but firmly insist she gives her performance. That being said, in general, emotional coaching is superior in dealing with emotions.

Emotionally coaching/dismissing mismatch predicts divorce!

One of Gottman's and Jacobson's most startling statistics was that a meta-emotion mismatch in parents—one parent is emotionally dismissing with kids, while the other is emotionally coaching—predicted divorce with 80 percent accuracy!

The superiority of emotional coaching styles extends into marriage quality. Emotionally coaching parents had better marital relationships, more empathy, and better problem-solving skills (they were more able and willing to get back to love).[16]

Showing up for a child or family member often requires understanding and empathizing with that person's inner life and interior world of feelings, thoughts, beliefs, desires, memories, and dreams. An emotionally dismissing style can block such attunement and empathic understanding, potentially leaving the other feeling socially isolated, misunderstood, or crazy.

I certainly felt crazy as a teenager, wracked with rage, sadness, shame, fear, loneliness, and sexual urgency. My culture said, "Just choose to feel better!", but I just couldn't do it! Part of what felt so magical about psychotherapy when I first experienced it as a teen was the emotional coaching atmosphere where such feelings were normalized, examined, accepted, and mysteriously transformed in the intersubjective intimacy between me and my therapist.

If you look back at all the material we've covered so far in this book, and at all the examples I've offered of couples doing well or poorly, you'll see that the happier couples are emotionally coaching, while unhappy couples seem to be emotionally dismissing. The takeaway? Learn emotional coaching and practice it with your spouse and your kids! Learn to notice when you are emotionally dismissing, and turn it around into emotional coaching. This is a wonderful example of turning toward your partner and kids in ways that leave them feeling known and loved by you.

EXERCISE: *Emotional coaching and dismissing*

Write at least one episode where you have been emotionally coaching and one where you have been emotionally dismissing with a child, spouse, or other family member. How did the child or family member respond, and how did you feel? Share this with your spouse or another parent.

Discuss with each other how you can help each other be more emotionally coaching, and what is a respectful reminder you would like from your partner if they experience you being emotionally dismissing. One of my favorite reminders is, "Could you please use a kinder tone?" Asking for kindness generally works much better than attacking meanness or dismissiveness.

In the future, if your partner asks for kindness respectfully, or says he or she feels cut off or not acknowledged, thank him or her and shift to emotional coaching—listen, understand, validate, and support. If you remind your partner respectfully and they make an effort, let that person know with your smiles, hugs, kisses, or caresses how grateful you are for their efforts!

Chapter 35

Growth Hierarchies and Dominator Hierarchies

Humans have existed in tribes of one sort of another for millions of years. We have multiple social instincts to guide us in such social groups. Examples are:

* Our instincts to relate with others, share with others, and care for others. These instincts are exhaustively documented in Lynne McTaggart's extraordinary book, *The Bond*.[17]

* Our instincts to have position on personally important social hierarchies. When you walk into a group, there is an area in your left hemisphere that determines where you fit into its social hierarchies and protests if you're not being treated appropriately.[18]

* Our instincts to pair bond, bond with our biological children, and nurture and protect our families.[19]

Social hierarchies are universal in mammals, and we humans are no exception! Every social group (which is two or more people connected in some fashion) has explicit and implicit hierarchies to maintain social order and protect and guide the group. With humans, there are two major forms of social hierarchies, *growth hierarchies* and *dominator hierarchies*.[20]

Growth hierarchies are fair, and designed to help everyone grow and develop. If there are problems, everyone's experience matters and the leaders receive influence to improve themselves and the system. Open-system families with authoritative parents tend to be growth hierarchies. People generally thrive and are happier in growth hierarchies. Countries with the highest levels of citizen happiness on the United Nations' happiness surveys tend to be social democracies like Sweden and Holland, where the political structures are consciously intended to be growth hierarchies.

Dominator hierarchies are when the top people retain power through fear and intimidation. They are not fair, and most participants feel coerced or oppressed rather than supported. Closed family systems and authoritarian parenting styles tend to produce dominator hierarchies. People tend to suffer and be less healthy in dominator hierarchies. Politically, former Soviet Eastern Bloc countries—and in general authoritarian regimes—have been among the least happy countries in the United Nations' happiness surveys.

Most of us have participated in both dominator and growth hierarchies, and under stress we can have instincts to dominate and fight in response to threat. Luckily, we can become more growth hierarchy people with effort and progress. (Growth mindsets!) We have instincts to cooperate when we feel secure and to coerce when we feel threatened. Cooperation is the gold standard and creates hierarchies that support growth. Coercion generally creates dominator hierarchies based on controlling (or being controlled by) people we fear, inevitably inhibiting growth.

Open systems, authoritative parents, and progressive democracies are growth hierarchies (also known as *liberation hierarchies*) where the explicit goals of the systems are to be fair, to share, to care for other members, and to help people grow. This leads to happy, healthy families and cultures.

Children and other family members want our approval, so many families use that yearning to approve of prosocial, healthy choices, and "effort and progress are beautiful" growth mindsets. Those are growth hierarchies. Remember that emotional coaching involves a caring parent in control by recognizing and honoring a child's feelings and then setting boundaries and solving problems. This is a hierarchical relationship—the parent is in control—but the explicit and implicit agenda is fairness and development.

Children have a profound sense of personal dignity, so it's wonderful to respect their inner world while providing healthy family structures like what I've been describing in this section. This gives kids a sense that you want them to thrive in a respectful environment, a growth hierarchy.

We also need to respectfully disapprove of children when they need it, which leads to prosocial shame reactions (as opposed to toxic shame reactions). The next chapter explores shame dynamics in more detail.

EXERCISE: *The growth/dominator hierarchy*

What's the best family you've ever known? What characterized them? Was everyone respected, cared for, and listened to? Did the purpose of the system seem to be supporting people's growth? Write details of this superior system and how it probably reflects a growth hierarchy.

What's the worst family you've ever known? Write what characterized them and how that probably reflects a chaotic or dominator hierarchy.

Now discuss what you've written with your spouse or a friend and talk about what you can do to create more growth hierarchies in your life.

EXERCISE: *Family of origin*

Reflect on your experiences growing up and write about the parenting styles of each of your parents (authoritative, emotionally coaching, etc.), as well as what kinds of family systems you were in—closed/open, growth hierarchy/dominator hierarchy, etc.

Now write the same about the family or families you are currently embedded in. It could be you, your spouse, and your kids, or relatives and friends where you are a participating member of some sort. Share this with your spouse or another parent. Talk with him or her about how you've been influenced by your past, as well as about improving the systems you currently are in. Especially focus on your couple relationship and family relationships with your children.

Talk about what you've written with your partner or someone else you trust, and then write about your conversation. What stands out as your growth edge for improving at this time? Do you want to become more emotionally coaching, or create more of a growth hierarchy in your family? As you identify goals, consider how you can make effort-and-progress changes to improve your family system.

Chapter 36

Secure Attachment
and Shame Dynamics

How we bond with caregivers when we're infants has profound effects on our lives and relationships!

In the middle of the last century, psychiatrist John Bowlby and therapist Mary Ainsworth observed that different parenting styles predicted characteristic attachment styles in infants. Those infants demonstrated attachment styles of being secure or insecure, and those styles tended to remain stable throughout life. Further research found that genetics had practically nothing to do with attachment style. Rather, it was almost entirely a function of parent-child attunements—especially with the mother.[21]

An attachment style is not just how you're likely to behave in relationships with an intimate other, but also how you calm yourself in distress, observe yourself in different emotional states, and how you hold your life stories, your autobiographical narratives, as more positive or negative, coherent or chaotic. In other words, attachment styles are astonishingly important in how we self-identify, live, and love. Bowlby and Ainsworth (and subsequent researchers) demonstrated that these attachment styles were in place by the time a baby was *12 months old!*

That's right! How we attach to our babies can affect their moods, relationships, and self-images for their entire lifetimes!

Secure attachment is best.

Briefly, the best attachment style is a secure parent creating secure attachment in a baby, consistently attuning to a child from birth onward. A secure parent is one who has what's called a *coherent autonomous autobiographical narrative*. A coherent autobiographical narrative is a life story that makes sense, has few dissociations, and has an adult at peace with his or her past, living mostly in healthy response to the present moment, and optimistic and realistic about the future.

When this parent attunes to an infant, the child tends to be secure. The baby, trusting that a sane parent is consistently available, explores the world, seeks soothing and receives it when distressed, socially references the trustable parent for guidance and comfort, and tends to create good relationships in adulthood. This baby has a *secure attachment style with that parent*. Fifty-five percent of U.S. babies are securely attached.

Preoccupied parents tend to create anxious ambivalent attachment in children.

Parents who are distracted away from the present moment, often preoccupied with past distress (or real or imagined problems), and have difficulties self-soothing, tend to have babies who are anxious and ambivalent (also called "angry resistant"). These babies tend to be needy, clingy, whiny, and hard to comfort. They have compromised abilities to self-soothe, and are often difficult to parent.

Emotionally dismissive parents tend to create avoidant attachment in children.

Parents who are emotionally dismissive, not particularly in touch with their feelings, and resistant to self-awareness, tend to have babies who are avoidant. The kids are emotionally self-sufficient (they can often function apparently well by themselves), but are also emotionally cut off from others and mildly hostile.

Extra-crazy parents tend to create disorganized/ disoriented attachment in children.

Parents who are seriously unresolved, extra crazy, emotionally out of control on a regular basis, and have lots of distress, tend to frighten babies. These babies often become disoriented and dissociated, and are more likely to be extra crazy themselves when they grow up. These kids can have angry resistant traits and/or avoidant traits, but are not organized in any coherent way to deal with caregivers or the world.

Showing up for babies

How do we create secure babies? Well, the short answer is to attune to yourself and your baby, and keep attuning no matter what.

More specifically, parents need to be *present, congruent/contingent,* and *marked,* so babies feel known, accepted, and protected. What does this mean?

* **Present** simply means to be around almost all the time. In some tribes, babies are held by safe adults *all the time* for the first six months of life.[22] It doesn't matter how great a parent you are if you're not around consistently.

* **Congruent/contingent** means being authentic and tuned into baby's moods. Babies can sense if you are being phony, and especially sense if you're not in harmony with him or her.

* **Marked** is baby talk, and, not surprisingly, baby talk is good for babies! Baby talk is parents exaggerating their tones and expressions just a little so babies know when you make a face and say, "You're *mad,*" that you're not mad *at them,* but instead you're empathizing with them being mad. "You're *sad.* You're *scared!*" You can hear the subtle shifts and emphases in attuned parents' voices when talking to their infants and toddlers. These marked tones say, "I get your distress, but I love you and am not distressed myself."[23]

When parents are present, congruent/contingent, and marked, babies feel known, accepted, and protected. They feel known because the marked attunement of parents communicates to their nervous systems that their inner states are visible and being adjusted to. They feel accepted because attuned parents project acceptance and caring intent. Acceptance and caring intent are the foundations of attunement. Babies feel protected because this big parent is present and attuned, but also because the attuned parent protects the baby from the crazy and extra crazy parts of the *parent*. If an attuned parent is furious, freaked out, grief-stricken, or totally fried, they tend to protect babies from their emotional pain, and *hardly ever* take their distress out on babies.

Nobody's perfect. Most every parent has characteristic attachment styles with babies that combine different amounts of secure/secure, preoccupied/anxious ambivalent, dismissive/avoidant, and unresolved/disoriented and disorganized. Secure parents are overwhelmingly anchored in coherent autonomous autobiographical narratives, and keep attuning to themselves and their infants *no matter what.*

One infant researcher, Ed Tronick, found that parents and infants frequently became miscoordinated in their moods—up to 70 percent of the time—but that secure parents, attuned to their babies, kept repairing miscoordinations back to attunement.[24] This process of noticing a rupture and routinely attuning back to harmony characterized secure parent-infant dyads. If you think about it, it's what characterizes happy couples too!

This is essentially *finding* the other emotionally. If my baby feels disconnected from me in a distressing way, I attune and baby feels *found* emotionally—known, accepted, and protected. If my partner feels disconnected from me in a distressing way, I attune and my partner feels *found* by me emotionally—known, accepted, and protected. You can see in this how secure attachment as an infant predisposes us to have secure attachment in our intimate relationships.

Always attune to yourself first

When we attune to ourselves we become more securely attached *intra*psychically with ourselves, which helps us attune *inter*psychically with others. This is where we can create cross-generational transmission of secure attachment styles. When we consistently attune to ourselves and then to our children, they develop more secure attachment with us, and are more likely to do so with their future spouses and children.

Attachment is primarily non-verbal, unconscious to unconscious. We are always communicating with infants from our non-linear, emotional, non-linguistic, holistic right hemispheres to their right hemispheres, which are dominant the first two years of life. Babies' nervous systems are literally programmed via these non-conscious communications (as well as their cardiovascular systems, metabolic systems, and neuroimmune systems). The right hemisphere is where our sense of self is centered, and secure attachment sets the stage for virtuous, prosocial, healthy development in our babies.[25]

EXERCISE: *Attachment*

When do you feel securely attached to an important figure like your spouse, a parent, or a special friend? You're likely to feel this when you feel safe, understood, and cared for, and you sense that person feels cared for and appreciated by you. If you have kids, when do they feel securely attached to you or another special adult? Write your answers in your journal.

When do you become preoccupied, dismissive, or unresolved? You know, you're lost in distress and not fully present, ashamed and "don't want to think about it," or impatient with emotion and just want to get on with your life. Write your answers. Share what you've written with your partner or someone else you trust. Write about your conversation.

What about shame?

But what about disapproving of children? What about shame?

Children under 10 months of age don't have enough self-awareness to feel shame. Children don't start blushing in embarrassment until this age, because babies have to have a sense of self observed by another to feel embarrassed, and this ability requires around 10 months of neural development.

At about a year old, children develop capacities to walk, feel the need for mom *as a separate being* to soothe them when they're upset, and to *feel shame* if they are disapproved of.

Shame is a social emotion that helps us learn how to be with others. When a parent disapproves of a securely attached 14-month-old, the baby blushes, freezes, looks down, and sometimes begins to cry. Jimmy hits baby sister Annie. Mommy says, "No! Don't hit your sister!" Jimmy freezes, blushes, looks down, and feels shame. Mommy picks Jimmy up, comforts him, and, within ten seconds, he feels fine, but social learning has taken place! It's not good to hit people; it's bad. This is a moral value being communicated to a kid mostly non-verbally with tone and expression—after all, a 14-month-old can only speak and understand a limited number of words, but does communicate via a vast array of tones and expressions.

All mammals have this capacity of disapproval-based social learning, but like everything, humans turn it into something much larger and more complex—a capacity that can grow to help us feel a moral responsibility to care for everyone and everything.[26]

Shame dynamics arise to support social development and social learning, but, since babies' nervous systems don't like shame, and parents aren't perfect, children also instinctively generate defensive neurological networks and intra- and interpersonal defensive patterns in response to shame. Kids might blame others when disapproved of (projection), attack someone else (scapegoating), deny wrongdoing (denial), or explain why they didn't do anything wrong (rationalization). These are only a few of the defensive habits we begin learning starting at one year old in response to disapprovals from others, and are what generate defensive states when we feel threatened.

In general, when a child does something that you believe is wrong, you need to *briefly* disapprove—strategically shame them kindly but unmistakably—and, when they shift into the shame response, hold them and love them immediately, communicating simultaneously that what they did was wrong, but that you love them.

It doesn't matter if toddlers don't understand the words. Your body and vibe will communicate as you hold them and speak to them.

This last reflects the fact that babies are born communicating nonverbally, and their nervous systems understand far more than was previously thought before the end of the twentieth century. For instance, infants whose parents consistently tell them how they appear to feel ("You seem happy," "You seem sad," or "You look hungry right now" are all examples) are more in touch with their feelings when they learn to talk. All of this social learning helps babies become more healthy and happy, and, along with all the love, play, and approval you shower them with, will help them have secure attachment styles.

Defensive states are based largely on implicit learning, often anchored in shame responses. Remember that implicit memories get cued and guide us, even though they don't *feel* like something is being remembered. Like every other aspect of our selves, defenses continue to develop throughout life, which means, with growth mindsets, we can keep growing our defensives to shift from denial, projection, rationalization, etc., to attuned self-awareness and effective interpersonal repair.

Age-appropriate communication of disapprovals, boundaries, and moral guidelines

Infants need parents to be present, congruent/contingent, and marked in a "You are the greatest!" world of constant approval.

Toddlers need strategic approvals and disapprovals to learn socially appropriate behaviors.

Two- to five-year olds can begin to self-observe, and parents can narrate approvals/disapprovals and boundaries like time-outs with statements like, "It's against the rules to unfasten your seatbelt when you are in the car." At three or four, it might feel moral to a child to break a rule if no one observes the violation. At five or six, children are more likely to feel guilty (a shame emotion), even if they break a rule and aren't observed.

Six- to eleven-year-olds become more communitarian and motivated to be "good." They discover roles of good boy, good girl, hard worker, soccer player, etc., and want to be true to those roles. They are black and white either/or thinkers (called concrete operational cognitively), and need clear rules with little ambiguity, like "Don't lie," "Be on time," "Never hit your sister," or "Always do your homework."

Parents help pre-adolescent kids regulate defensive states with boundaries, rules, and modeling. Grade-schoolers can participate in moral discussions like "What do you think is right?" when discussing misbehavior, but are still neurobiologically more limited than older children. Grade-school kids' brains are too immature to have deep insights such as, "When I feel ashamed, I look for some else to blame and then rationalize my angry thoughts and aggressive behaviors." Try explaining *that* to a seven-year-old!

Around adolescence, kids' brains are mature enough to perceive and integrate defensive states. Their brains have matured to the point they can engage in critical thinking and more self-observation. At this point some children can *consciously* progress on their integration-of-defenses line of development. They can be conscious of blaming another when they make mistakes, or denying responsibility and guilt when they hurt another person. These self-awareness and self-regulatory capacities often involve being able to process shame emotions more deeply and to refine the values that underlie all of them.

~~~~~~

EXERCISE: *Shame*

> *When was the last time you felt ashamed? See if you can identify the rule your nervous system thinks you've broken. Shame is some part of your unconscious Shadow self-observing when you break a rule and responding with a shame emotion like shame, guilt, embarrassment, chagrin, etc. When do you think you learned that rule, and from whom did you learn it? Is it a good rule? Can you make it a better rule? Write down your thoughts and share them with your partner or someone else you trust.*

Chapter 37

Executive Function
and Willpower

A human superpower is our ability to consciously focus attention. We all can do this at will. For instance:

* Send your attention to the sensations in your stomach and chest.

* Now focus on the nearest wall.

* Now direct your attention to the nearest living plant in your view.

* Focus on the last time you were at the beach. Feel the sand and sun.

* What feels good right now? Warmth? Coolness? A breeze? Music in the background?

* Focus on a good time you are planning for the future as if you're there right now.

* Imagine yourself floating in space, looking out at a universe of stars.

Inside (stomach and chest), outside (wall), nature (plant), past (the beach), present (what feels good right now), future (your fun plan), and fantasy (floating in space)—we can direct our attention at will to them all. This capacity to consciously direct our attention is called *executive function*.

Our attentional abilities are what give us the superpower of focused intent and action, in service of principle, and driven by resolve. This super-power is present in all of us, but to fully utilize it requires *willpower.*

Willpower and Walter Mischel's marshmallow experiment

Stanford researcher Walter Mischel was interested in willpower. He wanted to know how it developed and what it meant in our lives, so he decided to measure willpower in kids and then follow them throughout life.

He had four-year-olds come into his lab and sit down in front of a plate with marshmallows on it. He told them he was going to leave and come back, and that if they didn't eat one, they would get two marshmallows when he returned. He then left and let them sit in the room for a number of minutes in front of the plate until he returned. Some kids had the willpower to resist eating one, some didn't. The willpower of those young kids predicted future success and income more than any other variable, including I.Q. and future SAT scores. Apparently, willpower is a pretty big deal in living a successful life![27]

Luckily, we can amplify willower with practice! Any time you set a goal and insist on following your plan in spite of distractions, you are increasing your willpower. Willpower ebbs and flows, and diminishes with hunger and fatigue, so it's often harder to resist the doughnut at 8:00 p.m. than 8:00 a.m. That being said, the more we practice willpower, the stronger it gets.

Executive function and willpower

Executive function is how well we can plan and carry out plans, using will-power to stay focused and resist competing impulses that might interfere with our plans. Executive function and willpower are the drivers of most change processes, and most of the practices I've suggested so far in this book enhance both executive function and willpower.

Developing consciousness

Children's consciousness changes dramatically as they grow. Their minds and universes change with each developmental stage, with each stage including and transcending the previous one. At every age, executive func-tion and willpower correlate with success. Growth mindsets, emotional coaching, and open systems support the development of executive function and willpower.

Knowing all this, we can better attune to children and adjust our parenting as they pass through each developmental fulcrum. For instance, rough and tumble play with a strong dominant parent is prosocial and is good for little kids' neural development.[28] A strong, dominant parent "roughhouses," stays attuned, and de-escalates before anyone gets hurt or distressed. That tends to result in better impulse control and executive function in their child. A weak dominant parent lets the play accelerate until someone gets hurt/distressed, which creates less impulse control and less executive function.

EXERCISE: *Kid observation*

Observe or remember when your kid (or someone else's) seemed to be coming from a mature—even wise and caring—place. What do you notice about their willpower and executive function? Did they seem focused? Did they seem to have a clear intent? Describe this in your journal.

Now describe a time when this same kid seemed to be operating from an immature—even selfish or violent—place. What do you notice about their willpower or executive function? Write in detail what you observe and remember.

EXERCISE: *Kid communication*

If you have kids, or hang out with them occasionally, try the following experiment.

When the kid is in a mature state, start a conversation about what it's like for them when he or she is immature, selfish, or violent. Be curious as to what this child believes he or she feels, thinks, judges, or wants in that immature place. Offer no solutions unless the child asks for them, just inquire, listen, and communicate understanding, but not critical judgment or moralizing. Write about this conversation and share it with your partner or another parent.

During the next week, notice when you talk to children how much you listen without judgment until they feel heard and understood, and how often you leap to criticism or advice. See if you can notice differences in how the child responds to the different modes.

Listening supportively without critical judgment tends to increase both willpower and executive function.

Chapter 38

Step-Parenting

Less than 50 percent of American children grow up with both biological parents. That means that there are a lot of blended families and step-parents in this country, which can be particularly challenging.

Severn and Peter

Severn fell in love with Peter, who had three small children. Peter was cautious about Severn meeting the children throughout the first year of their relationship. Time with her alone and time with the kids alone on alternate weeks suited him. Both divorced, Severn and Peter worked hard to take care of their love, and eventually it felt right to both of them for Severn to start hanging out with the kids. When she did, she just played with them and enjoyed them, deferring to Peter for boundaries and limits. Over many months they became a blended family, supportive of the kids' biological mother, but participating in a sweet intersubjectivity that was all their own.

Severn and Peter took their time, kept improving their friendship and love affair, had shared values of attunement, and didn't push the pace of letting their blended family constellate. They worked together to help Severn be an effective and valued step-mother.

Jack and Sally

Jack married Sally, who was mother to six-year-old Janie. They all stayed together ten years, but escalating conflicts between Jack and Sally tormented them, and Sally refused therapy, so they divorced. Through those ten years, Jack participated in every way imaginable in Janie's life (her biological father was a useless narcissist). He adored her, and she bloomed under his attention and affection. After the divorce, Jack struggled to stay connected to Janie, but their relationship quickly became tenuous, with Janie becoming ambivalent about even letting Jack take her out to dinner.

This is one of the hazards of step-parenting—you fall in love with the children, but, if you can't keep you marital love affair and friendship growing and learn quick repair of problems, you risk losing them abruptly and forever.

I see this fragility of connection more with step-parents than with biological children, or even adopted children. Step-parents break up with a partner and risk losing a son or daughter in ways biological and adoptive parents are less likely to suffer.

On the other hand, blended families with step-parents have much in common with biological and adoptive parent families. You still want goodness of fit with kids, open systems, healthy family growth hierarchies, and emotional coaching communication styles no matter what kind of family you're in.

It *does* tend to be delicate integrating a new parental figure into a mother and kid(s) or father and kid(s) culture (the way Severn and Peter did so elegantly). Step-parenting is often one of the most challenging and vulnerable forms of parenting. It's especially difficult with step-fathers of step-daughters—where conflict is common. The principles of good parenting remain the same, but the relationships require more parental commitment, flexibility, and maturity for the step-parent to be consistently perceived as positive by the kids. Especially with discipline, the step-parent needs to be empowered by the biological parent and meticulously respectful and consciously empathic with each child.

In this sense, the gatekeeper—the key figure—in step-parenting is usually the biological (or adoptive) parent. This father or mother needs to empower the step-parent to guide, set limits, and be an advocate for everyone's development. As a wise step-parent once told me, "It's all about the agreements."

If your partner is a step-parent, you need to empower him or her with your children to support a prosocial open family system. You need to help your partner be authoritative, but not authoritarian; generous, but not permissive.

If you are a step-parent, in general you need to let the biological parent be the ultimate authority when dealing with the kids, but still offer influence to him or her to be a better person and parent, and be dedicated to attuning to yourself and the kids. (Of course, there are always exceptions to this with dysfunctional biological parents suffering from addiction, mental illness, impulse control problems, or other debilitating handicaps.) Remember the secure attachment principles of "present, congruent/contingent, and marked, so that each kid feels known, accepted, and protected."

~~~~~~

EXERCISE: *Have you ever been in some kind of step-parenting role?*

Did you have a step-parent? Do you have friends with step-parents or who are step-parents? Is your partner a step-parent to your biological children? Write what you believe is the most important aspect of this relationship for you and your partner, and the one aspect of your relationship that you believe is most important to each child. Share what you've written with your partner or another parent and write about your conversation.

Chapter 39

Parenting in Different Dimensions

In sixty years we've evolved from goodness-of-fit models into attachment-based mutual growth models. We recognize kids are different types, and attunement-based growth hierarchies involve parents leading children and children leading parents into progressively more coherence.

We know that open family systems work better, authoritative parenting is superior, and emotional coaching is the way to go.

We know we need to shame children appropriately, support them always, and stay attuned to ourselves and our kids, with quick repair when there are ruptures.

We know what secure and insecure parenting and attachment looks like, and how good it is for our children for us to be secure and to keep adjusting to attunement with them so they can develop secure attachment styles.

We know that willpower and executive function are crucial to later success, and that emotionally coaching parents who have authoritative parenting styles support the development of that function in children of all ages.

We know that "small t" and "big T" traumas exist and will occur in every family. We, therefore, need to make sure all aspects of the human experience—both pleasurable and painful—are safely "talkaboutable" in our families. That way, no one goes unsupported when experiencing trauma, or uncelebrated when experiencing success and triumph.

When you ask yourself the Fourth Star question, "Would this person show up appropriately as a parent or family member?", keep in mind that these are many of the dimensions that matter most in showing up. To some extent, reading this section and doing the exercises has deepened your adaptive unconscious' (your constructive Shadow's) abilities to show up yourself and discern others who are likely to do the same.

~~~~~~

EXERCISE: *Weaknesses, vulnerabilities, and bad habits*

Make two columns on a sheet of paper. In the first, write all your strengths as a parent as specifically as possible. For example, "When I'm tired late at night I can still be compassionate when my two-year-old wakes me up and wants attention."

In the other column, write your weaknesses or vulnerabilities as a parent as specifically as possible. For example, "I get contemptuous when my son gets parking tickets."

Each weakness or vulnerability will probably have a bad habit involved. For each one, write a good habit you'd like to replace it with and what the first thirty seconds of practicing that good habit looks like.

Make a schedule for a week of practicing at least one of these good habits, and put the schedule on a wall where you can see it daily. Share this with your partner, your kids, or another parent.

Section Endnotes

1 Felitti 1998	8 Dougherty 1997	15 Ibid	22 Liedloff 1979
2 Witt 2006	9 Chess 1965	16 Ibid	23 Bateman 2004
3 van der Kolk 2014	10 Nichols 2007	17 MacTaggart 2012	24 Tronic 2008
4 Nichols 2007	11 Baumrind 1966	18 Siegel 2005	25 Schore 1994
5 Weinhold 2008	12 Twinge 2009	19 Fisher 2004	26 Witt 2006
6 Cherlin 2009	13 Schore 2003	20 Wilber 2000	27 Duhigg 2012
7 Gilbert 2006	14 Gottman 2014	21 Siegel 1999	28 Panksepp 2007

Does this person have deep soul's purpose, while recognizing and admiring what is deeply meaningful to me?

In John and Julie Gottman's Sound Relationship House theory, making dreams come true and creating shared meaning is at the top of the house. (Google "Sound Relationship House." The Gottmans' work is amazing!) They and many others have demonstrated that shared values and a sense of the sacred are super-good for relationships.

This is not surprising! Happiness research shows that people with a spiritual orientation—a felt sense of where they fit into the cosmos and how they contribute to everyone else—are happier, healthier, and more likely to be in satisfying marriages.

Bill O'Hanlon, a charismatic therapist and lecturer about positive psychology, says that three keys to happiness are compassion, connection, and contribution—all of which involve a sense of the sacred, of making your life more than just about you.[1]

The first step toward answering, "Does this person have deep soul's purpose, while recognizing and admiring what is deeply meaningful to me?" is knowing the importance of deep soul's purpose.

Know this: Your life needs purpose and meaning. You need what's sacred and special to you to be recognized and honored by your most intimate others, and honoring deep purpose in another usually involves a hunger for deep purpose in yourself. This knowledge guides you as a seeker (and if you've made it this far in this book, you *are* a seeker!), and helps you recognize these qualities in others.

This section explores what deep soul's purpose is, how you can discover and refine your own deep purpose, and what qualities tend to sustain you in it. We all crave deep purpose and usually admire it in others. I've found it to be a foundation of respect and caring in happy relationships, and that's why "Does this person have deep soul's purpose, while recognizing and admiring what is deeply meaningful to me?" is the Fifth Star.

Chapter 40

What Is Deep Soul's Purpose?

Deep soul's purpose is a *feeling* that what I'm doing right now is important, and is an activity, mission, or vision in my life that is regularly characterized by that feeling of personal significance. Activities, interests, and passions change throughout life, but the *feeling of meaning*—that some quality, pursuit, or mission is important, even sacred—keeps a similar flavor throughout life.

One of my clients asked her five-year-old grandson to get off the computer and come to lunch. While he was investigating dinosaurs, he looked up and said, "I have to finish my work first!" Learning about dinosaurs felt important to him. Like a wise grandmother, she honored his sense of mission and let him finish his "work."

~~~~~~

EXERCISE: *Deep purpose model*

Think of someone you really admire. This can be a real or fictitious character. Does he or she have some mission in their life that seems bigger than just their own individual self? I find people like Steven Spielberg, Bill

*and Melinda Gates, Gandalf, Michelle and Barack Obama, and Stephen
Colbert admirable because they seem committed to service larger than
their individual successes. Write about your person and his or her mission,
and ask yourself what deep purpose in you is awakened by their service.*

*Write a brief imagined conversation with this person where you describe
how their mission has helped clarify yours. At least once imagine yourself
being that other responding to you, and write down the dialogue.*

*Ask your partner who he or she really admires, and ask him or her to
describe those qualities in themselves.*

Deep soul's purpose can be almost any service, project, mission, or commitment that feels personally significant to you.

I've had lots of missions in my life that felt sacred. The most central has been learning, practicing, and teaching psychotherapy over the last fifty years, but there have been many others. Learning Shotokan Karate, studying Taoist healing, tap dancing, surfing, songwriting, and playing tennis all have had the signatures of deep meaning. Loving my wife, Becky, doing my best to parent my two children, and living my values all feel sacred to me. Practicing my meditations and spiritual disciplines and dedicating myself to a lifetime of learning and spiritual growth are central to my personal sense of self and meaning. Writing this book has the feeling of deep soul's purpose.

But, be careful! Deep purpose is not always healthy! Without attuning to others, deep purpose can make a person feel entitled to rip them off. In 2013, there was a group of criminals in Orange County whose deep purpose was to cut holes in the ceilings of banks and rob them. Deep purpose for Europeans in the Crusades was to kill infidels and win the Holy Land back for Christians. Deep purpose in terrorists is to maximize body counts. Staying attuned to ourselves and others protects us from such crazy passions.

Purpose often involves service.

Ask people who feel a sense of deep soul's purpose where they discovered it, and it will often be through some form of service to others. One of the main ways to address depression or anxiety is to offer help to others, to commit to some project larger than yourself. Mother Teresa suffered from grinding depression, but regulated it by surrendering to serving the poor in India.[2]

I find it especially beautiful for partners to find deep soul's purpose in supporting their love, their children, and each other's personal evolution.

But a sense of purpose doesn't have to be service. Athletes can feel deep purpose in their sport, artists in their art, businesspeople in their businesses, seekers on their path, or competitors in their successes.

Almost any human activity can have the feeling of deep soul's purpose. Purpose is more a *feeling* about an activity than any activity itself.

In *The Teachings of Don Juan,* the Shaman Don Juan explains purpose to his student, Carlos Castaneda. Don Juan states that a warrior needs to be on a path with a heart. Carlos asks how to know which path has a heart, and where such a path leads.

Don Juan laughs and responds with a version of, "I've been on many paths with heart, and here I am in this desert with a crazy gringo! A path with a heart is what you do that feels sacred to you."[3]

Purpose often changes throughout life, but the *feeling* stays very much the same. That is the feeling of deep meaningfulness.

Spiritual teacher David Deida believes that deep soul's purpose is especially important for guys, because it organizes their mission in life and stabilizes their relationship with their chosen feminine partner. A woman doesn't want a guy to organize his life primarily around her. If he does, it tends to subtly diminish him in her eyes.[4]

A client of mine in her 40s, Judy, had a lover who made it all about her. "I want what *you* want" was his position with her. Eventually she became disgusted with him and split up. A later lover had purpose—his work and son—but also wanted her as his chosen partner. She respected him and continued to find him and his life attractive and admirable.

I've found guys more likely to be okay with a partner whose purpose is to support his and her love—especially if it involves family (though it can distress him if she is self-neglectful or self-derogatory), but I've found women to be put off by a guy who lives for her and has no sense of deeper meaning.

Flow guides us to purpose.

Mihaly Csikszentmihalyi has researched flow states where people become lost in activities and time compresses. Writing often takes me into flow: "My legs are asleep! Have I been sitting at the computer two hours?!" Any interruption—even praise—of a flow state can feel intrusive and irritating. Csikszentmihalyi maintains that meaningful activity is often characterized by flow states, and his work has been replicated by many researchers. Flow is total pleasurable absorption.[5] We often find purpose in those activities that deliver consistent flow states.

EXERCISE: *Getting into flow*

Sit in a quiet, beautiful place with your journal beside you, and attune to yourself. Start with awareness of breath in and out, and then continue to experience sensation, emotion, thought, judgment, and desire with acceptance and caring intent. As you settle into a mindful, attuned state, allow the words, "My deep soul's purpose is..." to hover in your consciousness, and attend to what arises in feelings, thoughts, images, judgments, and desires. Write whatever comes and share it with your partner, telling him or her why you are doing this to clarify and/or deepen your personal sense of deep soul's purpose. Ask your partner do the same, and listen with interest and respect as they relate their thoughts and experience. Write about your conversations.

EXERCISE: *Bigger than me*

Think of a time when you were engaged in something that felt larger and more significant than you personally. Maybe you were helping produce a play or were working on a political campaign. Write about that time with special emphasis on how you felt in your body. As you do this, expand to awareness of whatever sensory experience you associate with that sense of purpose. Are there flavors, colors, textures, images, people, or stories connected with this sense of purpose? Write these down, and share everything with your partner with the goal of clarifying and deepening your sense of purpose.

Think of a time when caring for your partner felt important and sacred. Maybe when she was sick, or when he lost his brother, or when she won the bridge tournament, or when he got a promotion. Think of a time your partner made it all about you when you really needed it. Write how these experiences felt, and share with your partner what you wrote.

Our best gifts

Purpose is often giving our best gifts, which other people can sometimes see better than we can ourselves.

Our best gifts are often those aspects of ourselves that we need to manifest in service or risk feeling distress and lack of fulfillment. They can be deeply embedded traits and qualities that don't seem that special to us. My neighbor Rosemary was so deeply kind to everyone that she glowed with goodness. My friend Bill automatically relaxes and engages whenever another person needs his attention. Two children lost in a game with love and laughter are demonstrating their best selves. When I point out such characteristics to people, they frequently make some dismissive remark such as, "That's no big deal; I'm just being myself." People often can't see the special beauty in these wonderful personal traits.

We are social beings who attune to one another constantly. Often what feels like an effortless quality in us is perceived as special by others. Has anyone ever complimented you on some quality—like kindness, friendliness, insightfulness, integrity, or acceptance—and you felt somewhat disconcerted, as if that quality in you is so natural that it is no big deal? Alternately, you might have felt embarrassed because *you* don't identify with this quality, or see your flaws and mistakes as more defining of you.

These deep, often effortless positive qualities can lead us into deep purpose, first through acknowledging them, and second through sourcing them to guide us. If I acknowledge my basic kindness, I can ask my kind self what to do when I'm hurt, angry, afraid, or confused. If we access our positive personal resources before conclusions or actions, whatever way we move through our professional and personal lives, we are contributing to the wellbeing of those around us. Contributions to others are often the hallmark of deep purpose.

EXERCISE: *Personal resource insight*

> *Ask your partner and one or two of your friends to tell you some aspect or aspects of you that they find particularly wonderful and don't get exactly from anyone else. Write everything down and look for themes, repetitions, and constellations of qualities. Write these insights down and share every-thing with your partner or someone you trust, looking for insight about how these aspects or qualities might inform your deep soul's purpose.*
>
> *Tell your partner the two or three most wonderful aspect of him or her and write about your conversation.*

Purpose can be found in suffering.

When I was between 14 and 15 years of age, I had a major depressive episode. This is a common time for such crises, as our nervous systems adjust from childhood toward the adults we are going to become. It can be a terrifying prospect to look ahead to an uncertain life. I was angry, lonely and despairing, fighting with my family, and beginning to have problems at school.

My parents sought help from a therapist who, after working with us some months, had me committed to a psychiatric clinic and given elec-troconvulsive therapy (ECT). ECT is just as extreme as it sounds. You are strapped to a table, given intravenous valium to protect you from the seizure to come, and electrodes are attached to the front of your skull deliver a jolt that convulses your body. This causes temporary amnesia and confusion, but also temporarily lifts the burden of depression.

In that clear space where, for the first time in several years, I was no longer maddened by emotional pain, I discovered I wanted to be a psycholo-gist and a martial artist. In retrospect, I was choosing the healer and warrior archetypes, as many young men do. When the emotional pain began to return, I was able to tolerate it and carry on in my karate classes and my studies of psychology. At 19, I was awarded my black belt in Shotokan Karate, and at 25, I earned my first license to practice psychotherapy and was training other therapists in Santa Barbara. I had found purpose through my suffering.

If often hurts when we don't feel a sense of purpose. We don't like pain and often try to escape with sensation (like food, drugs, alcohol, sex, work, or play). Spiritual teacher David Deida has suggested feeling the suffering and facing it to discover purpose. Over time you'll notice activities, thoughts, or experiences that don't feel like escape, but rather feel like they alleviate the suffering *by answering its call* in a significant positive way.[6]

In my twenties, when I was first working as a paraprofessional counselor at the UCSB student counseling center, I remember my first sessions as a therapist being exhausting and challenging, but also deeply satisfying and meaningful. Some part of me that had been urgently yearning for expression and meaning relaxed as I did my best to help my fellow students.

~~~~~~

EXERCISE: *Purpose in suffering*

Remember a particularly dark time in your life. It could have been being put down by others, suffering from illness or accident, or a loss of a person, place, or activity. Write about it in your journal. Now read what you've written, looking for what direction, meaning, or purpose emerged for you from dealing with this dark time. Talk about this with your partner or someone you trust and write about your conversation.

Talk with your partner about a time you shared a crisis. How did you show up for each other and how did it feel? Did the support aspects deepen your love? Did the negative aspects separate you? Talk about this with your partner, and discuss how you can get closer and more able to give and receive sacred support.

Purpose can be found in anger.

Similarly, what *really* pisses you off? What makes you so mad that you have to do something about it? In the 1970s and 1980s, the psychotherapy world was fragmented, with different approaches arguing with each other about whose system was best. Behaviorists despised psychoanalysts, who despised humanists. Family therapists denigrated individual therapists, and short-term therapists were critical of therapists who worked long-term. This all pissed me off and motivated me to look for cross-disciplinary systems with universal principles that I could bring to my therapy, teaching, and writing, leading to much of the work I've done since. It primed me to be lit up by Ken Wilber's Integral meta-theory when I first encountered it, which focuses on how everyone is at least partially right, and how to fit all the beautiful, good, and true perspectives together into coherent wholes.[7]

~~~~~~

EXERCISE: *Purpose in anger*

Get your journal and write down the one or two things you most deeply resent, and what you are called to do about them. Global warming? Social injustice? Some deeply unfair situation in your town or company? Share this with your partner.

If you have frustration at not having purpose or not being able to embody your purpose, sit in an attuned state and cultivate the frustration. Spend at least twenty minutes doing this. Keep focusing on the pain of not having purpose, and your tendencies to try to escape the pain. Write down your experiences. If you do have deep soul's purpose, remember a time you didn't, and then write about how you transitioned into having purpose. What happened? How did you feel different before and after? Share what you've written with your partner or someone you trust and write about your conversation.

Ask your partner if they have deep resentments that demand some healing action.

Chapter 41

What Are the Stories That Magnetize *Me?*

Favorite stories, books, movies, plays, music, art, or dreams often light us up and guide our path to deep purpose. J.R.R Tolkien's *Lord of the Rings* trilogy, C.S. Lewis' Narnia books, and Frank Herbert's *Dune* captured my imagination and felt sacred in mysterious ways I couldn't adequately articulate as a child and teenager.

As I studied Jungian texts and Joseph Campbell's work, I realized that all these books involved the epic journey narrative. The hero is called, resists the call, takes the call, defeats the threshold guardian, and passes through the threshold into the road of trials. Through struggling to transcend challenges, monsters, and his own inner darknesses, the hero reconciles with the divine feminine and masculine, receives a gift from Spirit, and returns through the threshold, transformed, with a mission to serve the community.[8] My fascination with these stories led me to listen for my calls and surrender to my epic journeys—all permeated with the feeling of deep soul's purpose.

EXERCISE: *Meaning in stories*

> *What are your favorite stories, books, movies, plays, music, art, or dreams? Write them down and look for themes that attract you. How does each inform your purpose at this moment? Write your insights and share with your partner or someone you trust. Write about your conversation afterwards.*
>
> *Ask your partner how themes and characters of their favorite stories, books, movies, etc. inform their sense of purpose. Write about your conversation.*

Meaning in dreams

Dreams are stories that your unconscious creates especially for you! Your dreams uniquely reflect you, your conflicts, your needs, and *your purpose.* They happen every ninety minutes when you sleep, and 60 percent of them are problem-solving dreams, presenting you with issues that are important to your deep unconscious and attempt to address your challenges.[9]

EXERCISE: *Purpose in dreams*

> *Try writing your dreams down every morning, as soon as you wake up, for a week. After writing each dream, ask yourself, "What is the message of this dream to me?" and then write the first thoughts, images, feelings, that arise. After a week, read what you've written and share any patterns or insights you've found with your partner or someone you trust. Write about your conversation afterwards.*

Chapter 42

Purpose Needs Attunement and Self-Knowledge

Attunement keeps us connected with our own interior experience, the humanity of others, and the importance of how we all influence each other. Purpose with no attunement can be a frightening thing. Focus, intent, and action, with no principled attuned foundation, driven by resolve, can be a nightmare—causing unspeakable horrors of war, violence, selfish greed, and thoughtless objectification of precious human beings.

The fifteenth-century missionary movements in South America, the Crusades, terrorism, and the Third Reich are all examples of purpose that objectified others. People on a mission who objectify others can feel morally justified in "doing what it takes," even if it involves causing suffering, ripping people off, or even killing them.

The financial crisis in 2008 was created by individuals passionately committed to creating personal wealth with no regard for the collective welfare of homeowners across the country. The war in Iraq was at least partially motivated by desires to influence and control Middle-Eastern oil, with reckless disregard for the consequences of war.

Attunement personalizes our attention because we focus on real human beings with human experiences. When we're attuned to others, it is more difficult to objectify them and engage in such excesses.

EXERCISE: *Reckless disregard*

Remember a time you were so enthusiastic, distracted, or impassioned that you didn't care about how you affected others. Were you so happy about your success that you didn't notice someone else's disappointment? Were you angry at some group or country that you supported hurting or suppressing them? Were you so disgusted at someone's behavior that you desired they lose rights or suffer some extreme punishment?

Write about that time, what happened, and how you think and feel about it now. Have you changed? If so, how? Have you learned from the experience? If so, what have you learned? How do these experiences currently inform your sense of personal meaning? Write about this and share it with your partner or someone you trust.

In retrospect, if you could go back and attune to others in the situation, what would you have done differently? What does all this teach you about your life's purpose? Write all this down and share it with your partner or someone you trust, and then write about your conversation.

Masculine and feminine qualities influence purpose.

We are all different types of people, and, especially in the sexual occasion, we are generally a more masculine or more feminine person. As I mention in Chapters 9 and 10, I consider the masculine and feminine to be meta-types that influence other types like introvert/extrovert or other personality types such as the nine Enneatypes or the Human Design types.

EXERCISE: *Sexual essence and meaning*

What are the three most meaningful activities in your life? Write them down. What are the three most meaningful aspects of your primary relationship? Write them down.

Now imagine you are your opposite sexual essence. To keep this simple, if you're a guy, imagine you're a woman, and if you're a woman imagine you're a guy. How do you think you might answer these questions differently? Write what you imagine.

What does this suggest to you about how masculine and feminine aspects and essence in you and others influence your sense of purpose? Share this with your partner and write about your conversation.

One unfortunate consequence of feminism and the Me Too movement is that conversations about masculine and feminine differences and similarities, or male and female differences and similarities, have often become emotionally charged, or even taboo. We are all unique individuals, but types have existence, and, just as I am more extroverted than introverted, I am more masculine than feminine in my sexual essence. Knowing this about myself helps guide me through the world and helps me understand my purpose in relationship to women and other men.

Knowing our sexual essences and aspects helps Becky and me organize the polarities of our life to deepen our friendship and love affair.

Relationships are asymmetrical in many ways.

Modern relationships have equal power, but they are asymmetrical by necessity because we are different types of people, have different roles and responsibilities in our shared lives, and especially, we are more masculine or more feminine types.

Spiritual teacher David Deida suggests that a more masculine person's life is likely to follow a pattern of success, failure, success, failure, success… death. He suggests a more feminine person's life is more likely to revolve around the pattern of love is happening, love isn't happening, love is happening, love isn't happening, love is happening…death.[10]

Now, of course, we all want success and love. None of us like failure and loneliness! But more masculine or more feminine people often have different emphases in their personal lives, families, and work. How might this apply to you?

EXERCISE: *Polarity and purpose*

I suggest you skim over the polarity chapters (9 through 16) and what you wrote in your journal doing the exercises. As you do, what do you discover about your sexual aspects and essence and your experiences of erotic polarity that inform your sense of self and deep soul's purpose? Write about what you discover.

Talk with your partner about their sense of sexual aspects and essence, and discuss how knowing this can help you love better.

Read everything you've written about purpose, and look for how your sexual essence and aspects seem to inform your purpose and write about what you discover. Write about your insights and share what you've found with your partner or someone you trust. Write about the conversation afterwards and what you learned from your talk.

Chapter 43

Love and Purpose Summary

The Fifth Star, "Does this person have deep soul's purpose, while recognizing and admiring what is deeply meaningful to me?", reflects the fact that for a couple to have shared meaning—a central aspect of happy relationships—each needs to know what deep soul's purpose feels like and be willing to honor the importance of it in themselves and their partner.

Whether we are in a relationship or not, we evaluate the world from our own understanding and principles. Often we best discern whether another has deep purpose by becoming intimate with our own deep purpose. Similarly, we often help our partner honor what's sacred to us by being interested in and appreciative of what's sacred to them.

Here's a summary of some of the main points of this section:

* Deep soul's purpose in yourself and others is a big deal, and it is a feeling more than a specific mission or activity.

* We can find purpose in what lights us up, pisses us off, eases our suffering of meaninglessness, or in what others find beautiful in us.

* We can find purpose reflected to us from our impacts on the world.

* We can find purpose in seeking closeness with spirit, or unity with God.

* We can discover purpose in perspectives, solutions, or ways of being that are so wonderful we must share them.

* We can also be called to purpose by events—our country goes to war, we discover a local river being polluted, etc.—and we must do something. Your community is not caring for some of its members and you are moved to become an activist. Your child becomes sick or injured and you are on a mission to get him or her the best care. All of these events call us to deep purpose.

* As we move through life, we discover purpose in many places, but it will always feel significant and important, which points us to a path with a heart. That feeling is one of our best guides.

* If we're in relationship, knowing and admiring what is sacred to our partner nourishes our love and supports our partner's personal evolution.

EXERCISE: *Absorbing this section's lessons*

Read everything you've written so far in this section, and write what you notice about your purpose, and your life.

Now write what you notice about your partner, his or her purpose, and your shared life.

Do you feel more able to answer the Fifth Star question of "Does this person have deep soul's purpose, while recognizing and admiring what is deeply meaningful to me?" Write how you are better at answering this question. Show what you've written to your partner and write about your subsequent conversation.

EXERCISE: *Mind map summary*

Use this opportunity to create a deep soul's purpose mind map!

* *Get a big sheet of paper, put a three-inch circle in the center, and write "My deep soul's purpose" in the center of the circle. If you have determined a specific current purpose that organizes your life, put a few words to describe it in this inner circle. For instance, if I'm mind-mapping my psychotherapy, "Love heals" is in the center circle.*

* *Using this section's responses as guides, write or draw relevant aspects of your deep purpose (including experiences, commitments, practices, objects, problems, and people) around the center circle and draw wavy, different colored lines connecting the center with them. Also draw lines connecting them with each other if you are so moved.*

* *You can illuminate this mind map with drawings, pasted-in photos or images, brief phrases, or anything else that helps it feel more beautiful, good, and true to you. Put the mind map on your wall where you can see it daily and add to it at will. Explain your mind map in detail to your partner or someone you trust, and then write about your conversation in your journal.*

* *Ask your partner to draw a mind map of deep soul's purpose that you two can look at and discuss. If your partner doesn't want to draw a mind map of their own, ask them what they would put in the center and around the edges, and write about your conversation.*

Section Endnotes

1 O'Hanlon 2007   4 Deida 1997   7 Wilber 2000   10 Deida 2006
2 Graham 2016   5 Csikszentmihalyi 1990   8 Campbell 1949
3 Castaneda 1968   6 Deida 2006   9 Kaufman 2013

Bringing It All Together

We're reaching the end of the *Loving Completely* journey, and I hope you've enjoyed the trip!

This last section returns to some core principles and practices, contemplating how you can use this material to change your life and the lives of everyone close to you.

Intimacy is a wild ride on which we're all destined to career up and down from conception to death (and maybe beyond death—who knows?). The *Loving Completely* system gives you tools to *be* a good partner, *choose* a good partner, and *grow and maintain* outstanding relationships. It also gives you criteria you can use to evaluate whether a relationship will work for you or not, and how to discern and address *your* parts of relationship problems.

These last three chapters revisit some central themes, and further discuss mastery, receiving influence, and exploring your own virtues and vulnerabilities in relationships.

Chapter 44

Relationships Everywhere

This book began with the premise that everything is relationships, and that we grow in relationships with ourselves and others throughout our lives. Our relationship with our chosen other revolves around our friendship, love affair, and capacity to effectively repair the injuries and ruptures that are a natural part of a primary relationship.

I hope that your understandings of your relationships with all the different parts of you in your past, present, and future, as well as your relationships with your chosen one, others, nature, and meaning, have changed or expanded as a result of the perspectives I've shared with you. Your understandings also may have changed from what you've discovered yourself by reading this book and doing the exercises.

To recapitulate:

Everything is relationships.
Asking the Five Star questions about others predisposes us to choose better partners and be a better partner. Noticing the Five Stars in ourselves guides us to personal growth in these central dimensions of existence. Noticing the

Five Stars with our partner guides us in understanding and maintaining our friendship and love affair with him or her, and helps us repair ruptures in the relationship when they inevitably occur.

The Five Stars are:

* ✷ Is there erotic polarity, a spark of attraction, between me and this other person?

* ✷ Does this person maintain their physical and psychological health?

* ✷ In conflict, would this person be able and willing to do what it takes to get back to love?

* ✷ Does this person show up appropriately as a parent or family member?

* ✷ Does this person have deep soul's purpose, while recognizing and admiring what is deeply meaningful to me?

EXERCISE: *Identifying change*

Ask the Five Star questions about people you meet and consciously observe, and then record the Five Stars in them and yourself for the next couple of days. If you're in an intimate relationship, observe the dimensions in you and your partner. Write about your experiences in your journal, and then compare them with your initial answers when we first explored the Five Stars in the beginning of this book.

What has changed, deepened, or shifted in your experience and understanding? Write these insights in your journal, along with any action steps you could take to embody these insights into your daily life. Share this with your partner and write about your conversation.

Mastery

Humans learn according to social and neurobiological principles that have been observed and studied. We've talked about George Leonard's "mastery curve" of effort plus feedback leading to progress, plateau, progress, plateau. His findings have been replicated by researchers studying talent,[1] intelligence,[2] and grit.[3]

George Leonard's mastery curve says that initial learning leads to quick progress that stabilizes into a plateau period where continued effort *doesn't appear* to be creating more progress. This is often where students wanting quick progress drop out and give up. If the student persists, receiving influence from their teacher and tolerating the frustration of not having quick results, there is a tiny dip in competence followed by another burst of learning. No matter how inexperienced or expert his students were, Leonard observed them repeating this pattern throughout training.[4]

Mastery obviously fits with growth mindsets. We enjoy learning, receive influence, continue working (focusing on effort and progress), and enjoy visible payoffs when they show up, but don't insist on rewards or quick victories to keep working.

Daniel Coyle, in his excellent book *The Talent Code,* looked at hotbeds of mastery around the world and found common elements in high achievers and their learning experiences. He found ignition, deep practice, and master coaching to be universal characteristics. What do they involve?

* Ignition was finding a goal, *deep purpose*, that you were passionate about. Most of us are passionate about having superior relationships, and I hope that *Loving Completely* has ignited you to commit to loving better throughout your life.

* Deep practice was breaking skills into bits you studied, working with them as whole constructs, and doing them faster and slower in time. I've broken down the Five Stars into systems of component perspectives and practices to help you develop mastery in each dimension.

* Master coaches stayed attuned to you and kept you moving on effort and progress mindset paths toward mastery. I've encouraged you to use this book, your partner, and wise guides to receive caring influence to grow and flourish.

Coyle found these commonalities while studying areas that produced great soccer players, musicians, and artists, among many other disciplines. He interviewed and studied students and master coaches and kept finding the same components over and over again.[5]

John Gottman, studying the "masters and disasters" of relationship, found similar forces at work. Masters of relationship were motivated to love, grow, and receive caring influence, and they kept working on their relationships through hardship and troubles.[6]

Mastery involves attuning to yourself and your activity and reaching for coherent flow states. I believe you'll find this applies to you personally in loving and being loved well and improving throughout life.

~~~~~~

EXERCISE: *Mastery*

In what specific areas do you crave more mastery? Pay special attention to relationship areas you wish to improve. Write these down.

In these areas, what are the habits and practices that you're already doing that are wonderful and you want to sustain? Write these down.

Who are your best guides in these areas—teachers, therapists, coaches, or friends? How are they helping you with your mastery curves? Write about this in your journal.

Map out a possible program over the next thirty days that will result in more effort and progress—the gold standards of growth mindsets and mastery—to further extend your mastery of these habits and practices. Check this out with your guide(s) and consider committing to this program for a month. Write about your conversations.

Put this program on a calendar, with daily commitments as important as dentist or doctor appointments, and put it on a wall where you can see it daily. Share all this with your partner or someone else your trust and note on your calendar each day whether you are following your program or not. At the end of thirty days review everything, write about what you've experienced, and share this with your helper, your partner, or someone else your trust.

Chapter 45

Receiving Influence

We've talked a lot so far about the importance of receiving influence in intimacy, growth, and happiness.

When asked what the main characteristic of a happy couple was, John Gottman said it was the husband's ability to receive influence from his wife. In psychotherapy, the clients I work with who best receive caring influence from me and others generally grow the fastest, have the fewest problems, and experience the most successes.

Receiving influence is supremely important because we are all social and make social adjustments back and forth in order to optimize relationships. Can you remember a conversation where the person you were talking with *completely refused* any influence from you? This is a situation where nothing you said or did had any discernible impact on his or her opinions or attitudes. How did you feel in this situation? Frustrated? Angry? Helpless? Frightened? These are not comfortable, prosocial experiences! This is what others are likely to feel when *we* refuse influence.

Receiving and offering positive influences is crucial to growth and love, and you can get better at it! Here are some steps that are often effective at giving and receiving positive influence, which are very similar to the steps of quick repair we've practiced in previous chapters:

* The first step is *noticing* when you or the other is blocked off and unavailable to be influenced.

* The second step is soothing yourself and offering soothing influence to the other, often simply by attuning.

* The third step is offering compassionate understanding to the other.

* The fourth step is reaching for how both of you can be right.

* If none of this recruits the other into mutual influence, then you shift from relating—looking for shared understanding and productive dialogue—into handling. Handling a person locked in a position involves setting compassionate boundaries while staying attuned. One useful form of boundary is respectful withdrawal from an impasse, "I don't think we're making progress. Let's talk about this tomorrow morning at eight." You'll notice that this uses a respectful tone, not blaming the other for your lack of progress, and setting a specific time to continue the talk. Another useful boundary is asking for a kind tone (usually absent in gridlock), as in, "Could you please make your point again, but this time with a kinder tone? I think it will help me listen better." Again, you're not attacking the person or their tone, but asking for more kindness.

Relating and handling are universals.

The relating/handling dichotomy is a universal in social relationships. When mutually influencing dialogue fails, human instincts are to attack, coerce, defend, collapse, or flee—all usually counterproductive. Recognizing yourself refusing influence gives you the choice of self-soothing and looking for what is valid in the other's points. Recognizing the other refusing influence gives you the choice of switching to handling—first soothing and asking for kinder mutuality, and then respectfully disengaging with reassurances that important issues will be dealt with soon at a specific time.

You can see in this how discerning and setting boundaries for negative influence (both in yourself when you're acting badly and for others when they're acting badly) is crucial for safe relating, and can prevent any number of regrettable incidents. Regrettable incidents often arise from escalating conflicts where neither partner is receiving or offering caring influence.

~~~~~~

EXERCISE: *Receiving influence*

When have you been profoundly influenced positively by another person, especially your partner? Remember a specific incident. How did it feel? How were you different afterwards and what did you have to do to receive and keep receiving this positive influence? Write your answers in detail and share them with your partner or someone else you trust.

Receiving caring influence amplifies wisdom and love.

Two central, powerful, transformative practices are receiving caring influence from wise others and offering caring influence (never hostile or coercive, always respectful and compassionate) to those we love. Of all the qualities I've discussed thus far in this book, giving and receiving caring influence are most necessary for optimal growth and joyful relationships. More than any other single capacity, offering and receiving caring influence can dial us in to optimal love, success, and development.

~~~~~~

EXERCISE: *Influence wish list*

Make a list of the people and resources that you want influencing you. It might be this book, your parents, spouse, best friend, wise teacher, change program, religious assembly, sponsor, or child. Write what you have to do to receive and act on their loving input, especially when you don't feel like it. Write what it would take for you to regularly seek out and receive wise and caring influence from these sources and people you admire and respect. Share this with your partner and especially with any person you want to influence you.

Virtues and vulnerabilities

Receiving caring influence from ourselves involves rigorous honesty about who we are and what is happening *right now*. There isn't room for false modesty or denial of faults in rigorous honesty right now. So let's look at your virtues and vulnerabilities.

Virtues

Knowing your strengths is at least as important as knowing your vulnerabilities. Often in therapy, it's harder to help people see how brilliant and beautiful they are than to help them find their conflicts and weaknesses. When I asked Ken Wilber what stood out in the people who were drawn to the Integral community in Boulder that began forming around the turn of the century, he told me one striking characteristic they seemed to share was that they didn't seem to realize how beautiful and talented they were.

Many years ago, I was working with a couple in their 30s. The husband had been wildly successful in a business he created, and his brilliant wife was helping him with a new venture. He had criticized her unfairly for her help, and she was angrily telling him how important he and his work were to her. She saw me smiling and asked, "What?"

I said, "I'm noticing how brilliant and effective you are and thinking how lucky your husband is to have you as an ally and guide." Her husband immediately softened as this resonated with him, looking at her with love and appreciation. She became confused. She didn't feel brilliant and effective at that moment, but she was. Me focusing on both their virtues made those virtues more visible to them, disarmed them, and led to productive dialogue.

Often our biggest blocks to growth are lack of awareness of, or gratitude for, our strengths.

EXERCISE: *A list of virtues*

Create a chart of your virtues. Read all your journal entries and make a list of your strengths and virtues. Put them all on a big sheet of paper and illuminate them with colors, photos, and anything else that's fun for you. Put it on your wall and show it to your partner. Ask for him or her to help you expand and refine it, adding new virtues and clarifying others. Write in your journal about your conversation.

Encourage your partner to do the same, and, if they choose not to, have a conversation about his or her virtues where you share your appreciation and admiration for them.

Vulnerabilities can be turned into opportunities.

We have tendencies to avoid what we fear and are ashamed of in ourselves. This disconnects us and blocks integration and growth.

With growth mindset attitudes, we can turn weaknesses and vulnerabilities into opportunities for development and deeper strength and resilience. Years ago, I found myself frequently feeling deep shame when I was tired or burned out, looking for personal flaws and mistakes I'd made. I became interested in this reaction, and began to research it, leading to my book, *The Gift of Shame*. My research led me to more deeply understand and even redefine shame and humor, sexual shame, shame as necessary in healing pathological narcissism, and shame as a spiritual guide. Gradually my shame (and others' shame) became more interesting and instructive to me. I began to see how listening and acting on shame accelerates growth, leading eventually to understanding shame as an evolutionary driver.

To benefit from my vulnerability to shame when I was tired and burned out, I had to first recognize it and choose to address it. What are your vulnerabilities?

~~~~~~

EXERCISE: *A list of vulnerabilities*

Create a chart of your vulnerabilities. Read all of your journal entries again and make a list of your weaknesses, vulnerabilities, and characteristic defensive states. List them on one side of a big sheet of paper and after each, write what you could do each day to grow in this area. Again, illuminate it with colors, photos, or anything else you'd like. Put it on the wall next to your chart of virtues you created in the last exercise and share it with your partner, asking him or her for caring influence to help you with this project.

Chapter 46

Thrive and Love Well!

Thank you for reading this book! Thank you for considering all of the ideas and exercises I've found so useful and transformative in loving and being loved over the years.

One big takeaway I want you to get from *Loving Completely* is that *you matter!* How you live, love, and grow influences way more people than you can possibly know. As you commit to choosing Five Star people and being a Five Star person, you influence all of us for the better. This is a meta-purpose on top of all our deep soul's purposes—to live and love well to support all of us living and loving well!

Let's finish with two integration exercises.

~~~~~~

EXERCISE: *Study your journal for insight and direction*

Take some time and read all your journal entries. Sit in front of your mind maps and charts and reflect on your goals and experiences. Relax and open yourself for insight, direction, images, and associations. Write

*down anything that comes, and then share it with your partner or
someone you trust.*

~~~~~~

EXERCISE: *The integration chart*

*If there are one, two, three, or more insights, practices, or relationships
that have emerged from this book process that you especially want to
implement in your life, write them down, organize them how you want,
and put them on a big chart that you illuminate with colors and images.*

*Put this chart on the wall and share it with your partner or someone you
love. Look at it every day for the next two weeks, hopefully developing
a habit of checking it out daily for months and years to come searching
for guidance, insights, and validation of your life and purpose. As you
continue your life and relationships, edit and alter this chart as you see fit.*

*I encourage you to implement your program and share your experiences,
both triumphs and letdowns, with your partner. Help him or her soothe
you in defeat and celebrate your triumphs. Do this for you, for the people
you love, for all your teachers, and for the world.*

Much love to you,

Keith Witt

Section Endnotes

1 Coyle 2009   3 Duckworth 2016   5 Coyle 2009
2 Kaufman 2013   4 Leonard 1991   6 Gottman 2015

Bibliography

Achor, Shawn. (2011). *The Happiness Advantage*. Penguin/Random House: NYC, New York.

Armstrong, Alison. (2007). *Making Sense of Men*. 417 W. Foothill Blvd. Glendale, CA. UnderstandMen.com.

Barash, David. P. and Lipton, Judith Ever. (2009). *Strange Bedfellows: The surprising connection between sex, evolution and Monogamy*. New York: Bellevue Literary Press.

Barash, Susan. (2008). Little White Lies, Deep Dark Secrets: *The Truth About Why Women Lie*. St. Martin's Press: NY, NY.

Barratt, Barnaby. (2005). *Sexual Health and Erotic Freedom*. Philadelphia: Xlibris.

Bateman, Anthony, and Fonagy, Peter. (2004). *Psychotherapy for Borderline Personality Disorder: mentalization-based treatment*. Oxford: Oxford University Press.

Baumeister, R. F. and Leary M. R. (1995). *Desire For Interpersonal Attachments as a fundamental human motivation*. Psychological Bulletin, 11. 7. 497-529

Baumeister, R. F. (2011). *Willpower: Rediscovering the Greatest Human Strength*. New York: Penguin.

Baumrind, D. (1966). *Effects of Authoritative Parental Control on Child Behavior, Child Development, 37(4)*, 887-907.

Beck, Don Edward, and Cowan, Christopher C. (1996). *Spiral Dynamics; mastering values, leadership, and change*. Malden, MA: Blackwell Publishing.

Bergner, Daniel. (2009). What Do Women Want? *The New York Times Magazine,* Jan 25, 2009.

Berreby, David. (1998). Studies explore love and the sweaty T-shirt. *Science,* June 9, 1998.

Blanchard, R. (1997). H-Y antigen and homosexuality in men. J. *Theor. Biol.* 185 (3): April, 1997.

Bleyer, Jennifer. (2015). Good in Bed. *Psychology Today:* October, 2015.

Brogan, Kelly. (2016). *A Mind of Your Own*. New York: Harper/Collins

Buss, D. M. (2003). *The evolution of desire: Strategies of human mating* (Second Edition). New York : Basic Books.

Buss, D. M., & Shackelford, T. K. (1997). Susceptibility to infidelity in the first year of marriage. *Journal of Research in Personality, 31,* 193-221.

Buss, D. M. (1999). *Evolutionary Psychology: The New Science of Mind.* Boston, MA: Allyn and Bacon.

Campbell, Joseph. (1949). *The Hero With a Thousand Faces.* Princeton: Princeton University Press.

Camperio-Ciani. (2004). Evidence for maternally inherited factors favoring male homosexuality and promoting female fecundity. Proc. Biol. Sci. 271 (1554): November, 2004.

Castaneda, Carlos. (1968). T*he Teachings of Don Juan.* New York: Simon and Schuster.

Chapman, Gary. (2015). *The Five Love Languages.* Chicago: Northfield Publishing.

Cherlin, Andrew. (2009). *The Marriage-Go-Round.* New York: Vintage.

Chess, Stella, Thomas, Alexander, Birch, Herbert. (1965). *Your Child is a Person: A Psychological Approach to Childhood without Guilt.* The Viking Press, New York.

Childre, Doc. Rozman, Deborah, (2006). *Transforming Anxiety.* New Harbinger Publications: Oakland, CA.

Christensen, Beth, Maslin, Mark. (2008). Rocking the Cradle of Humanity: new thoughts on climate, tectonics and human evolution. *Geotimes,* Jan. 2008.

Clark, Russell & Hatfield, Elaine. (1989). Gender differences in receptivity to sexual offers. Journal of psychology and human sexuality. V2(1) 1989. The Haworth Press.

Cloniger, Robert C. (2004). *Feeling Good, the Science of Well-Being.* Oxford University Press.

Coyle, Daniel. (2009). *The Talent Code.* New York. Bantam.

Cozolino, Louis J. (2002). *The Neuroscience of Psychotherapy.* New York: W.W. Norton & Co.

Csikszentmihalyi, Mihaly. (1990). *Flow: the Psychology of Optimal Experience.* New York: Harper & Row.

Danielou, Alain. (1994). *The Complete Kama Sutra.* Rochester, Vermont: Park Street Press.

Darwin, Charles. (1872). *The Expression of Emotions in Man and Animals.* London: John Murray.

------. (1859), *On the Origin of Species.* The president and fellows of Harvard College. Boston: Mass.

Davidson, Richard. (2012). *The Emotional Life of your Brain.* New York: Penguin.

Deida, David. (2004). *Enlightened Sex.* Boulder, Colorado: Sounds True (audio recording)

------. (1995). *Intimate Communion.* Deerfield Beach: Health Communications, Inc.

------. (1997). *The Way of the Superior Man.* Austin: Plexus.

------. (2006). *David Deida, live, volumes 1, 2, 3.*

Dossey, Larry. (2013). *One Mind.* Hay House Inc: New York, NY.

------. (2009). *The Power of Premonitions.* Hay House Inc: New York, NY.

Doherty, William. (1997). *The Intentional Family.* Avon Books/Harper Collins: New York, NY.

------. (2013), *Take Back Your Marriage*. Guilford Press: New York, NY.

Duckworth, Angela. (2016). *Grit: The Power of Passion and Perseverance*. Simon and Schuster, New York, NY.

Duhigg, Charles. (2012). *The Power of Habit*. New York: Random House.

Dunbar, Robin. (2010). *How Many Friends does one Person Need?* Harvard University Press: Cambridge, Massachusetts.

Dweck, Carol. (2006). *Mindset*. New York: Ballantine.

Evans, M. E. (2013). *The Big Cheat: The Truth about Italian Men*. Surviving in Italy Blog. April 8, 2013.

Felitti, Vincent J: Anda, Robert F (1998). "Relationship of Childhood Abuse and Household Dysfunction to Many of the Leading Causes of Death in Adults: The Adverse Childhood Experiences (ACE) Study," *American Journal of Preventive Medicine*. 14 (4): May, 1998.

Fisher, Helen. (2004). *Why We Love: the Nature and Chemistry of Romantic Love*. New York: Henry Holt.

------. (2009). *Why Him? Why Her? Finding real love by understanding your personality type*. New York: Henry Holt.

------. (2002). The Anatomy of Love. Presented at *Anatomy of Intimacy Conference*, Life Span Learning Institute. Available through www.lifespanlearn.org.

Fosha, Diana. (2008). *Transformance: Recognition of Self by Self, and effective action*. In K. J. Schnieder (ed.), *Existential-Integrative Psychotherapy: Guideposts to the core of Practice*. New York: Routledge.

Fowler, J. H. Christakis, N.A. (2008). Dynamic spread of happiness in a large social network: longitudinal analysis over 20 years in the Framingham Heart Study. BMJ. 2008 Dec 4.

Gable, Shelly. (2006). "Will you be there for me when things go right? Supportive responses to positive event disclosures." *Journal of Personality and Social Psychology: V. 91. #5.*

Gilbert, Daniel. (2006). Does Fatherhood make you Happy? *Time Magazine,* June 19th, 2006.

Gilligan, Carol. (1993). *In a Different Voice: Psychological Theory and Women's Development*. Cambridge, Mass.: Harvard University Press.

Glass, George. (2014). *Blending Families Successfully*. Audio Studios: Whispersync for Voice ready.

Goldberg, Elkhonon. (2009). *The New Executive Brain*. Oxford University Press: NYC, New York.

Gottman, John, M., Silver, Nan. (1999). *The Seven Principles for Making Marriage Work*. New York: Three Rivers Press.

------. (2007). Meta-Communication, *Presented at the conference, "The Healing Power of Emotion."* By the Lifespan Learning Institute, www.lifespanlearn.org.

------. (2001). *The Relationship Cure, a 5 Step Guide for Building Better Connections with Family, Friends, and Lovers.* New York: Crown Publishing.

------. (2015). *Principia Amores: the new science of love.* New York: Routledge.

Gottshall, Jonathon. (2012). *The Storytelling Animal.* Houghton, Mifflan, Harcourt: New York, NY.

Graham, George. (2016). Unholy Bound: Mother Teresa's Battles with Depression. Oxford University Press Blog, April, 2016.

------. (2016). Trivers' Pursuit. Jan 7, 2016 issue of *Psychology Today.*

Jowett, B. (1911). *The Dialogues of Plato: Translated into English, with analyses and Introductions Vol.I.* Charles Scribner's Sons, New York.

Jung, Carl G. (1961). *Memories, Dreams, and Reflections.* New York: Random House.

------. (1959). *The Archetypes and the Collective Unconscious.* Princeton: Princeton   University Press.

------. (1959). *The Basic Writings of C. G. Jung,* ed. Violet Staub De Laszlo, New York: The Modern Library.

------. (1957). *C. G. Jung: The Collected Works.* Princeton University Press.

Kahneman, Daniel. (2011). *Thinking Fast and Slow,* Penguin Books

Kaufman, Scott, Barry, (2013). *Ungifted: Intelligence Redefined.* Philadelphia, Basic Books.

Kegan, Robert. (1982). *The Evolving Self: Problems and Process in Human Development.* Cambridge, Mass: Harvard University Press.

Langer, Ellen J. (1997). *The Power of Mindful Learning.* Cambridge, MA: Da Capo Press.

LeDoux, Joseph (2015), *Anxious.* New York: Viking.

Lehmiller, J. J. (2009). Secret romantic relationships: Consequences for personal and relational well-being. *Personality and Social Psychology Bulletin,* 35, 1452-1466.

Leonard, George. (1991). *Mastery.* New York: Penguin.

Levine, Judith. (2002). *Harmful to Minors.* Minneapolis: University of Minneapolis Press.

Liedloff, Jean. (1975). *The Continuum Concept.* Reading Mass: Addison-Wesley Publishing Company, Inc.

MacTaggart, Lynne. (2007). *The Intention Experiment: Using Your Thoughts to Change Your Life and the World.* New York: Free Press.

MacTaggart, Lynne. (2012). *The Bond.* New York: Free Press.

Marks-Tarlow, Terry. (2008). *Psyche's Veil: Psychotherapy, Fractals, and Complexity.* New York: Routledge.

Masterson, James F. (1981). *The Narcissistic and Borderline Disorders, an integrated developmental approach.* New York: Brunner/Mazel.

Marano, Hara Estroff. (2009). Love's Destroyer. *Psychology Today:* July/August, 2009.

------. (2016). Love Interruptus. *Psychology Today:* July/August, 2016.

McGonigal, Kelly. (2012). *The Willpower Instinct*. New York: Penguin Books.

Mekel-Bobrov (2005). *Ongoing adaptive evolution of ASPM, a brain size determinant in Homo sapiens*. Science: Sep 9;309(5741): 1720-2.

Mellick, Jill. (1996). *The Art of Dreaming: Tools for Creative Dreamwork*. Canari Press Books.

Meltzer, Andrea. (2017). Quantifying the Sexual Afterglow: The Lingering Benefits of Sex and Their Implications for Pair-Bonded Relationships. *Sage Journals*, March 16, 2017.

Murdock, Maureen (1990). *The Heroine's Journey*. Boston, Mass. Shambhala Publications Inc.

Mushashi, Miyamoto. (1974). *A Book of Five Rings*. Woodstock, New York: The Overlook Press.

Nichols, Michael. (2007). *The Essentials of Family Therapy*. New York: Pearson.

Northrup, Chrisanna, Schwartz, Pepper, & Whitte, James. (2013). *The Normal Bar: The surprising secrets of happy couples and what they reveal about creating a new normal in your relationship*. New York: Harmony.

O'Hanlon, Bill. (2007). *Positive Psychology*. J&K Seminars. www.JKSeminars.com.

Orstein, Peggy. (2016). Dutch Masters of Sex ed. *L.A. Times*, April 10, 2016.

Pace, Thaddeus. (2009). Effect of compassion meditation on neuroendocrine, innate, immune and behavioral responses to psychosocial stress. *Psychoneuroendocrinology*, Volume 34, Issue 1, January, 2009.

Panksepp, Jaak. (2007). The Emotional MindBrain: The Foundational Role of Core Affects in Consciousness and Psychotherapy. Lifespan Learning Institute conference, *The Healing Power of Emotion*. Lifespan Learning Institute.

Paris, Wendy. (2010). Still doing it. *Psychology Today*: May/June 2010

Pearce, Joseph Chilton. (2002). *The Biology of Transcendence: A Blueprint of the Human Spirit*. Rochester, Vermont: Park Street Press.

Perel, Esther. (2006). *Mating in Captivity*. New York: Harpers.

------. (2017). *The State of Affairs*. New York: Harpers.

Pillemer, Karl. (2012). *Thirty Lessons for Loving*. Penguin: New York, NY.

Pink, Daniel. (2007). How to make your own luck. *Fast Company*, December, 2007.

Porges, S. W. (2006). Presented at a conference, *The Embodied Mind: Integration of the Body, Brain, and Mind in Clinical Practice*. UCLA, March 4 and 5.

Porges SW (2011). *The Polyvagal Theory: Neurophysiological Foundations of Emotions, Attachment, Communication, and Self-regulation*. New York: WW Norton.

Prigogene, Ilya. (1996). *The End of Certainty*. Free Press/Simon and Schuster: New York, NY.

Radin, Dean. (2006). *Entangled Minds: Extrasensory Experiences in a Quantum Reality*. New York: Paraview Pocket Books.

------. (2007). Theater of the Mind Interview with Dean Radin. *Podcast by Kelley Howell.*

Real, Terry. (2017). Relational Life Training Series with Terry Real. Sounds True, Boulder, CO.

Robinson, Marnia. (2009). *Cupid's Poisoned Arrow.* North Atlantic Books: Berkeley, CA.

Rutter, Virginia. (2014). Love and Lust. *Psychology Today,* July/August 2014.

Sapolsky, Robert. (1994). *Why Zebras don't get Ulcers.* New York: Henry Holt.

Schreiber, Katherine. (2013). From Desire to Doing it. *Psychology Today:* July/August, 2013.

Siegel, Daniel J. (1999). *The Developing Mind.* New York: The Guilford Press.

Schore, Allan. (2006). Presented at the UCLA Lifespan Learning conference, *The Embodied Mind: Integration of the Body, Brain, and Mind in Clinical Practice.* UCLA, March 5.

Schore, Allan. (2003). *Affect Regulation and the Repair of the Self.* New York: W.W. Norton and Company.

------. (1994). Affect Regulation and the Origin of the Self. Lawrence Erlbaum Associates. New York.

------. (2014). Affect Regulation and Healing of the Self. Affect Regulation and Healing of the Self (full audio program) 2014 Annual Interpersonal Neurobiology Conference full conference. Available through Lifespan Learning.

------. (2009). Lecture in Lifespan Learning Institute conference, *Current Approaches to the Treatment of Trauma.* Lifespan Learning Institute.

------. (2009). Lecture in Lifespan Learning Institute conference, *Current Approaches to the Treatment of Trauma.* Lifespan Learning Institute.

Shetty, Priya. (2008). Monogamy gene found in people. *Daily News,* September 1, 2008.

Siegel, Daniel J. (1999). *The Developing Mind.* New York: The Guilford Press.

Siegel, Daniel J. and Hartzell, Mary. (2003). *Parenting from the Inside Out.* New York: Penguin

Siegel, Daniel J. (2005). *The Mindsight Lectures: cultivating insight and empathy in our internal and interpersonal lives.* Mind Your Brain, Inc.

Siegel, Daniel J. (2007). *The Mindful Brain.* New York: W.W. Norton and Co.

Singer, Jerome. (1976). *Daydreaming and Fantasy.* New York: Routledge.

Stanton, Sarah. (2013). The Michelangelo Phenomenon: How Your Partner Sculpts a Better (or Worse) You. The Science of Relationships.

Symons, D. (1979). *The Evolution of Human Sexuality.* New York: Oxford University Press.

Taylor, Shelley E. (2002). *The Tending Instinct: How Nurturing is Essential to Who We Are and How We Live.* New York: Henry Holt and Co.

Thomas, Alexander, Chess, Stella, and Birch, Herbert. (1970). The Origin of Personality. *Scientific American,* pp 102-109, 1970.

Thomson, Paula. (2008). Mommy and Me: Shared Trauma During Prenatal Development. Conference, Adult Attachment in Clinical Context. Available through Lifespan Learning.

Tronic, Ed. (2008). Recorded panel discussion at UCLA conference: Towards a new psychology of interpersonal relationships. Lifespan Learning Institute.

Tronic, Ed. (2007). *The Neurobehavioral and Social-Emotional Development of Infants and Children.* Norton: New York, NY.

Twinge, Jean, M. and Campbell, W. Keith. (2009). *The Narcissism Epidemic: Living in the Age of Entitlement.* New York: Free Press.

van der Kolk, Bessel. (2002). Presented at a conference, *The Anatomy of Intimacy.* Foundation for the Contemporary Family. UC Irvine, Nov. 5 and 6.

van der Kolk, Bessel. (2006). *Clinical Implications of Neuroscience Research in PTSD.* Annals of N.Y Acad. Sci. 1071: 277-293Boston University School of Medicine, The Trauma Center, Brookline, Mass. 02446.

------. (2014). *The Body Keeps the Score.* New York: Penguin.

------. (2016). Intensive Trauma Treatment Course. Anthony McFarlane. How PTSD Affects Mind, Brain and Biology. PESI continuing education 11/14/1016.

Ware, Bronnie. (2011-2012). *The Top Five Regrets of the Dying.* Balboa Press.

Weinhold, Janae. (2008). *The Flight from Intimacy.* New World Library: Novato, CA.

Weintraub, Pamela. (2016). The 10 Second Take. *Psychology Today,* June, 2016.

Whitbourne, Susan, Strauss. (2012). Is Red the Color of Sexual Desire? *Psychology Today,* Dec. 2012.

Wilber, Ken. (2000). Sex, Ecology, Spirituality, the spirit of evolution. (revised from 1995). Boston: Shambhala Publications.

------. (2000). *Integral Psychology.* Boston and London: Shambhala.

------. (2000). *A Brief History of Everything.* Boston: Shambhala.

------. (2003). *Kosmic Consciousness.* Boulder: Sounds True (audio recording).

------. (2006). *Integral Spirituality.* Boston: Shambhala.

------. (2004). *The Simple Feeling of Being.* Boston: Shambhala.

------. (2013). *Address in The Integral Living Room.* Boulder, Nov. 1, 2013.

------. (2015). Personal communication.

------. (2016). *Full Spectrum Mindfulness.* Integral Life.

Winon, Guy. (2017). Solutions for the Solitary. *Psychology Today:* July/August.

Witt, Keith. (2006). *The Attuned Family: How to be a Great Parent to Your Kids and a Great Lover to Your Spouse.* Santa Barbara Graduate Institute Publishing/iUniverse.

Witt. Keith. (2006). *The Gift of Shame: Why we need shame and how to use it to love and grow.* Santa Barbara Graduate Institute Publishing/iUniverse.

Witt, Keith (2015). *Integral Mindfulness: from clueless to dialed-in.* Integral Publishers. Tucson: Az.

Witt, Keith (2016). *Shadow Light: Illuminations at the Edge of Darkness.* Integral Publishers. Tucson: Az.

Witt, Keith (2017). *Shadow Light Workbook.* Integral Publishers. Tucson: Az.

Witt, Keith. (2006). *Sessions, All Therapy is About Relationships integrating toward unity.* Santa Barbara Graduate Institute Publishing/iUniverse.

Witt, Keith. (2005). *Waking Up: Psychotherapy as Art, Spirituality, and Science.* Santa Barbara Graduate Institute Publishing/iUniverse.

Witt, Keith. (2015). Loving Completely. Audio class available through IntegralLife.com.

Wormser, Gary. (2010). Voice indicator of male strength. *Santa Barbara News press,* July 25, 2010.

Young, Larry, J. and Wang, Zuoxin. (2004). The neurobiology of pair bonding. Nature neuroscience 7. Published online: 26 September

Zimmerman, Eilene, (2012). Modern Romance. *Christian Science Monitor,* February 13, 2112.

Zinn, Jon Kabat, (2009). *Letting Everything Become your Teacher.* Delta Trade.

Index

Going Deeper

Now that you've read the book, go even deeper
by accessing bonus resources at

www.lovingcompletely.com

Join Loving Completely Web Course

Use the special promotion code
LOVINGBOOK to get a 10% discount on
Dr. Witt's in-depth Loving Completely
online course, with hours of audio and
guided practices to support great
relationships throughout your life!

or

Join Dr. Witt's FREE 7-part Email Course

CPSIA information can be obtained
at www.ICGtesting.com
Printed in the USA
FSHW01n0753090918
52155FS

9 780998 984063